Simmel

Classic Thinkers

Richard T. W. Arthur, *Leibniz*
Terrell Carver, *Marx*
Daniel E. Flage, *Berkeley*
J. M. Fritzman, *Hegel*
Bernard Gert, *Hobbes*
Thomas Kemple, *Simmel*
Dale E. Miller, *J. S. Mill*
Joanne Paul, *Thomas More*
A. J. Pyle, *Locke*
James T. Schleifer, *Tocqueville*
Andrew Ward, *Kant*

Simmel

Thomas Kemple

polity

First published in 2018 by Polity Press

Polity Press
65 Bridge Street
Cambridge CB2 1UR, UK

Polity Press
101 Station Landing
Suite 300
Medford, MA 02155, USA

ISBN-13: 978-1-5095-2110-4
ISBN-13: 978-1-5095-2111-1 (pb)

A catalogue record for this book is available from the British Library.

Library of Congress Cataloging-in-Publication Data

Names: Kemple, Thomas M., 1962- author.
Title: Simmel / Thomas Kemple.
Description: Medford, MA : Polity Press, [2018] | Series: Classic thinkers | Includes bibliographical references and index.
Identifiers: LCCN 2018020993 (print) | LCCN 2018031201 (ebook) | ISBN 9781509521142 (Epub) | ISBN 9781509521104 (hardback) | ISBN 9781509521111 (pbk.)
Subjects: LCSH: Simmel, Georg, 1858-1918–Political and social views. | Sociologists–Biography. | Social sciences–Philosophy.
Classification: LCC HM479.S55 (ebook) | LCC HM479.S55 A58 2018 (print) |DDC 301.092 [B]–dc23
LC record available at https://lccn.loc.gov/2018020993

Typeset in 10.5 on 12 pt Palatino
by Toppan Best-set Premedia Limited
Printed and bound in Great Britain by CPI Group (UK) Ltd, Croydon

For further information on Polity, visit our website: politybooks.com

Contents

Illustrations   vii
Abbreviations   viii
Preface and Acknowledgements   xi

1   Introduction: The Problem of Fitting in and
    Standing Out   1

    Excursus on Social Evolution: Simmel without
    Spencer and Freud   19

Part I Philosophy of Money   23

2   The Price of Freedom   27

    Excursus on Social Quantities: Simmel before
    Durkheim and Tarde   39

3   Functional Values and Personal Worth   43

    Excursus on Cultural Capitalism: Simmel with
    Weber and Sombart   56

4   The Lifestyles of Fast Capitalism   59

    Excursus on Class Conflict: Simmel beneath
    Marx and Engels   71

Part II Sociology of Metropolises 75

5 Privacy and Secrecy in Mass Society 79

Excursus on Maternal Feminism: Simmel between
Marianne Weber and Gilman 91

6 The Cosmopolitan Worldview and Urban Fashion 96

Excursus on Sociological Vitalism: Simmel through
Bergson and Mannheim 110

7 The Propertied and the Poor Person in the Big City 114

Excursus on Race Relations, Strangers, and Other
Marginals: Simmel behind Park and Du Bois 126

Part III Cultures of Modernity 133

8 The Ruin and Renewal of Life 137

Excursus on Sustainability and Surplus: Simmel
alongside Veblen and Mauss 149

9 Adventures in Space and Time 153

Excursus on Spatiality and Temporality: Simmel after
Martineau and Tocqueville 166

10 Conclusion: The Tragedy of Individuality 170

Excursus on Identity and Difference: Simmel across
Mead and Husserl 185

Suggestions for Further Reading 188
References 190
Index 202

Illustrations

Open house in Berlin's Westend, summer 1914   x

Table 1 Simmel's life and work   2–3

Figure 1 Between fitting in and standing out   16
Figure 2 Outline of the *Philosophy of Money*   30
Figure 3 Money as a matter of necessity and chance   46
Figure 4 Consumer culture and the money economy   62
Figure 5 Outline of *Sociology*   82
Figure 6 The metropolis and mental life   100
Figure 7 The mutual recognition of the propertied and
the poor person   118
Figure 8 Outline of *Philosophical Culture* and *View of Life* 141
Figure 9 From everyday experience to the adventure   156
Figure 10 Between self and other, beyond subject
and object   174

Abbreviations

I use the following abbreviations in this book when citing the most readily available or recent editions of Georg Simmel's writings. Whenever I modify an English translation, I also cite the German edition according to volume and page number – e.g. (S: 43; GSG 11: 25). References in the text with dates but no author are by Simmel and are given in the reference list – e.g. (1968). See the Suggestions for Further Reading and table 1 for more information on various editions of Simmel's works.

GSG = (1989–2015) *Georg Simmel Gesamtausgabe* [Georg Simmel Collected Works], 24 vols, ed. O. Rammstedt et al. Frankfurt am Main: Suhrkamp

ISF = (1971) *Georg Simmel: On Individuality and Social Forms*, ed. D. N. Levine. Chicago: University of Chicago Press

PM = (2004) *The Philosophy of Money*, trans. T. Bottomore and D. Frisby. London: Routledge

S = (2009) *Sociology: Inquiries into the Construction of Social Forms*, 2 vols, ed. H. Helle, trans. A. J. Blasi, A. K. Jacobs, and M. Kanjirathinkal. Leiden: Brill

SC = (1997) *Simmel on Culture*, ed. D. Frisby and M. Featherstone. London: Sage

VL = (2010) *View of Life: Four Metaphysical Essays with Journal Aphorisms*, trans. J. A. Y. Andrews and D. N. Levine. Chicago: University of Chicago Press

For Martha Garland

I have had to convince myself that only a few people know Goethe as a whole, that is, as the unity of his parts; these parts, to be sure, are known to many. But their sum does not yet by any means yield the 'whole' Goethe – for him one must look beyond the particulars.

From a letter Georg Simmel wrote to Marianne Weber, 9 December 1912, to whom he dedicated his book *Goethe* (GSG 23: 146; facsimile in 1959: 241. Courtesy of Arnold Simmel)

Open house in Berlin's Westend, summer 1914
(courtesy of Cornelia Hahn Oberlander)

Preface and Acknowledgements

An old black and white photograph captures a moment in time, as if to freeze the flow of events under the aspect of eternity (*sub specie aeternitatis*). A woman and two men in their Sunday best are standing in a lush garden, the one on the left talking animatedly and gesticulating with his hands to the man in the dinner jacket and the woman in the large hat and fur stole. They are all smiling, if only for the photographer, but must be very hot in the summer heat. They are evidently not strangers but appear to be familiar with one another, a trio related through friendship, through family, or in other ways. The handwriting on the back of the photograph notes that the man speaking is the philosopher and sociologist Georg Simmel, and that the setting is an open house in summer 1914 at the home of the economist and historian Ignaz Jastrow, at 14 Nussbaumallee in Berlin's Westend. Jastrow is standing in the centre next to Simmel's wife, Gertrud, and the inscription points out that she wrote books of philosophy under the pseudonym Marie Luise Enckendorff. Simmel is making one of his 'characteristic gestures', as if to grasp an idea from the air and twist it around in his hand. The people in the picture are not at a formal lecture or a scripted seminar at the university, of course, but simply taking part in a sociable gathering and an improvised conversation. As Simmel's son Hans later recalled, exchanges like this one were a regular feature of social life among these circles of colleagues, families, and friends: 'He was a master of conversation, but not interested in "discussion" in the usual sense of the term …. What he found essential and interesting was to fasten on to a word or opinion that would expand the conversation, … or to offer remarks with some constructive new point of view' (H. Simmel 1958: 254; similar remarks are made by students, in Stewart 1999: 7; Gassen and Lassmann 1958: 160, 228).

The date, summer 1914, is significant for both personal and historical reasons. Simmel and Jastrow, who met in the late 1880s and became best friends and neighbours, had recently been separated when the Simmels moved to Strasbourg a few months earlier (GSG 23: 349–50, 356n). After almost thirty years as a popular lecturer at Berlin University, and despite publishing many well-regarded books and articles, Simmel had finally been called to take up his first post as a full professor. His friend continued to lecture at Berlin University where they had been colleagues, but he had recently been dismissed from his teaching position at the Commercial College he had co-founded, an injustice Simmel vehemently protested in a newspaper editorial as a violation of academic freedom (GSG 17: 115–18, 463–5). Just a few weeks after this photograph was taken, the lives of these individuals and of many others in their social circle would be decisively transformed with the outbreak of the First World War in August 2014. As Simmel reflected melancholically in a letter to the Jastrows almost exactly a year later, 'the war placed a period where I had at first only expected a semicolon. I am convinced that a new world era is beginning ... & that I shall belong to the old' (quoted in Goodstein 2017: 338; GSG 23: 534–5).

This book is intended to serve primarily as a short introduction to the work, life, and legacy of Georg Simmel (1858–1918) for undergraduate students and general readers. I try not to assume any prior knowledge of Simmel's work, his social and intellectual circles, or technical issues in philosophy and sociology. Because Simmel often responds to the academic, cultural, and political issues of his time, I situate his work within important historical and cultural events and in the larger field of classical sociological and modern philosophical thought. And since one of the lasting lessons of his work concerns his perspective on what is unique about the modern experience, this book also offers an assessment of the significance of his ideas for understanding some current intellectual debates, cultural issues, and everyday phenomena. Although I cannot present more than a snapshot of Simmel, I invite readers to look beyond the particulars and to imagine the unity of his life and work for his time and for ours, just as Simmel himself had hoped to accomplish in his book on the novelist, poet, playwright and natural scientist Johann Wolfgang von Goethe (1749–1832) (see the epigraph above).

A distinctive feature of my approach consists in connecting the most familiar and influential themes of Simmel's writings which have been the main concern of scholars for over a century – on money, metropolises, and modernity – to lesser known topics and texts that have come to light in the recent reception of his work. Following Simmel's own method of seeing the whole through the parts, I select key works featured in most English-language anthologies and commentaries, especially his masterpiece on the *Philosophy of Money* (1900, revised in 1907), his famous lecture on 'The Metropolis and Mental Life' (published as an essay in 1903), and the chapters of his monumental *Sociology*, including his often cited piece 'The Stranger' (1908). At the same time, I bring these works into conversation with writings that have received less attention: from his early aesthetic, ethical, and philosophical publications to his later metaphysical, sociological, and cultural writings, especially the provocative essays collected in *Philosophical Culture* (1911) and the challenging chapters that make up his *View of Life* (1918). In my Introduction, and in the opening remarks to each of the three parts of this book, I present some relevant details of Simmel's biography and intellectual milieu insofar as they illuminate the life of the thinker within the development of his thought. For example, I consider his popularity and influence on students; his relations with leading cultural figures and artistic movements; the importance of travel, family life, friendships, and colleagues in shaping his ideas; his struggle for institutional recognition and professional security; and his personal tastes and political opinions. In my Suggestions for Further Reading, I offer some practical suggestions on using this text in the classroom or for further study: in conjunction with accessible selections from Simmel's work, with short pieces by other classical and contemporary thinkers, or with useful resources listed in the References.

Simmel's life and work are therefore the main *focus* of this book, but they also serve as *a frame* for rethinking his pivotal place within the 'classical age' of social scientific thought in the 150-year period between 1789 – the French Revolution, which inspired the rise to the modern social sciences – and 1939 – the beginning of the Second World War, which provoked a period of critical rethinking concerning the relevance and scope of philosophy and sociology. An appreciation of the significance of Simmel as a classic thinker is enhanced when he is understood in light of certain key texts, core concepts, and main themes from other classic writers, above all the classic sociological 'trinity' of Karl Marx (an important influence on Simmel's ideas), Max Weber (a valued colleague and friend), and Emile Durkheim (his contemporary and occasional rival). I also touch on the ideas of some young thinkers who studied with him and followed their own intellectual paths later on, particularly the radical cultural philosophers Georg Lukács, Siegfried Kracauer, and Ernst Bloch. I show that his writings complement the work of his contemporaries in sociology as well, including Herbert Spencer, Charlotte Perkins Gilman, W. E. B. Du Bois, Karl Mannheim, Marcel Mauss, Robert Park, and George Herbert Mead. Rather than distract from the core issues and texts by Simmel that are my main concern, I address these thinkers in pairs in a few brief digressions or 'excurses', a device Simmel himself used in tracing thematic connections, examples, or departures from his main topic of study. These excurses highlight Simmel's remarkable influence in Europe, the United States, and elsewhere (astonishingly, his work was extensively translated into English, French, Russian, Polish, and Italian in his own lifetime). They also help us trace his importance for later developments in urban sociology and social network analysis, phenomenology and metaphysics, cultural criticism, and the study of everyday life in the modern world.

Although my aim is to provide a conventional reading of the life and work of this important modernist thinker, I also hope to capture some of the innovative spirit of Simmel's unique method of thinking and observing as well as his original way of reading and writing. In each chapter I display some key concepts and main themes in a series of simple diagrams that take the shape of objects and images that he himself uses as simple examples and analogies, such as a door, a vending machine, a mirror, and a bridge. I present these figures as ways of thinking through Simmel's theoretical problems in verbal and visual ways, or to borrow from Simmel's description of his own method of forming concepts, as 'geometrical sketches' that take 'the unavoidably accidental and crude form of all drawings' (S: 24; ISF: 31).* Presenting Simmel's life and work in this book reveals a tension with the approach he takes in his writings on Rembrandt and Rodin, Schopenhauer and Nietzsche, or Kant and Goethe.

---

*The figures are meant primarily to provide a quick overview of the key concepts discussed in the chapters rather than to make a separate point or an original argument on their own. Figures 1 and 10 present the frame of the book as a whole, and figures 2, 5, 6, and 8 give chapter outlines of the main works by Simmel on which I focus in each of the three parts. All diagrams depict the relationships between significant ideas, analogies, or images that Simmel uses in the works under discussion and therefore serve as 'thinking pictures' (Swedberg 2016). To make my sources more accessible for the general reader and to the student new to Simmel, I use parenthetical references rather than footnotes, and each excursus can be read either on its own or in connection with the topics discussed in the chapter.

For him, these artists, writers, and thinkers are embodiments of the modern worldview, and to some extent they also present portraits of himself, just as Simmel sometimes serves this purpose for me in this book (and in Kemple 1995: 224–6; 2014: 206–8). My aim is not to present his life and work merely as exemplary instances of the aimless wanderer (the philosophical *flâneur*) or the intellectual tinkerer (the sociological *bricoleur*), as some commentators have argued (Frisby 1986; Weinstein and Weinstein 1991). Even though I cannot present the whole Simmel in this book, my aim is to approach his work as a model for how systematic study and methodical thought can address the deepest problems of modern experience.

* * *

I owe an incalculable debt to many undergraduate students over the years, including those in my social theory classes, in my Arts One seminars, and especially in my course on Simmel and social media, where the outlines of this book were first worked out (unbeknownst to me or them). Rayka Kumru, a student in that class, led me to the photograph of Simmel presented above after befriending an old woman by chance on the ski slopes of Whistler, British Columbia: Cornelia Hahn Oberlander, the renowned landscape architect and Ignaz Jastrow's granddaughter (Herrington 2013). I am grateful to Mrs Oberlander for permission to reproduce this photograph and to Arnold Simmel for permission to use his grandfather's letter to Marianne Weber. My undergraduate research assistant, Jastej Luddu, has given me valuable feedback on making this manuscript more accessible and interesting for newcomers to Simmel, as have my former undergraduate students Babak Amini, Andrew Brown, Jennifer Diep, and Justin Kong, among others. As always, many graduate students and teaching assistants have offered me their encouragement, critical insight, and expertise in making these ideas useful for further study and in helping me draw my diagrams, especially Caitlin Forsey, Heather Holroyd, Mo Ismailzai, Katherine Lyon, and Rachael Sullivan. (All figures are drawn by me, and images taken from internet websites such as www.ecosia.org are free to share, modify, or use commercially.) My colleagues Sylvia Berryman, Dawn Currie, Brandon Konoval, Renisa Mawani, Carla Nappi, Gavin Paul, and Mike Zeitlin offered compelling advice at the right moments as I considered alternative approaches to this book.

I am grateful to Mike Featherstone, Couze Venn, Scott Lash, Nick Gane, and other members of the editorial board of *Theory,*

Culture & Society for their valuable support and suggestions on two special issues on Simmel (Kemple 2007; Harrington and Kemple 2012). Austin Harrington and I have sustained an inspiring friendship and productive collaboration through our shared interests in Weber, Simmel, and Berlin (Harrington and Kemple 2013; Kemple and Harrington 2016), and he has generously shared the draft of his forthcoming collection of translations of Simmel's writings on art and aesthetics along with his extensive introduction. Bryan Turner invited me to edit *The Anthem Companion to Simmel*, which led to a collegial relationship and wonderful friendship with Olli Pyyhtinen, who opened my eyes to the expanding world of Simmel studies beyond the English-speaking world (Kemple and Pyyhtinen 2016; Kemple 2016), in addition to giving me scrupulous comments on this manuscript. Through Olli I was able to connect with Natália Cantó-Milà, Gregor Fitzi, Nigel Thrift, and many other inspiring new Simmel scholars. A belated reading of the excellent book by Ralph Leck (2000) gave me a new perspective on Simmel's intellectual, political, and personal milieu, as well as a new friend. I never met the late David Frisby personally, although his work on Simmel and theories of modernity infuses much of the approach I take here (Kemple 2010), and I am grateful to the late Donald Levine for inviting me to the conference on Simmel's legacy in Chicago after reading my papers in the *Journal of Classical Sociology* (Kemple 2009 and 2011). Stimulating discussions at colloquia in Montreal, Irvine, Edinburgh, Oñati, and Vancouver (the last in a pivotal paper co-authored with Zohreh Bayatrizi) led to articles in the *Journal of Historical Sociology*, *UC Irvine Law Review*, and *Sociologie et sociétés*, several ideas from which have made their way into the present book (Kemple 2014a and 2013; Bayatrizi and Kemple 2012). Through the hospitality of Sanjeev Routray and Ravinder Kaur, I was able to present some of these ideas to graduate students at the Indian Institute of Technology in Delhi, and I also benefited from stimulating discussions with Hubert Knoblauch, Arnold Windeler, Nina Baur, and above all Robert Jungmann at the Technische Universität in Berlin during my summer there as a DAAD fellow. I thank the reviewers at Polity Press, and my editor George Owers, who has been patient and helpful in pushing me to clarify the ideas and simplify the presentation of this book through several iterations, each (hopefully) better than the preceding one.

My intersecting circles of friends – especially David Chacon, Gilles Beaudin, Scot Ritchie, and Wolf Drägestein – keep me in touch with all things strange and familiar in Vancouver. As always, Stephen Guy-Bray is the heart and soul of everything I do.

1

Introduction: The Problem of Fitting in and Standing Out

In the summer of 1904 Georg Simmel took his young son Hans on a trip to the Swiss Alps, in the course of which the father told some of his signature stories. When they returned home Hans wrote out one of the more fanciful of these fairy tales, which Simmel himself later expanded on (Simmel 2009–10; GSG 20: 302–3, 547–9, 618–27; Hans Simmel 1958: 255). It recounts the life of little Grülp, a colour who cannot find his complement anywhere in the world, not even in the rainbow. A magician, an old owl named Colorum who could only see at night, is also unable to find a place for little Grülp, declaring him 'the colour that doesn't exist'. Eventually little Grülp visits the Paris studio of the painter Clixorine, who is delighted to make use of him in his work. But when Clixorine can no longer sell his paintings he starves to death. In despair, little Grülp visits the Opal's house, where he finds a home among other colours that do not exist. But, at this point, our storyteller breaks off, unable to understand the name that little Grülp was given in his new family.

Besides offering an amusing glimpse into Simmel's own family life, this odd tale expresses some of Simmel's own ideas and can stand as a charming portrait of the man himself. In this regard, it bears some resemblance to Simmel's famous short piece on 'The Stranger', which many have argued is partly autobiographical. They note that Simmel himself is like the one who 'comes today and stays tomorrow', settling into various social and intellectual circles while remaining both an insider and an outsider in each of them (S: 601–5; ISF: 143–9, 296–330; Levine et al. 1976; Goodstein 2017: 296–330; Coser 1965: 29–42). Although I consider the theme of

Table 1 Simmel's life and work

Date	Simmel's Life	Simmel's Works	Intellectual-Historical Context
1858 to 1890	◆ Born 1 March 1858 in Berlin, the youngest of 7 ◆ Father dies (1874); Julius Friedländer sponsors his university studies in history, psychology, Italian, and philosophy ◆ Lecturer [*Privatdozent*] at Berlin University (1885)	◆ Dissertation on yodelling rejected; doctorate later granted for his prizewinning essay on Kant's *Physical Monadology* (1881) ◆ 'Psychological & Ethnological Studies of Music' (1882) ◆ 'Dante's Psychology' (1884) ◆ Post-doctoral lecture-essay on Kant's theory of space-time rejected, later accepted (1885)	◆ Durkheim (born 1858) ◆ Darwin's *Origin of Species* (1859) (dies 1882) ◆ Schopenhauer (d. 1860) ◆ Weber (b. 1864) ◆ Marx's *Capital* (1867) (d. 1883) ◆ Nietzsche's major works published; suffers a nervous breakdown in 1889 (d. 1900) ◆ Franco-Prussian War (1870–71), economic boom (*Gründerzeit*)
1890 to 1900	◆ Marries Gertrud Kinel (1890), who later writes under the pseudonym Marie Luise Enckendorff; son Hans born (1891) ◆ Appointed Extraordinary Professor of Philosophy without salary at Berlin University (1900); colleagues with Dilthey	◆ *On Social Differentiation* (1890) ◆ *Problems in the Philosophy of History* (1892; revised 1905) ◆ *Introduction to Moral Science* (1892–93) ◆ Writings for *Jugend* (1897–1907) and other avant-garde and scholarly journals ◆ *Philosophy of Money* (1900; revised 1907)	◆ Spencer, Durkheim, Weber, Tönnies, Tarde, Veblen, Gilman, Du Bois, and Cooley publish early sociological writings ◆ *American Journal of Sociology* (founded 1895) and *Année sociologique* (founded 1898) publish translations of Simmel's early work ◆ Berlin Trade Exhibition (1896)

Years	Events	Works	Context
1900 to 1908	• Exchanges with Rilke, George, Ernst, Rodin, Buber, Husserl, Rickert, Bergson, and other major cultural figures • Park, Hiller, Stöcker, and others attend popular Berlin lectures • Heidelberg Professorship rejected, despite Weber's support	• 'The Metropolis and Mental Life' (1903) • Kant (1904) • Kant and Goethe (1906; revised 1916) • Religion (1906; revised 1912) • Schopenhauer and Nietzsche (1907) • Sociology (1908)	• Freud's Interpretation of Dreams (1900) • Husserl's Logical Investigations (1900–01) • Weber's Protestant Ethic and the Spirit of Capitalism (1904–05) • Bergson's Creative Evolution (1907) • Expressionist, Naturalist, Feminist, and Activismus movements gain in prominence
1908 to 1918	• Lukács, Bloch, Kracauer, and others attend salons in Berlin Westend home • Appointed Professor at Kaiser-Wilhelm University in Strasbourg (1914) • Simmel dies of liver cancer 26 September 1918 in Strasbourg	• Main Problems in Philosophy (1910) • Philosophical Culture (1911) • Goethe (1913) • Rembrandt (1916) • The War and Our Spiritual Decisions (1917) • Fundamental Questions of Sociology (1917) • View of Life (1918)	• First meeting of German Sociological Association in Frankfurt (1910) • Logos journal founded (1910) • Durkheim's Elementary Forms of Religious Life (1912) (d. 1917) • World War (August 1914–November 1918)

the stranger in later chapters, the tale of little Grülp's efforts to find his complement might serve just as well as a statement of Simmel's struggles to find a place in the university, if not also my own attempt here to fit him into the history of classic thinkers. Simmel's life and work are likewise mirrored in the attempts of the old owl Colorum to explain the unexplainable and to account for what does not seem to exist in reality. His frustrations with academic life are also reflected in the ambition of the obsessive painter Clixorine to produce some unknown masterpiece out of materials which have not yet been discovered, and even to represent the unrepresentable (Kemple 1995: 113–25). As a philosopher and sociologist, and as a theorist of art and life who was also a popular writer, Simmel often appears strange from the perspective of established academic disciplines or out of place with respect to recognizable literary genres. Like a colour we cannot name, or which at first might not even seem to exist, his work does not appear as a substantial contribution to any one field. His uniqueness and originality are thus a bit like little Grülp, who at first either stands out or seems invisible but may unexpectedly find a home somewhere.

In this introductory chapter I give an overview of Simmel's life and work by considering his career-long concern with combining sociological observation and philosophical speculation on modern experience. After reviewing some of his own personal struggles with fitting in and standing out in the academic world, I consider how many of his most interesting ideas are announced or antici-pated in his early writings. These works from the 1890s include his first book, *On Social Differentiation*, his two-volume *Introduction to Moral Science*, and several shorter pieces that attempt to bridge philosophy and social science. Without abandoning his academic training in philosophy, Simmel developed his own approach to social life in the years when sociology was just beginning to estab-lish its own journals, professional associations, and university departments. Later on, he expands on the relationship between 'association and differentiation' as his main problem (*Hauptproblem*) or basic question (*Grundfrage*), which the philosophers Immanuel Kant (1724–1804), Georg W. F. Hegel (1770–1831), and Friedrich Nietzsche (1844–1900), as well as the sociologist Herbert Spencer (1820–1903), first inspired him to formulate: 'How is society possi-ble?' (S: 40–52; ISF: 6–22). Simmel's question concerns how people, events, and things stand out from one another as singular, unique, and purposeful, and also how they fit together as types, members, and parts of a whole. To situate his early work in the context of other major intellectual trends of the late nineteenth century, I include a short excursus on how Simmel's approach to 'social evolution' contrasts with that of other major thinkers of his day, namely Spencer and Sigmund Freud (1856–1939). The key themes that I highlight in my discussion of these early writings are anticipated in the chapters that follow on the complications of the money economy, the complexities of metropolitan society, and the unintended consequences of modern life.

Early Life and Work

Although Simmel himself resisted writing out the details of his personal life, we can identify a number of significant events and turning points that illuminate the development of his ideas and the evolving shape of his work (see table 1). Since there is no complete biography of Simmel, these notes are based on letters, memoirs written by others, public documents, and other materials relating to his life (especially Helle 2013: 181–7; Köhnke 1996; Landmann 1958: 11–14; Pyyhtinen 2018: vii–x; and H. Simmel 1958). Thus we could at most call them 'biographemes' or mere fragments of a biography (Barthes 1989: 9). Simmel was born on 1 March 1858, the last of seven children, in a house that stood on the northwest corner of Friedrichstrasse and Leipzigerstrasse in central Berlin. As he grew up, the world around his childhood home changed rapidly in the wake of the Franco-Prussian War of 1871–2, which inaugurated a period of tremendous industrial and political development and led to the foundation of a unified German nation and the economic boom called the *Gründerzeit*. The opera, theatres, concert halls, museums, parliament, churches, markets, the castle, and the university, as well as countless restaurants, bars, and new venues of mass entertainment – all were within walking distance. As his good friend the poet, philosopher, and literary critic Margarete Susman (1872–1966) later reflected, 'not just the time but also the place of his birth were decisive for his life and thought, a Berlin already on its way to becoming a lively and bustling metropolis' (Susman 1992: 32).

Simmel's parents had migrated to Berlin from Breslau shortly after marrying, and both came from Jewish families that had converted to Christianity. Simmel was baptized a Protestant and regularly attended services until his final years, when he chose to pursue a more private and independent expression of his faith. His father, who co-founded a successful chocolate factory, died in 1874 when

Simmel was just a teenager. A close family friend and wealthy sheet-music merchant, Julius Friedlander, was appointed his legal guardian and sponsored Simmel's studies in history, psychology, Italian, and philosophy at Berlin University. There he took classes with some of the most illustrious academics of the day, including the eminent historians Theodor Mommsen and Heinrich von Treitschke; the pioneers of social psychology (*Völkerpsychologie*) Moritz Lazarus and Heymann Steinthall; and the well-known economic historian Gustav Schmoller, who would publish some of Simmel's first works in his journal and book series. Simmel's difficulties in defending his doctoral and post-doctoral dissertations have become legendary, and they are often cited as early indications of his status as both an insider and an outsider to the academy. His doctoral thesis on the psychology and ethnology of music, which used an empirical case study of yodelling, was rejected by the examining committee as too stylistically sketchy and poorly proofread to be acceptable. Eventually his examiners agreed to accept his prize-winning essay on Immanuel Kant's physical monadology instead. A few years later, at his post-doctoral lecture on Kant's theory of space and time, Simmel ridiculed a senior faculty member's suggestion that the soul has a physical location in the brain (a belief also held by the seventeenth-century philosopher René Descartes). The examination was suspended and the candidate was asked to reflect on his breach of academic etiquette, although his work on Dante's psychology was later accepted in its place. Finally, in 1885 Simmel was appointed lecturer (*Privatdozent*) at the university that had grudgingly granted him his degrees, although his position was paid out of student fees rather than a fixed salary.

Although his career was only just beginning, Simmel's life and ideas began to take off after around 1890 (Köhnke 1996). Friedlander's death in 1889 left him with a considerable inheritance, although fluctuating returns on investments meant that his financial independence was never entirely secure. Nevertheless, he would continue to go his own way as a lecturer, thinker, and writer. In 1890 he married Gertrud Kinel (1864–1938), whom he had met through the artistic and literary circles with which he had become acquainted, and a year later their son Hans (1891–1943) was born. In addition to their shared cultural interests, the couple was an intellectual match, with Gertrud later writing her own philosophical books under the pseudonym Marie Luise Enckendorff (Leck 2000: 146–56). Simmel published a number of academic articles and journalistic pieces in these early years, as well as three major books in philosophy and social science: *On Social Differentiation* (1890), *Problems in the Philosophy of History* (1892), and *Introduction to Moral Science* (1892–3). The last of these has an unintentionally ironic title, since this 'introduction' was actually a massive two-volume work! Even as he continued to lecture and write on a wide range of scholarly topics, Simmel remained a free thinker, and his views on art and politics were often culturally subversive. He published creative and stylistically innovative pieces for the avant-garde journal *Jugend*, for example, and associated with counter-culture groups with such names as 'The Unrestrained' and 'The Unbridled' (Rammstedt 1991; Leck 2000: 38–45). Despite his growing list of publications and his popularity among students, he was able to secure a permanent position as an unsalaried professor (*Extraordinarius*) at Berlin University only in 1900, after submitting applications to several other universities as well.

Several factors seemed to have contributed to the young Simmel's relatively marginal place in the late nineteenth-century world of academia. The one often cited by commentators is the perception of his Jewishness in a German intellectual culture often marked by various forms of overt and covert anti-Semitism. In a lecture on 'Science as a Vocation', Simmel's friend and colleague Max Weber (1864–1920) quotes the notice at the gate to hell from Dante's *Inferno* as a warning to any young Jewish academic attempting to enter a full-time career in the university – '*lasciate ogni speranza* [abandon all hope!]' (Weber 2004: 7). In these remarks from 1917, Weber may have been recalling the recommendation he gave to his friend in 1908 for a professorship at the University of Heidelberg. Simmel's hopes were dashed when Weber's conservative colleague Dietrich Schäfer confidentially circulated a damning denunciation of the young Berlin academic who supposedly advocated 'life- and world-views ... that are clearly distinct from our Christian-classical culture' (quoted in Goodstein 2017: 93; GSG 24: 286–8). Schäfer also seems to have objected to Simmel's disregard for academic conventions and disciplinary boundaries, singling out the lecture he gave in Dresden in 1903 on 'The Metropolis and Mental Life' for inadequately accounting for the political, economic, and intellectual conditions of city life (Frisby 2001: 131–9). Perhaps just as significant in keeping Simmel from securing a university post, his transgressive and bohemian sympathies attracted large numbers of unconventional students, including non-academics, foreigners, and women, who attended his lectures but could not formally enter the university until 1907. Even open-minded and otherwise supportive colleagues, such as the famous philosopher of the cultural sciences Wilhelm Dilthey (1833–1911), may have felt some resentment at Simmel's astonishing productivity and popularity. As Ralph Leck argues, 'it is less the case that there is anything characteristically Jewish in his writing or thinking than that anti-Semitism coded him as cosmopolitan, anti-bourgeois, and therefore as an outsider and cultural pariah' (Leck 2000: 82). In any case, the usual custom of not promoting one's own graduates also meant that Simmel had little chance of becoming a full professor at Berlin University.

In the final decades of the nineteenth century, when Simmel was a young graduate student and university lecturer, a number of unorthodox writings were circulating among a new generation of intellectuals looking for alternatives to the generation of scholarship represented by Kant, Hegel, and Arthur Schopenhauer (1788–1860), including Charles Darwin's *Origin of Species* (1859); Karl Marx's *Capital* (1867); and Friedrich Nietzsche's *Unfashionable Observations* (1876), *Thus Spoke Zarathustra* (1883), *Beyond Good and Evil* (1886), and *On the Genealogy of Morality* (1887) (Scaff 1988: 7–13). Also appearing at this time were the early sociological writings of Herbert Spencer in England; Emile Durkheim and Gabriel Tarde in France; Max Weber, Werner Sombart, and Ferdinand Tönnies in Germany; and, in the United States, Thorstein Veblen, Charlotte Perkins Gilman, Charles Horton Cooley, and W. E. B. Du Bois (whose ideas I discuss elsewhere in this book). Simmel's distinctive perspective on social science caught the attention of the University of Chicago's Albion Small, who founded the *American Journal of Sociology* in 1895, and of Durkheim and his colleagues, who founded the *Année Sociologique* in 1898. Both journals were quick to feature translations of Simmel's early writings. In an era when sociology was often readily associated with dangerous ideas such as socialism, and sometimes identified with subversive avant-garde cultural and political movements such as feminism, a prolific scholar like Simmel who sympathized with these tendencies naturally had a hard time finding a place in traditional educational institutions. An influential comment by Lewis Coser summarizes the double-edged perception among colleagues of Simmel as a scholar who could hardly fit in because he stood out so much: 'Simmel, the marginal man, the stranger, presented his academic peers not with a methodical, painstakingly elaborate system but with a series of often disorderly insights, testifying to amazing powers of perception' (Coser 1965: 36–7). Although these views may be exaggerated or unfair, they defined Simmel's career and the reception of his writings in his lifetime.

They would also determine his posthumous reputation, as I note in my introductory comments to each of the three main parts of this book.

In an expansive article on 'Tendencies in German Life and Thought Since 1870', published in English in 1902, Simmel offers his analysis and diagnosis of the political, cultural, and intellectual world in which he grew up (1994a; Frisby 1986: 42–5). The unification of the German nation-state had propelled the development of the technical and objective side of the country's material culture, he argues, but failed to cultivate the inner life and spiritual well-being of the individual. During this period, the economic conditions of the middle classes improved and there were significant advances in technology and communications, including the telegraph and the telephone. As industrial progress accelerated, international competition intensified, and crowding in the big cities led to a decrease in the 'natural' distance between rich and poor and a corresponding intensification of class conflicts. In responding to these social problems, social democrats and socialists demanded social equality, while counter-culture activists, including many in the emerging women's movement, pushed for more individual freedoms. A culture of consumerism promoted mass entertainment and public spectacles but ignored the moral cultivation and mental refinement of individual citizens. As a result of all these developments, Simmel concludes, the modern age is increasingly characterized by feelings of nervous excitement leading to mental exhaustion and cultural decadence. Individuals long for originality or to 'be otherwise' at any cost, but they do not thereby become more dignified or wise. Technical innovations such as photography are displacing the traditional arts, and the sciences are becoming experimental and empirical, leaving artists and scientists wondering whether life has any meaning or purpose. In the course of these tumultuous years, 'Germany has become the classic land of *the theory of knowledge*' (1994a: 26), although a comprehensive theory of life and a practical understanding of human action and its significance are still sorely lacking.

A Doorway to Simmel: How are History, Society, and Nature Made Possible?

Simmel devoted his life's work to providing some answers to the questions raised by the academic and cultural world that produced him. In his final years he made a few attempts to draw up what he called a 'balance sheet' of his most original ideas and to sketch an 'unambiguous portrait' of his spiritual and intellectual individuality (GSG 24: 71–2). The most elaborate of these autobiographical sketches seems to have been written around 1910 or perhaps earlier, probably as an introduction to a work he was planning to write on metaphysics (GSG 20: 304–5, 549; see Goodstein 2017: 61–95; and Helle 2013: 189–91). Today, the most familiar of Simmel's contributions are his sociological studies of the forms of **association** (*Vergesellschaftung*). Like many German scholarly terms, this one has meanings which are technical – and so might be translated with the awkward 'societalization' or the invented word 'sociation' – as well as colloquial – including 'socialization', when applied to children growing up in families, for example, or to medical institutions managed by the state. Although Simmel's use of this word is both specialized and commonsense, I prefer the ordinary English word 'association', since it conveys his understanding of social life more as a dynamic process than as a completed substance (Kemple and Pyyhtinen 2016: 8n1). For Simmel, *association* is the process by which things, events, and people are gathered into groups and given meaning, often voluntarily but sometimes unconsciously. Human beings (and even non-human things, we might add) *associate* with one another by following patterns through which they become related and by exhibiting durable forms that persist over time. This theme, which I highlight in Part II of this book, becomes especially evident in Simmel's sociology of cities and in his studies of social interaction and individual experience more generally.

Another insight for which Simmel claims credit in his autobiographical fragment concerns how sociological investigations of social interactions between individuals led him to a broad metaphysical understanding of the nature of truth, value, and objectivity. Reality emerges as a product of reciprocal **interaction** (*Wechselwirkung*), he argues, or, more precisely, it results from 'the living reciprocity of elements' (quoted in Goodstein 2017: 59; GSG 20: 304). Like 'association', this key term is difficult to translate and could be rendered with somewhat more opaque expressions such as 'exchange effect', 'reciprocal action', or even 'reciprocal cause and effect'. Recent thinkers have formulated this idea with the slogan 'the real is relational' (Bourdieu 1998: 3–5), by developing a method for 'tracing associations' (Latour 2005: 159–64), or with the thesis that 'relations are one with the essence or substance of a thing' (Pyyhtinen 2018:

40). The important point for Simmel is that everything is connected to everything else and that the whole of existence, not just human interaction, is related in the broadest imaginable sense (an idea that Gabriel Tarde developed around the same time, as I note in chapter 2). The concept of reciprocal *interaction* (or *reciprocal cause and effect*, as I sometimes translate the term) does not mean that reality, objective truth, and value are relative in the sense that they are merely human products, historically changeable, or socially constructed. Rather, this expansive idea encompasses the dynamic make-up of natural as well as cultural life, as Simmel shows with the example of how money mediates all kinds of relationships among people and things (as I discuss in Part I). At first glance his point seems rather abstract, speculative, and even mystical, and Simmel himself says that his 'relativism' is a cosmic 'absolute' that is the basis for his philosophy of religion as well (GSG 20: 305). More concretely, however, he illustrates this metaphysical concept of reciprocal *interaction* with examples emerging from the everyday **culture** (*Kultur*) of the modern age. He focuses especially on ordinary experiences of how unfettered individualism (subjectivism) leads to a radical uncertainty (scepticism) and a deep distrust (cynicism) regarding anything that seems to be a restraint on life (these are themes I introduce in Part I and expand on in Part III).

Simmel's key concepts of *association, interaction,* and *culture* stem from the intellectual breakthrough he achieved in his early studies of Kant (GSG 20: 304). Where Kant was concerned with the prior necessary conditions (the transcendental-logical *apriorities*) by which *nature* could be grasped scientifically in the mind, Simmel extends this idea to include the conditions that make possible our experience of *society* and perhaps even our knowledge of *history* as well. Thus his *apriorities* can be called experiential-immanent, since they are inherent in interactions and not just constructed in the mind of the observer. For Kant as for Simmel, no knowledge can be an exact replica, mirror, or photographic copy of reality. Simmel develops his own version of this argument throughout his writings, but especially in his lectures on Kant first published in 1904 (which expand on his doctoral and post-doctoral studies), his 1905 chapter 'On the Immanent Limits of Historical Inquiry' (from the *Problems in the Philosophy of History*), and his 1908 chapter on 'The Problem of Sociology' (which introduces the book *Sociology*). The question concerning what makes nature, society, and history possible – as objects of experience and knowledge – also informs his later work, including *Main Problems of Philosophy, Philosophical Culture,* and

Fundamental Questions of Sociology. Throughout his working life he did not think of sociology only as a scientific method, and he did not approach philosophy merely as an academic field or a disciplinary commitment. Rather, what he calls his 'philosophical sociology' or 'sociological metaphysics' is concerned with the fundamental sources and widespread cultural forms that give shape and direction to life itself (Harrington and Kemple 2012). If philosophy and sociology are his preferred ways of understanding the world, they are also his topics of investigation, occasions for critical reflection, and motives of inquiry in their own right. Simmel's great theme was *the mental experience of the modern money economy and metropolitan life* (in German: *das Geistesleben der Geldwirtschaft und der Großstädte*), an experience that he considers to be both a philosophical problem and a sociological question. In short, modern experience entails leading a *philosophical life* and a *sociological life*, at times as a matter of personal and cultural urgency.

Simmel poses his basic question 'How is Society Possible?' in a digression inserted into the introductory chapter of *Sociology* on 'The Problem of Sociology' (ISF: 6–22; S: 40–52). The question might seem strange at first, since we usually assume that social life is possible because it is necessary, or because we simply take for granted that we are essentially social beings. But Simmel is asking what makes society possible as *a reality, an experience,* and *an object of knowledge*. Social, historical, and natural life is therefore a *problem* in the sense of being both a topic of study and a subject of concern for people in their everyday lives. This dense yet short piece seems at first to focus on human interactions, but it can also serve as an introduction to Simmel's thought as a whole, including his philosophy of nature and history and his metaphysics of culture and society more broadly. Kant argues that nature exists as an object for the scientific observer or the ordinary spectator, although it does not simply reveal itself to us and ultimately exceeds human comprehension. By contrast, Simmel notes that social life does not usually need an observer in order to be perceived as a reality or to be understood as a unity: 'it is directly realized by its own elements because these elements are themselves conscious and synthesizing units' (ISF: 7; S: 41). To some degree, every individual is already a kind of amateur sociological thinker or intellectual tinkerer insofar as everyone strives to find unity and make connections out of the fragmentary impressions of experience. Just as we piece together our perceptions of natural life for various aesthetic, ethical, or scientific purposes – in order to turn a flower into a work of art, protect the rainforest, or explain a solar eclipse – so too social life is assembled from various bits of experience and formed out of manifold impressions. Simmel's question thus goes beyond Kant's philosophy by expanding on a *social theory* of *human interactions and historical changes* and developing of a *philosophy of life and its limits*. The 'apriorities' he identifies can be understood as establishing the terms for his sociological and metaphysical inquiry into the relationships between self and other, the familiar and the foreign, as well as subjectivity and objectivity as a whole.

I shall try to provide a clear and useful summary of Simmel's apriorities, in part by drawing upon as well as departing from similar attempts made by others (especially Cantó-Milà 2013: 10–12; Helle 2013: 82–4; O'Neill 1973; Pyyhtinen 2018: 39–43). Like all such quick overviews, mine must remain tentative and incomplete. And since these ideas often seem very abstract, it may help to think of an ordinary encounter with a particular person in a specific place and time – say, if we can picture meeting Simmel himself at the garden party in the summer of 1914 (as depicted in the illustration, p. x). In my view, these necessary conditions that make social life possible can be thought of as *axes of association* along which individuals and groups are predisposed to interact, along horizontal (x), vertical (y), and diagonal (z) dimensions. For example, we can think of how the people in the photograph relate to one another both in their generic roles as friends, colleagues, and spouses and as unique persons in ways that are different from how they would converse with others outside their little group. I also think these apriorities suggest *thresholds of reciprocal interaction* through which the elements of life as a whole are connected to or separated from one another, embracing both natural objects and human subjects. Here we might imagine how the garden, the fashionable clothes, and even the tea about to be served all become elements in the conversations among these individuals. Simmel's primary aim in 'How is Society Possible?' is to describe the conditions under which human subjects relate to each other in society. At the same time, these apriorities can be understood to describe the conditions under which humans relate to things and how things are connected in space and over time. In more technical terms, we can say that his apriorities sketch out a *theory of reality* (ontology) as well as a *theory of knowledge of relationships* (epistemology), if not also a *theory of appearances and essences* (phenomenology).

Since Simmel enumerates just three of these axes or thresholds (though he acknowledges there could presumably be more), we might go a bit further to picture them as dimensions in space ('here and there') or even as points in time ('before and after'). For instance, the first apriority describes how one's experience of another person becomes coherent and meaningful somewhere after the initial perception of someone simply as part of a group and as one among many others, and then subsequently through the intimate knowledge one acquires of the other person as a completely unique individual:

> We conceive of each person – and this is a fact that has a specific effect upon our practical behavior toward that person – as being the human type that is suggested by that person's individuality. We think of the individual in terms not only of his or her singularity but also in terms of a general category. (ISF: 10; S: 44; GSG 11: 48; here and elsewhere I avoid the use of sexist pronouns whenever I think they distract from Simmel's deeper point)

Our relationships with other people are not given to us all at once. Rather, they emerge over time and are more or less skilfully assembled together through a 'practice of life which is based on those modifications and supplementations, on the transformation of given fragments into the generality of a type'. We may think of a lover or a friend, a spouse or a colleague, as having a singular personality with a distinctive face and name, but the prostitute or the Jew (to take Simmel's examples) are more likely to be perceived in terms of a general category or even a stereotype. In any case, there is no social life without individuals, and to some degree individuals can be located along what may be called the *horizontal dimension of typification*.

Since no person can be entirely unique or entirely typical while still being part of a group, a second apriority of social life describes the reality of being to some extent both included and excluded:

> The fact that in certain respects the individual is not an element of society constitutes the positive condition for the possibility that in other respects he or she is; the way in which a person is associated is determined or co-determined by the way in which he or she is not. (ISF: 13; S: 45; GSG 11: 51)

Not all elements of social life can be fully integrated into a seamless and self-sustaining whole. Some links, connectors, or relay points are needed to determine who can be admitted as full or as partial members, who can enter when and from where, what allows someone or something to remain within a group while others are forced out, and so on. Simmel notes how the criminal, the pauper, and the stranger are relatively excluded from normal social life to a greater extent than those who are part of groups that are more law-abiding, propertied, or established, such as the educated middle classes of his day. Generally speaking, the degree to which people are included in some social circles while simultaneously being excluded from others depends upon where they fall along the *diagonal dimension of membership*.

Simmel goes on to point out that these first two apriorities do not just describe realities of everyday and institutional life. They further suggest personal values of autonomy, as well as social ideals of solidarity, and therefore can be understood as patterns of involvement and detachment. For social life to be possible, individuals must also be free from one another to some extent, and yet at the same time they must somehow be bound to social life more broadly, as Simmel states with his third apriority:

> The nexus by which each social element (each individual) is interwoven with the life and activities of every other, and by which the external network of society is produced, is a causal nexus. But it is transformed into a teleological nexus as soon as it is considered from the perspective of the elements that carry and produce it – individuals. (ISF: 22; S: 51; GSG 11: 61)

This double perspective – both causal and teleological – is concerned with how social life may hold together as a whole or fall apart into its individual pieces. On the one hand, all parts of the system need to play their role or serve an objective function, but in order to do so each must also have some space and time to realize its own subjective aims, inclinations, and intentions. For example, individuals may strive to pursue their own aspirations, talents, and convictions in the vocation they choose (or that is chosen for them). On the other hand, their personal calling must also serve some specialized function in the social division of labour if it is to be sustained over time. For example, an artist, a scholar, or a genius may be committed to following his or her purpose in life or inner conviction in contrast to a bureaucrat or government official who is compelled to fulfil an external function. In general terms, everyone survives or thrives along a continuum between social control and personal agency, and thus somewhere within the *vertical dimension of commitment*.

In figure 1, I have depicted these dynamics of association and interaction in the shape of a door, partly as a way of imagining how human and non-human beings follow patterns of exit and entry and how they are subject to certain cultural technologies of opening and closing (Siegert 2015: 191–205). In a wonderful piece called 'Bridge and Door', published a year after he wrote 'How is Society Possible?', Simmel explores what might be interpreted as the metaphorical and material implications suggested by his apriorities. The examples of the door and the bridge (I return to the latter in my concluding chapter) demonstrate how, 'in the immediate as well as the symbolic sense, in the corporeal as well as the spiritual sense, we are at any moment those who separate the connected or connect the separate' (SC: 171). A closed door separates the outside world of nature from the inside world of social life, just as an open door can be an invitation for family members and guests or pets and vermin to come and go (the apriority of membership). In a modern money economy, of course, cash can make all the difference in

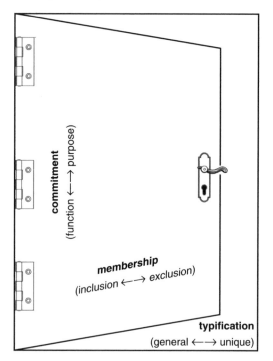

Figure 1 Between fitting in and standing out

determining who is included or excluded: 'Whoever knocks with the *taler* [or dollar] has all doors opened for him' (PM: 275). Likewise, just as the doorframe both connects and separates the space between here and there, it also marks the interval of time between where I came from (past) and where I am (present). These spatial and temporal distances therefore mark off differences between vivid perceptions of what is nearby and vague impressions of what is remote (the apriority of typification). Finally, consider the asymmetrical construction of a conventional door – how one side turns on a hinge while the other has a handle and a lock so that the door may be left open or fastened shut. This ingenious design displays in a palpable way how the material technology of hinges and locks (what Simmel will call 'objective culture') and the personal need for protection or privacy (a feature of 'subjective culture') are bound up with another yet also function independently (what I am calling the apriority of commitment).

As Simmel writes in the exhilarating final lines of this brief essay, the door marks off not only what is inside from what is outside but also a third order that is between or even beyond that threshold: 'Just as the formless limitation takes on a shape, its limitlessness finds its significance and dignity only in that which the nobility of the door illustrates: in the possibility at any moment of stepping out of this limitation into freedom' (SC: 174). Following Kant, he emphasizes that we never have a *pure impression of nature* just as we are never bound by an *immediate experience of social and historical life*. Our perceptions and knowledge of the physical, cultural, and historical worlds are always mediated and assembled in some way. At the same time, Simmel extends Kant's efforts to free the mind from objective nature by liberating thought from social constraints and historical forces as well. In this way, he frees his own thinking from the restrictions of both subjective idealism, where everything is a construction of the mind (so-called neo-Kantianism), and social evolution, where all life is reduced to mere nature (social Darwinism), two theoretical models that profoundly influenced him and many of his contemporaries (see the 'Excursus on Social Evolution', pp. 19–21).

As with the other 'geometrical sketches' I display in this book, the figure of the door offers an example and an analogy for illustrating certain key concepts that Simmel uses to open up his distinctive perspective on life. It displays an idea in the form of a figure and it is a metaphorical image that is also a material object. In the three main parts of this book, I try to deepen this understanding of the play between idea and image in Simmel's work and to show how he combines systematic thought with improvised analogies, often by implicitly using other 'master tropes' as well (Burke 1989). Part I considers the method Simmel developed in his early philosophical work on money of 'finding in each of life's details the totality of its meaning' (PM: 52) – that is, of seeing the whole in the part and perceiving the particular in the general (the trope of synecdoche). Part II focuses on Simmel's sociological account of how fragments of human experience are associated, transformed, or reduced to one another when they form a temporal series, a relationship of cause and effect, or a special link between the outer surfaces and inner depths of social life (the trope of metonymy). Part III takes up his metaphysics of modern life by examining how appearances may hide realities, how representations can distort reality, or how illusions often provide indirect pathways to the truth of cultural experience (the trope of irony). In each of these discussions, I draw loosely on the apriorities that Simmel outlines in 'How is Society Possible?', showing, for example, how money mediates between a view of people and things as general or particular (typification); how the metropolis is made up of social circles that intensify individual exclusion or inclusion (membership); and how modernity frees individuals and objects to pursue their own purposes while also binding them more tightly together within the flow and flux of life (commitment). Besides introducing readers to Simmel's ideas by discussing the works where he elaborated them, I consider how these ideas take shape through a practice of writing and a literary style that are unique to him (Green 1988; Goodstein 2002; Blumenberg 2012).

In addition to locating his thought within his own personal, historical, and intellectual contexts, my aim in this book is to follow Simmel in showing how social life is not always or entirely social and in reflecting on how life itself is never completely alive. These non-social and non-vital aspects of existence mark the limits of Simmel's ideas which he himself sometimes recognized but could not always surpass. Only rarely did he step back to offer an overview of his ideas or summarize his programme of study, and even then he could offer only a brief sketch or an amusing allegory. For example, in the closing lines of his 'Introduction' to *Philosophical Culture*, he recites the fable of an old peasant on his deathbed who tells his children there is a treasure buried in his field. After a year of digging away, they do not find any treasure, although the field yields a triple harvest. From this tale Simmel wants us to draw a lesson for his own approach to metaphysics: 'We will not find the treasure, but the world we have dug through in search of it will bring a triple harvest of the spirit, even if in reality there was no treasure at all but only the fact that this excavation is the necessary and inner determination of our minds' (SC: 36). Like the children of the old peasant, I hope that readers rummaging around in Simmel's field of the spirit will yield a triple harvest of insights into the money economy, metropolitan experience, and modern life. They may also be rewarded with a renewed sense of the value of the life of mind, and some unexpected perspectives on the worlds in which we now live.

Excursus on Social Evolution: Simmel without Spencer and Freud

Simmel's early writings up to the mid-1890s can be read in part as a response to the challenge Charles Darwin posed to the next generation of social scientists. Darwin himself seemed to consider the sociological implications of his biological studies by opening *On the Origin of Species* (1859) with a chapter not on natural selection but, rather, on the analogous case of artificial selection. His focus there is on 'variation under domestication', using the example of the selective breeding of the rock pigeon in England. By considering how humans intervene in biological processes, Darwin implies that evolution may be socially induced as well. This concern with how human culture is an agent of natural evolution can also be detected in many early theoretical works of the 1890s (including those by Tarde, Gilman, Durkheim, Veblen, Weber, and Bergson discussed in later excurses). One of the classic thinkers who demonstrates the influence of evolutionary biology on social scientists, including Simmel (Frisby 1992: 7–8, 206–7), is Herbert Spencer, whose *Principles of Sociology* was published in several volumes from 1876 to 1896. Ironically, Darwin made more extensive use of Spencer's characterization of the *Origin* as a thesis about 'the survival of the fittest' than Spencer did of Darwin's ideas on species change or natural selection. For this reason, it may be more accurate to call Darwin a 'biological Spencerian' than to characterize Spencer as a 'social Darwinist' (Francis 2007: 2; Shapin 2007: 76). In any case, Spencer explains social and natural development as an unstable and 'moving equilibrium' where species emerge by responding to flows of energy and motion in their environment. Despite the conflicting forces of militancy and industry in human history, he remains optimistic that social evolution will result in a social state where each individual works in order to live rather than lives in order to work (Spencer 1972: 165).

Simmel's doctoral dissertation takes issue with Darwin's thesis that language evolves from music, citing the example of yodelling as a form of social communication that is not simply an art form or a physiological reflex. In his first major book, *On Social Differentiation*, Simmel also rejects Spencer's tendency to naturalize society as a super-reality existing above and evolving independently of its individual parts. At the same time he generalizes and radicalizes what can be called Spencer's *principle of differentiation* as the basis for modern social science. Where Simmel treats individuals and their relationships as his beginning and end point, however, Spencer seems to hesitate before the Unknown world of singular lives that are not simply parts of some larger social organism (Du Bois 2000). And where Spencer hopes to moderate antisocial aggression through the corporate regulation of collective life, Simmel sees individualism as an indispensable way of cultivating personal authenticity. In his *Introduction to Moral Science* of 1892–3, he describes human development as a dynamic process brought about through conflict and competition rather than through the peaceful realization of social potentialities or an orderly unfolding of collective energies (Helle 2013: 58–63).

Although Simmel rejects the more reductive aspects of social evolutionism, he conceives of life as a vital process that is perpetually subject to change. Where Spencer thinks of evolution more narrowly in terms of how individual and social organisms adapt to their environments, Simmel emphasizes how biophysical processes play out on the socio-cultural plane through association ('fitting in') and differentiation ('standing out'). In this regard, he also approaches and then parts company with the young Sigmund Freud, who focuses on how social and psychological processes are 'bound to' or 'propped upon' natural and biological processes. In the *Project for a Scientific Psychology* written in 1895, Freud outlines his plan to discover the neurological foundations for the psychology of consciousness and memory. He tries to account for how the 'fraying' of nerves (*Bahnung* in German) sets the scene for the formation of a psychic economy in which desires are deferred, drives are restrained, and ideas are repeated or kept in reserve through 'an incessant and increasingly radical invocation of the principle of difference' (Derrida 1981: 84). In *The Interpretation of Dreams*, published in 1900 (the same year as Simmel's *Philosophy of Money*), Freud elaborates on this thesis by investigating how 'dream-displacement and dream-condensation' determine the force and intensity of different psychic values and energies (Freud 1976: 416).

In short, from Spencer to Freud, the social and psychological sciences were becoming progressively 'denaturalized' – that is, freed from the rules that govern the observation of the physical world. And yet both thinkers were often tempted to treat the natural order as their ultimate object of study and to adopt the methods of natural science for investigating cultural and individual life. By contrast, in the same period Simmel forged his own path towards a philosophical sociology and a sociological metaphysics of life, ultimately *without* appealing to biology as his scientific ideal or treating nature as his metaphorical model.

Part I

Philosophy of Money

In the diary Simmel kept up to the final years of his life, he reflected modestly on the incalculable influence that his work might have on later generations: 'I know that I shall die without spiritual heirs (and this is good). The estate I leave is like cash distributed among many heirs, each of whom puts his share to use in some trade that is compatible with his or her nature but which can no longer be recognized as coming from that estate' (VL: 160; GSG 20: 261). His choice of metaphors here is certainly not accidental, since the *Philosophy of Money* is among the best known of his works. But even though the book is often referred to as his masterpiece it is also among the least read and sparsely cited of his writings. Its hundreds of dense pages can be difficult to read, although it is worth the effort. Fortunately, Simmel was mistaken in believing that he would leave no appreciable intellectual legacy or that later thinkers would neglect to draw upon his many rich ideas. As he anticipated, a few influential readers of his great book would take up and develop his ideas according to their own interests, sometimes without naming him as their source. When he wrote up a balance sheet of his most significant contributions in the last year of his life, he took pride in having made 'an entirely novel first attempt to represent the entire psychic development of human culture through a single symbol' (GSG 24: 72). But at the same time he expressed regret that his book on money had not become better known or been very fruitful in generating further studies.

In the *Philosophy of Money* Simmel expands on themes from his university lectures and early essays on ethics, logic, art, and socialism and introduces some of the key ideas that accompanied him in his later writings on sociology, philosophy, and aesthetics. His arguments in this book convey certain messages to his contemporaries and successors in his own distinctive way – about the inevitability of *change*; the *interpretation* of reality; the nature of *interaction*; the modern character of *alienation*, and so on (Helle 2013). Looking back on his earlier writings, he remarked that he had lost interest in most of them since it seemed they could have been written by anyone, and so only the *Philosophy of Money* 'is really *my* book' (PM: xlvii). Perhaps he meant that for the first time he had fully developed his own original arguments independently of his teachers, predecessors, and contemporaries. Or maybe he was suggesting that this book expresses his personal reflections on a worldview that was only now becoming clear to him or that he had only recently come to embrace. Unlike the English translation of the book's title, Simmel's original German humbly avoids putting either a definite or an indefinite article before '*Philosophie*', as if to mark his hesitation over what it means to reflect on money as a symbol of the whole of human culture. It is as if money is not just an object of everyday experience and intellectual reflection but also a thing with certain 'philosophical' properties of analysis and synthesis of its own.

There is no doubt that money became an object of both practical concern and theoretical contemplation for Simmel in the decade leading up to the appearance of the first edition of the *Philosophy of Money* in 1900 (a second revised edition was issued in 1907). His position at Berlin University remained precarious until the year of its publication, when he was finally promoted from unsalaried lecturer to extraordinary professor, although the student fees he earned from his increasingly popular lectures were still considerable. As his son Hans later recalled, the inheritance from his legal guardian's fortune was worth almost a million Marks, and so at least for a while 'there were no longer any monetary worries for the Simmels' (H. Simmel 1958: 249). On the whole, Simmel seems to have enjoyed relative economic independence in the years he was working on his book on money. Although he would never be considered rich by the standards of Berlin's elite, the booming economic conditions of the day certainly shaped his aesthetic tastes and intellectual interests. For the most part, Simmel could lead the life of the mind and inhabit a world of creative thought without having to concern himself too much with financial pressures.

To a significant degree, Simmel's writings during this period converge on the general problem of how interactions (*Wechselwirkungen*) – in the broad sense of reciprocal causes and effects – unfold in time and space, and in particular how these relationships can be illustrated in terms of the cultural and psychological processes of social and monetary exchange (*Tausch*). Interestingly, the German word *Wechsel* (in the compound word *Wechsel-wirkung*) can mean change in the general sense of transformation, but it can also refer both to the exchange of goods and to change in contrast to paper money or a promissory note. With the emergence of finance and consumer culture in the industrial cities of nineteenth-century Europe, the money economy presented Simmel with an intellectual and cultural dilemma concerning how the world was changing. Among the questions he considers are whether the artistic perception of beauty, the scientific discovery of truth, and the ethical pursuit of justice can survive in a world that seems to cherish money, economic success, and industrial productivity above all other values. In the 'Preface' to the *Philosophy of Money*, Simmel emphasizes that his aim is not to contribute to economic theory or to follow the methods of any particular empirical science, including economics. Rather, his reflections on money are more ambitiously intended to offer a philosophical understanding of life as a whole: 'The unity of these investigations does not lie … in an assertion about a particular content of knowledge and its gradually accumulating proofs but rather in the possibility – which must be demonstrated – of *finding in each of life's details the totality of its meaning*' (PM: 55, emphasis added). Instead of formulating hypotheses that can be tested with observations and verified with empirical evidence, he wants to present a comprehensive view of the whole of reality by examining the meaning and significance of certain aspects of it. Following the general sense of Simmel's first apriority (discussed above), in the following chapters I examine his distinctive approach to how *typical interactions* play out in social and material relationships in the money economy and how interactions take shape through particular life experiences (*Erlebnisse*) and unique perspectives on the whole of existence.

In order to make this massive work more accessible and to show its connection with Simmel's other writings from this period of his career, I highlight a few shorter essays that he published in advance of the first edition of 1900 (see the list in PM: 531). I also expand on the comments he makes about trade exhibitions, sex work and mental work, and the psychology of the miser and the spendthrift. In each chapter I insert a short excursus that shows how Simmel's ideas relate to some important contemporaries, especially Durkheim and Tarde, Weber and Sombart, and two of his most influential predecessors, Marx and Engels. My aim is to convey a sense of the whole of Simmel's most systematic and perfect work – his masterpiece – by puzzling through some of its most interesting parts. In some ways, this well-structured book on the money economy anticipates and even exceeds his later studies in the philosophy of culture, the sociology of the metropolis, and the metaphysics of life.

2

The Price of Freedom

A character in a play by Oscar Wilde jokes that a cynic is a person who 'knows the price of everything and the value of nothing' (Wilde 1985: 92). Georg Simmel, a contemporary of Wilde, goes even further by characterizing cynicism as one of the most prevalent features of contemporary culture. He notes that nowadays it seems that the classic values of honour and conviction, talent and virtue, beauty and the salvation of the soul, can all be exchanged for money. Even the supreme ideals of modern life such as the freedom of the individual may be reduced to the common denominator of their market price and bought and sold for cold cash on the market. Echoing earlier literary writers and political critics of the day, Simmel calls stock exchanges 'the nurseries of cynicism' since they treat even the most time-honoured ideals with derision and denigrate every virtue with ridicule (PM: 257; Kemple 1995: 164–70). The stock market provides the 'geometric focal point of all these changes in valuation' that characterize today's world, with its 'sanguine-choleric oscillations between optimism and pessimism' (PM: 512). Quoting the early sixteenth-century poet and playwright Hans Sachs, Simmel suggests that markets have now replaced churches as the dominant cultural institution in modern society: 'money is the secular God of the World [*Gelt ist auff erden der irdisch got*]' (PM: 237–8; GSG 6: 307).

This chapter considers Simmel's sobering account of how money assigns numerical values to qualitative differences and also how relationships among people and between things are calculated and quantified in terms of their price or value in exchange. I describe the symmetrical outline of the *Philosophy of Money*, noting how his argument as a whole can be glimpsed in each of its parts. Against the panorama of this larger picture, I then focus on some interesting details from passages in chapters 1 and 4 from the book's two main parts and show their place within Simmel's overall philosophical framework. To illustrate the 'problem of numbers' that concerns him throughout the *Philosophy of Money*, I discuss related points he makes in his book *Sociology* about the quantitative determination of both small groups and complex social settings such as markets and crowds. Simmel's approach to 'who and what counts' in a money economy offers an interesting contrast to the views of his contemporaries Emile Durkheim and Gabriel Tarde on how numbers are used in social statistics generated by science and the state, as I note in a digression. These general considerations also provide a backdrop for Simmel's account of how the money economy enhances individual freedom by increasing social interdependencies, as he argues in a lecture he gave on 'Money in Modern Culture' and in a short newspaper article, 'On the Berlin Trade Exhibition'. I conclude by noting how Simmel treats the theme of the 'price of freedom' in a humorous way by suggesting that money alone doesn't make us happy.

How Values Emerge from Exchange

Although the opening paragraphs of the first chapter, on 'Value and Money', can be forbidding even for a well-trained reader, a few simple points can be picked out of Simmel's long sentences and shown to illuminate his larger perspective. He himself found this chapter the most troublesome, at one point writing to a colleague that he had reached a 'dead end', and he later revised these pages extensively for the second edition in 1907 (see Frisby in PM: 524). He begins by observing that, since we are not always satisfied with the equal and uniform place that things seem to occupy under 'the law of nature', we arrange them in a hierarchy according to 'the law of value'. In other words, *natural things* and *cultural values* form two separate series that may overlap but cannot really coincide: 'The value of objects, thoughts, and events can never be inferred from their mere natural existence and content, and their ranking according to value diverges widely from their natural order' (PM: 56). Nevertheless, the natural impulses that give rise to economic transactions – such as how much we want something, whether someone is greedy or extravagant, and our sense of whether a resource is useful or scarce – may be 'released' from their physiological and psychological basis in order to circulate as monetary and cultural values. Likewise, physical work can be broken down into the bodily energy and material products needed to perform it in order to be submitted to the logic of markets – that is, bought for a price, sold for wages, and exploited for profit. In a capitalist money economy, all things, as well as actions, events, and ideas, can potentially be converted into the value they have in exchange and integrated into the cash nexus. Although 'valuation' is not a part of the natural world, Simmel points out, it is 'rather the whole world viewed from a particular vantage point' (PM: 57). As also he notes repeatedly throughout the book, the cultural process by which things are valued through exchange may itself appear paradoxically as a natural fact that cannot be altered. In short, natural realities and cultural values are like two different ways of seeing the world: they may be temporarily coordinated but often come apart 'as if we had an imperfect visual faculty' (PM: 59).

These arguments already offer an initial glimpse into Simmel's plan for the book as a whole. The value that things take on when they are exchanged for money can be viewed from a strictly economic perspective, in terms of how much they cost, for example, or they can be treated more broadly as a philosophical problem about human values and desires. Simmel alludes to this more comprehensive view in his 'Preface', where he uses the topographical metaphor of an 'upper' and a 'lower boundary' beyond which the topic of money can be seen to take on a philosophical character (PM: 51–4). Both above and below the specialized inquiries of economics, philosophy strives to comprehend the totality of life, the infinite exchanges and interactions that take place between everything in existence, and the general culture and individual vitality of human beings. Simmel adds that, on 'either side' of the science of economics, he wants to analyse the particular conditions and causes that give rise to money exchanges and to arrive at a synthetic understanding of the consequences and effects of the money economy on social relations between people and their inner feelings. In any case, he is not primarily concerned with examining the historical preconditions of the modern money economy – the rise of new markets, the emergence of the industrial division of labour, the concentration of people in urban centres, the coinage of currency by the state, and so on. Nor is he mainly interested in developing a psychology of money calculations or a sociology of relations between producers and consumers.

A glance at the table of contents of Simmel's book, as displayed in figure 2, draws our attention to the focal points of this philosophical perspective. Two symmetrical parts are each made up of three chapters (and each chapter is itself divided into three parts): a first 'analytical part' (the three panels on the left) zooms in on picking apart the basic functions, materials, and means by which money is exchanged, and a second 'synthetic part' (on the right side) is concerned with piecing together the value and significance of money for the freedom, personal worth, and lifestyle of individuals. (This arrangement also guides my own approach in this chapter, where I focus on chapters 1 and 4, and in the following two chapters, where I discuss chapters 2 and 5 and then 3 and 6, respectively.) As Simmel describes his outline of the book: 'The one part seeks to make the essence of money intelligible from *the conditions and connections of life in general*; conversely, the other part seeks to make the

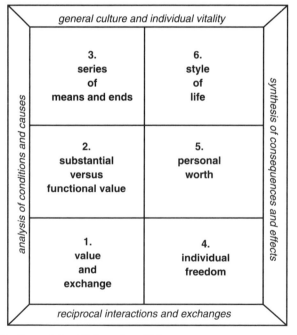

Figure 2 Outline of the *Philosophy of Money*

essence and organization of the latter intelligible from *the effectiveness of money'* (PM: 52, emphasis added). This philosophical framework is much like a picture frame around a work of art, which 'closes itself off against everything external to itself as a world of its own' (1994b: 11). In a similar way, Simmel's philosophical work on money tends to close itself off from considering the outer world of actual commercial transactions and economic facts, adopting a non-economic standpoint on values and relationships that would be viewed quite differently from a strictly economic, empirical, or pragmatic perspective (PM: 54).

Simmel's rather controversial equation between value and price in chapter 1 of the *Philosophy of Money* offers a useful illustration of this philosophical approach. Where a strictly political economic analysis (such as Karl Marx's) or a broadly social-cultural perspective (such as Oscar Wilde's) would emphasize how value and price diverge, Simmel's philosophical viewpoint sees them as essentially the same. From this perspective, price is simply a numerical expression of what it would take to acquire something that is *desirable* and therefore valuable or worthy of purchasing. In other words, the price of something is the calculable *sacrifice* required to engage in an exchange in order to acquire something deemed valuable on the market. In giving something up and handing something over for money, the process of exchange that takes place through these activities has a distinct reality of its own (*sui generis*): 'Exchange is not the mere addition of two processes of giving and receiving, but *a new third phenomenon*, in which each of the two processes is simultaneously cause and effect' (PM: 88, emphasis added). Simply put, things become valued and defined by their price *within and as a consequence of* exchange and as a result of a process of give and take. Goods and services are deemed useful or wasteful, abundant or scarce, and so on, only through exchange. Their price is just another way of saying that they need to be measured in order to *function* as values in exchange.

'Subjective valuation' is therefore a way of looking at objects and distinguishing or ranking them according to whether they are desirable or useful, beautiful or ugly, good or bad, and so on. This analytical distinction between the *valuing subject* and the *object valued* is key to what Simmel means by doing a *philosophy* rather than the psychology, sociology, or economics of money. Enjoying a delicious meal may be psychologically pleasurable, socially demanding, or economically costly, for example, but these facts alone do not convey the philosophical dimension of the *value* of the meal. Rather, value emerges 'from the *separation* between the subject and the content of enjoyment as an object that stands *opposed* to the subject as something desired and only to be attained by the conquest of distance, obstacles, and difficulties' (PM: 63–4, emphasis added). Again, to put this more simply, valuation is the ability to notice distances, to feel deprivations, or to sense deficiencies *and thereby* to strive to overcome these obstacles. Objects become valuable when they resist or elicit subjective desire, or, in other words, when they are 'thrown toward or in front of' us but are not yet enjoyed. (Note that *jacere*/throw and *ob*/towards in Latin make up the word 'ob-ject'.) This concept of value leads Simmel to make a seemingly paradoxical formulation: 'Objects are not difficult to acquire because they are valuable, but we call those objects valuable that *resist our desire* to acquire them' (PM: 64, emphasis added). Although we often take for granted that valuable things are by definition difficult to acquire, in fact they become valuable in large part because they are hard to get.

Value expresses a relationship of desire not just between subjects and objects ('I want something') but also between subjects ('he wants me', or 'she and I want the same thing') and between objects themselves ('that thing is worth wanting more than that one'). Money is a way of *measuring* these differences, difficulties, and distances, as well as a *means* of overcoming them (Dodd 2014: 28–9). Even though Simmel's prose does not become any easier to read at this point, his examples from the everyday world of buyers and sellers, producers and consumers, and his general ideas on 'exchange as a form of life' are illuminating (PM: 79–92; also in ISF: 43–69). He argues that both objective measurement ('how much?') and subjective valuations ('definitely worth it!') emerge from and are presupposed by exchange ('let's make a deal'). Exchange is therefore partially detached from 'the subjective-personal substructure' of feelings and desires, while objects become independently valid for subjects only through exchange. In effect, 'every interaction has to be regarded as an exchange: every conversation, every affection (even if it is rejected), every game, every glance at another person' (ISF: 43–4; PM: 78). Interaction (*Wechselwirkung*) is therefore the broader concept, since it includes all kinds of relationships between objects and subjects, while exchange (*Tausch*) applies more specifically to relationships that are primarily social and human. Exchange sets the pace of social life and establishes how the order of things is understood by a human group, along with their particular value and significance for individual members: 'The same synthetic process of mind that from the mere juxtaposition of things creates a with-another and for-another ... has through the category of exchange seized that naturally given rhythm of our existence and organized its elements into a meaningful nexus' (ISF: 44; PM: 80). In short, the properties of nature and culture are made to merge in the mind and to intersect in reality through the process of exchange.

Exchange is thus the core concept that Simmel recovers from this abstract discussion of value and then illustrates with concrete examples from the practical world of money. At the same time, he wants to argue more broadly that a radically new *relativistic worldview* is emerging from the money economy, one that sees reality more in terms of movement and interconnected relationships than as a set of stable substances and fixed entities. If we imagine how this longer view might look through the frame of the *Philosophy of Money*, we can picture a landscape where everything has meaning in relation to everything else and absolute realities recede endlessly into the horizon: 'The fact that what we perceive as absolute is nevertheless relative can only be resolved by admitting that the absolute signifies a road stretching into infinity whose direction is still marked out no matter how great the distance we cover' (PM: 111–12). Monetary values are simply the most obvious manifestation of this relativistic – or rather *relational* – worldview, where everything can be exchanged for and related to everything else (Cantó-Milà 2005; Pyyhtinen 2018: 16–26). From this perspective, even the classic values of truth, beauty, and justice are valid not in spite of being relative but precisely because they are relative. Money is the purest expression and symbol of a world characterized by the paradox of eternal movement and fluctuating permanence.

Figure 2 takes the shape of a window in order to highlight Simmel's way of locating his position 'outside' the concerns of economics and yet 'inside' a set of philosophical concerns. In the piece 'Bridge and Door' (discussed in the previous chapter) he notes that the window is like the door in connecting the inside world with the outside world. But the window is more one-sided and transparent, since it is designed mainly for looking out onto the world rather than for moving back and forth between inside and outside. Unlike the door, the window frame directs a path for the eye alone rather than for the whole body (SC: 173). By extension, we could say that Simmel's *Philosophy of Money* constructs a kind of philosophical window for looking out onto this emerging modern world. The book treats money as the primary symbol and quintessential example of this new 'world picture' characterized by 'indifference', 'infinite transformation', and a 'relativistic interpretation of being' (PM: 54). Viewed through this philosophical framework, the surface phenomena of monetary exchanges – where anything and everything may be bought and sold – are understood to have their sources in the deepest currents of life. Even the superficial appearances of the money economy reflect some ultimate value and deeper significance (PM: 52). In a sense, by 'following the money' as it comes into contact and interacts with multiple people and things, Simmel leads us into complex networks, webs, and labyrinths of relationships (Dodd 2014: 29; Pyyhtinen 2018: 76–7).

Before considering how the analytical points in chapter 1 about subjective desire and objective value are understood in social and personal terms in chapter 4 of the *Philosophy of Money*, it is worth reflecting for a moment on how money functions as the medium and measure of exchange. As Simmel remarks later, 'the democratic leveling where everyone counts as one and no one counts as more than one' is a result of 'this measuring, weighing and calculating exactness of modern times' (PM: 444). A money economy is obviously impossible without procedures for financial accounting in industry and statistical calculations by the state. In some ways, the dominant tendency of a modern society is to transform social and personal qualities into monetary and mathematical quantities. In his discussion of 'The Quantitative Determination of the Group' in the second chapter of *Sociology* (examined in more detail in Part II), Simmel also considers the opposite tendency, namely, the ways in which social quantities give rise to qualitative effects. In particular, he notes how the numerical size of a group can determine how interactions take place and how exchanges play out (S: 53–60). The common saying 'two's company, but three's a crowd' suggests that there is a significant difference between the experience of a solitary individual and an intimate couple, or between an independent group and two groups subjected to a third party, who may have an interest in judging them impartially or in dividing or uniting them (Pyyhtinen 2009). Whether there are 'a few' or 'many' people determines how groups may fuse into masses or fission into their atomistic elements, and whether there are 'some' or 'several' things can shape either how they relate to each other and change through addition and subtraction or how they organize themselves by multiplication and division (Naegele 1958: 581). In other words, *the problem of numbers is an intrinsic property of social groups* and not simply the invention of an outside observer. Rather than making a cynical point about how people and things are reduced to the numerical values of prices and variables, Simmel's 'social arithmetic' of individuals (monads), pairs (dyads), and groups of three (triads) expresses the deep structure of all interactions and exchange relationships (see the 'Excursus on Social Quantities', pp. 39–42).

Why Individual Freedom Emerges from Interdependence

Simmel's rather abstract discussion of the concepts of value and exchange in chapter 1 of the *Philosophy of Money* is illustrated with some concrete examples in chapter 4, which opens the 'synthetic part'. Here he takes up a classic theme discussed by many thinkers before him who treat the modern money economy as the great liberator of people, resources, and energies. Where earlier writers from Thomas Hobbes to Karl Marx view the rise of a market society as a steady march towards civil war or personal liberty, or as a class struggle leading to economic exploitation or collective emancipation, Simmel advances his own novel thesis (which, incidentally, resembles Durkheim's argument about the modern division of labour). Rather than describing recent history as progressing from coercion to liberation, he argues that *the increase in social ties* facilitated by monetary exchanges intensifies *the possibilities for individual freedom*: 'the money economy makes possible ... a specific kind of mutual dependence which, at the same time, affords room for a maximum of liberty' (PM: 295). It is not simply the case that wage work 'liberates' the worker from the despotism of traditional authorities or from powerful owners of the means of production; or that private owners can purchase or sell property and exchange products as they wish; or that consumers can choose freely between goods on the market. More importantly, Simmel argues, money creates conditions for discovering and cultivating the potential of the individual. Money makes people free by enhancing their essential human capacity to exchange goods and services, and in doing so they objectify themselves and one another. By creating more subjective ties and objective bonds between groups of people, trade and commerce actually enhance rather than inhibit the ability of individuals to become more equal, more free, and more themselves. In short, the price of freedom is the interdependence created by the money economy.

Imagine a lone settler in the German forests or a homesteader on the American frontier who mostly relies only on her- or himself for

survival (PM: 301). He or she is at most 'non-dependent' but otherwise bound to the daily demands and seasonal rhythms of nature.
The inhabitant of a modern metropolis, by contrast, must rely on
countless workers and operators, many of whom are unseen or
unknown, and who typically relate to one another in a distant and
objective way that is ultimately mediated by money: 'the individual
is more and more dependent on the achievements of people, but
less dependent on the personalities that lie behind them', Simmel
argues, introducing a theme that will become central to his sociology of cities (PM: 298–304). The personal touch that waiters, sales-
people, and bank tellers may extend to their customers, whether
voluntarily or as required by their professional training, is inciden-
tal to the paid services they provide and secondary to any bonus,
satisfaction, or tip they might acquire from doing so. For city dwellers, the apparently flexible and divisible character of the many roles
that individuals can assume in a money economy is made possible
by the objectivity and indifference that characterizes their daily
interactions with one another: 'The personality as a mere holder of
a function or position is just as irrelevant as that of a guest in a hotel
room' (PM: 297). As this example shows, money divides particular
tasks from the total personality while commercial transactions
widen the separation between households and businesses. Money
standardizes the anonymity of everyone in a way that intensifies
the freedom of anyone.

From Simmel's perspective as a philosophical sociologist of the
social interactions and cultural competences of modern life, the
money economy makes people more interdependent, more equal,
and more the same while at the same time creating more room for
people to express themselves freely and creatively. In a lecture on
'Money in Modern Culture' that he gave in 1896 in Vienna to a
gathering of economists, he outlines a clear version of his thesis that
the money economy paradoxically expands social equality while
fostering individual liberty:

> The streams of modern culture rush in two seemingly opposing
> directions: on the one hand, *towards leveling, equalization, the produc-*
> *tion of more and more comprehensive social circles* through the connection
> of the remotest things under equal conditions; on the other hand,
> *towards the autonomy of the most individual matters, the independence of*
> *the person, the autonomy of its development.* Both tendencies are sup-
> ported by the money economy, which makes possible, first, a com-
> pletely general interest and a means of connection and communication
> which is equally effective everywhere. Second, it permits the most

pronounced reserve, individualization and freedom for the personality. (SC: 247, emphasis added; also GSG 24: 634–5)

This contradictory double movement within modern culture leads to both a general flattening of the social terrain and a heightening of personal distinctions to an unprecedented degree. The enlargement of groups and the increase of populations – in crowds, public spaces, workplaces, cities, and nations – enhance individual differences just as the expansion of the money economy increases social interdependencies while creating space for the cultivation of a more complex inner life: 'money brings about the differentiation of elements in society just as much as in the individual' (PM: 352). In a sense, money completes in the economic sphere what the increase in population facilitates in the social sphere, namely the development of individuality. As people become more connected they are also encouraged to pursue their own desires in their own way, not by avoiding others but by coordinating their interests and activities.

Simmel's point here is vividly described in a short article also published in 1896, 'The Berlin Trade Exhibition'. Over the course of an eight-week exhibition in his home city, people could view a bewildering variety of the latest consumer goods and manufactured products (Frisby 2001: 101–7). This remarkable event impressed Simmel with a sense of how Berlin had been transformed from a metropolis (*Großstadt*) into a model world city (*Weltstadt*) that 'can represent itself as a copy and a sample of the manufacturing forces of a world culture' (SC: 257). By placing commerce before industry and consumption ahead of production, the exhibition conveys something distinctive about the modern spirit. The commodities on display mirror relationships between individuals in consumer culture, each competing with the others in an attempt to depreciate their value: 'on the one side, the individual is only the element of the whole, only a member of the higher unity; on the other, the individual claims to be a whole and a unity' (SC: 257–8). Here Simmel grasps a significant aspect of the early rise of commercial advertising and promotional culture, in particular how 'the shop-window quality of things' generates new wants and creates new values: 'The production of goods under the regime of free competition and the normal predominance of supply over demand leads to goods having to show a tempting exterior as well as utility' (SC: 257). By representing commodities and displaying the culture of things in so spectacular a fashion, the Berlin trade exhibition accentuates both the pragmatic core and the seductive surface of a money economy where almost anything can be bought, sold, and possessed but also appreciated from a distance and held out as a temptation.

In the *Philosophy of Money* Simmel elaborates on some of the wider implications of how money transactions become the agent of both individual freedom and social interdependence. In the regular course of human life, 'having' and 'being' mutually reinforce each other so that 'there is a chain from being to having and from having back to being' (PM: 308). However, the modern money economy dissolves this dependency between the object owned and the person of the possessor, who is 'confronted with an infinite number of objects the enjoyment of which is equally guaranteed by public order' (PM: 310). On the one hand, the possession of money places demands and exerts effects on the individual, so that possessions can sometimes feel like a shackle (PM: 311). On the other hand, money enhances the autonomy of the object that makes demands on the individual while also increasing the independence of the person who makes demands on the object. Subject and object are now afforded an expanded domain for action and expression, and both can go on to develop 'according to their own laws of life' (PM: 314). While the object expresses itself through the medium of money, for the owner, 'freedom is the articulation of self in the medium of things' (PM: 322). Acquiring property creates the conditions that release certain emotions and impulses of the soul and that allow the self to be extended into external objects. Just as the painter's passions flow into the brush or the violinist's into the bow, 'objects must enter into the Ego, and the Ego enters into objects' (PM: 333).

Simmel began his discussion of individual freedom in the money economy by noting in general terms that 'the development of each human fate can be represented as an uninterrupted alternation between bondage and release, obligation and freedom' (PM: 283). He does not assume that money is simply an instrument of emancipation, but notes that financial transactions introduce a new and distinct variation into these alternating patterns. From 1897 to 1907, the decade when he was writing and later revising his *Philosophy of Money*, he takes up many of the themes discussed in that book in a series of short pieces published in the journal *Jugend*, which featured the unconventional work of writers, graphic artists, musicians, and ambitious cultural leaders associated with the *art nouveau* or *Jugenstil* movement who hoped to transform the world into a 'total work of art' (*Gesamtkunstwerk*) (Rammstedt 1991). Most of Simmel's pieces were published anonymously or under a pseudonym and depart from the conventional genres of the philosophical monograph and the scholarly essay that make up the rest of his work, including playful short stories, poems, satirical fairy tales, fables, aphorisms, and a brief series of epigrammatic sketches he called 'Snapshots under the Aspect of Eternity' ('Momentbilder *sub specie aeternitatis*') (2012: 262–78). One of these snapshots, 'Money Alone Doesn't Bring Happiness', offers a humorous take on some of the issues I have been discussing. An unnamed narrator reports on overhearing a snippet of after-dinner conversation in which one group argues that money is a means of achieving the greatest cultural pleasures, both social and solitary, while another points out that money enslaves us by entangling us in things that endanger our sanity, salvation, and happiness. A clever and earnest man interrupts them with a profound declaration that seems to reconcile the two positions: 'Money alone doesn't bring happiness; you also have to have it!' (2012: 273). From this curious remark our narrator concludes that 'the eternal aspect of things' lies 'beyond any question of having or not having'. Sensuous things such as a delicious meal or a fine wine are destroyed when we enjoy them, but intellectual things such as a landscape painting bring aesthetic pleasure even to those who do not own them. There is thus a lesson here about the essentially relative character of values, if not also about aristocratic versus plebeian ways of viewing the world: someone might have something without thereby being happy, but someone may be happy without necessarily having something.

Excursus on Social Quantities: Simmel before Durkheim and Tarde

Simmel did not conduct empirical research in any sustained way or draw systematically from the emerging statistical studies of his day. His doctoral dissertation, an ethnological and psychological study of the history and culture of yodelling in the Swiss Alps, was designed to include a fifteen-question survey but was rejected by the members of his examining committee, who instead asked him to submit his previous prize-winning essay on Immanuel Kant's theory of simple substances and singularities (monadology). Nevertheless, he later developed an approach to the underlying quantitative aspects of social life that in many ways offers an important critical perspective on the role of statistics and empirical research in the social sciences. As he points out in the *Philosophy of Money*, social standardization in the form of weights and measures is 'the first step towards that objectivity in the free exchange of property between individuals which is the essence of exchange' (PM: 97; ISF: 67–8). It is also an important basis for the rationalization and calculability of modern life more generally. In *Sociology*, Simmel notes that standardized financial and demographic statistics compiled by states, companies, and scholars cannot grasp 'chronically lonely existences' (S: 79), although they may reveal significant patterns that characterize 'the quantitative determination of groups'. Although he sidesteps the problem of rigorously distinguishing primary conditions from secondary consequences and avoids assigning numerical values to independent and dependent variables, he analyses how interactions – *Wechselwirkungen* in the broad sense of reciprocal causes and effects – are determined by quantifiable characteristics (Lichtblau 1991).

Statistical and empirical questions were a major concern of many of Simmel's contemporaries, such as Emile Durkheim (1858–1917) and Gabriel Tarde (1843–1904), with whose work Simmel was well acquainted in his early career. Durkheim published translations of Simmel's work in the journal *Année Sociologique* soon after it was founded in 1895 and wrote a critical review of the *Philosophy of Money* in 1901. He considered the first analytical part of the book 'by far the clearer', although the account of the facts is 'unfortunately imprecise and unwarranted' (quoted in PM: xlviii–ix). In particular, he criticizes Simmel for not distinguishing between how metallic versus paper currencies are regulated, and thus for not adequately accounting for the moral and intellectual influence of money on individuals and groups. The book as a whole is 'interesting and in places suggestive' though 'laborious', and its philosophical questions 'endlessly overflow the framework' of economic sociology. Simmel's earlier study of social differentiation in many ways anticipated Durkheim's book on the specialization of functions in *The Division of Social Labour* (1893). Nevertheless, Durkheim eventually rejected Simmel's style of 'bastard speculation' and accused him of spinning out 'loose metaphors' and 'mere variations on social life' without offering any logical solutions or empirical explanations (see Goodstein 2017: 71–8). Durkheim's *Suicide*, for instance, published in 1895, takes a strictly scientific approach to the study of social life by displaying statistical tables that draw clear analytical distinctions between, on the one hand, the independent variables of social forces affecting suicide, including religion, occupation, education, and marital status, and, on the other, the dependent variables that are correlated with patterns of suicide, such as climate, mental illness, and race. His concern is less with how relationships between people and things drive or inhibit individuals to kill themselves than with aggregate factors that affect the rates and ratios of incidents of suicide. In the end, Durkheim interprets statistical data as indicators of the superindividual reality of 'society' as it emerges from the 'reciprocal and radiating influence' of social interactions (Durkheim [1895] 1951: 120–2).

More amenable to Simmel's expansive conception of sociology are the writings of Durkheim's older rival Gabriel Tarde, who managed the Bureau of Statistics from which Durkheim drew much of his data. Simmel reviewed Tarde's *The Laws of Imitation* the year it was published in 1888 (GSG 1: 248–50), expressing his appreciation for the way it examines· individual actions and infinitesimal interactions, beliefs, and desires by tracing a variety of 'inventions and the imitative editions of inventions' (Tarde 1969: 211). Tarde analyses a large corpus of social statistics in order to follow the curve of imitations within various groups and then contrasts these patterns with other statistically generated curves. This data is plotted on graphs that display 'mountainous' patterns such as the rapid rise, unstable plateau, and gradual decline of complex phenomena across the social 'terrain'. Simmel might also have found Tarde's later work, 'Monadology and Sociology', appealing for the way it places all reality under the sociological microscope by arguing that *every thing is a society*, and every phenomenon is a social fact' (Tarde 2016: 43). For Tarde as for Simmel, a group can potentially assemble all kinds of beings, while human as well as non-human or organic as well as inorganic elements can make up a 'society', broadly speaking. For each thinker, there is no reality apart from the infinitely minuscule parts that compose it and no unity apart from their myriad differences from one another: 'To exist is to differ; difference is truly in a certain sense the substantial side of things, that which is both most unique to each of them and most common to all' (Tarde 2016: 50). Both adhere to the principle that social quantities must be understood in terms not just of their volume and density but also of their *intensity and differences*.

In certain respects the conflicts between Simmel and his doctoral examining committee, and the dispute between Durkheim and Tarde concerning the validity of social statistics and the numerical character of social life, mirror later debates over the merits of quantitative versus qualitative methods in the social sciences. Like many social scientists today, Durkheim criticizes his older colleagues for lacking a scientifically rigorous means for measuring social reality and for confusing the instrument with the object being measured. Simmel and Tarde are more interested than Durkheim in what can be called the 'measured measurement' – that is, in how an actual state of affairs is determined by its numerical size or quantitative expansion. In contrast to Simmel, however, both Durkheim and Tarde are concerned with the 'measuring measurement' – that is, with how statistical instruments, criteria, and formats can calculate, assess, model, and display patterns of social life in terms of absolute numbers and relative proportions (Latour and Lépinay 2009: 15; Bayatrizi and Kemple 2012). In a significant way, Simmel's point about how numerical values and calculable quantities constitute social life can be understood as a logical presupposition that comes *before* any statistical representation of social reality.

3

Functional Values and Personal Worth

In the previous chapter I noted that cynicism is one prevalent attitude fostered by the money economy. In an essay on 'Socialism and Pessimism' published in 1900, the same year as the first edition of the *Philosophy of Money*, Simmel discusses two other responses to modern capitalism. He argues that socialism and pessimism are each concerned both with the problem of balancing suffering and enjoyment and with finding a 'just proportion' or 'equitable distribution' between happiness and misery. A pessimistic outlook assumes that the value of life increases with the happiness of the individual but tends to see the worst side of things and ultimately loses hope in the future. Pessimism also places a premium on cultivating conscious feelings and emotional awareness: 'In a sense we don't just want to be happy but also to know that we are' (GSG 5: 555). A socialistic worldview, by contrast, assumes that the value of human life depends upon the distribution of goods and looks with hope to a future in which resources are communally controlled and consciously managed (GSG 5: 554). Socialism embraces the highest and lowest human faculties in a contradictory way, as Simmel notes at the end of his discussion of individual freedom in the *Philosophy of Money*: 'on the one hand, socialism is the final developmental product of the rationalistic money economy, and on the other it is the embodiment of the most basic instincts and emotions' (PM: 348). In short, pessimism and socialism represent opposing responses to the modern struggle for social equality and the pursuit of individual distinction in a capitalist society (Leck 2000: 73–4). While pessimism envisions the creation of a spiritual aristocracy that would value individuality above all else, socialism sees intellectual work as a means of achieving social equality for all. Despite their differences, each worldview is both impelled and imperilled by the money economy.

This chapter presents Simmel's insights into how the money economy makes a 'claim upon society' at large while also providing a measure of personal worth. As pessimists and socialists each acknowledge in their different ways, modern individuals are distinguished from one another by their monetary value and social worth but are also thrown into debt and unequal structures of wealth and power. Simmel argues that in modern societies monetary currencies are increasingly unmoored from their material basis as relations between people become more abstract and efficient. The decreasing use of metal coins as a form of currency, for example, shows how the social and symbolic functions of money can be fulfilled by a variety of materials. Simmel's somewhat technical discussion of how money serves as a universal medium of exchange in chapter 2 of the *Philosophy of Money* can be illustrated with the examples of prostitution and intellectual work examined in chapter 5 of that book. In each case, certain intimate or unique aspects of a person – the body and the brain – are defined in terms of their monetary equivalents and exchanged for cold cash. In contrast to his argument about individual freedom, here he imagines the flip side of the coin, so to speak: money also subjugates the individual (a theme he takes up in chapter 3 of *Sociology* as well). As I note in an excursus, Simmel's ideas on the subjective meaning of economic transactions and social domination had a profound influence on his friend Max Weber's ideas on legitimate authority, power, class, and status; and their colleague Werner Sombart held similar views on the cultural values of the bourgeoisie in particular and on the spirit of capitalism more generally. Finally, I consider how Simmel's approach to power and wealth sheds light on the financialization of everyday life in ways that have become even more evident in the century since he wrote about the dematerialization and personalization of money transactions.

Money as a Claim on Society

It can be overwhelming to think of the many materials that have served as money in different societies throughout history – from shells, grain, and stones to copper, silver, and gold; and from cattle, salt, slaves, tobacco, and hides to bills of exchange, treasury bonds, personal cheques, and bank notes. Solving the puzzle of the *value of money* may appear to be either impossible (because too complicated) or simple (because so self-evident). Chapter 2 of the *Philosophy of Money* addresses the paradox that the substance of money seems to be both necessary and accidental, and that the value of money appears to be either intrinsic to the material that embodies it or merely symbolic of its essential functions. Simmel himself seems to have appreciated the difficulty of conveying this paradox when he advised a friend 'to skip over chapter 2 or at most to flick through it ... This chapter is the most technical one in the book and will hardly interest you as a whole' (quoted in PM: lxiii). And yet the fascinating historical and economic details he discusses raise cultural and philosophical questions that interested many of Simmel's early and most avid readers and that, in important ways, are still relevant to us today.

If we follow the zig-zag path between the analytical and synthetic parts of the book that I mapped out in the previous chapter, a simple example can provide a glimpse into these otherwise complex and specialized issues: the coin toss, heads or tails (see figure 3). Obviously, a metal coin is meant to serve primarily as money – that is, as a *means of exchange* or *a measure of value* for buying and selling commodities under certain conditions. But a coin might also be *stored* away for later use or *saved* in a collection of rare, old, or foreign currencies. It may also be taken out of circulation and tossed in the air to get a sporting event started or to resolve a dispute, in which case it no longer serves as money as such. A coin toss presupposes various contingencies and possible outcomes, the 50:50 probability of one side winning and the other losing. For the outcome to be meaningful, the act of tossing a coin assumes that some necessary ground rules have been laid out in advance – that is, a prior agreement that tails signifies one thing and heads another. In short, the coin toss connects certain social conventions between people with the physical properties embodied in an object. For this reason, it offers a useful analogy of the play of chance and the work of necessity that determine the circulation of currency and the conduct of commerce in the money economy.

Consider, for instance, how the tails side of a 20 Mark coin minted in 1901 with the imperial seal of the eagle of the 'Deutsches Reich' symbolizes its use in the exchange of goods between individuals and communities within the territory of Germany at the turn of the century. On the heads side, the profile image of 'Wilhelm II Deutscher

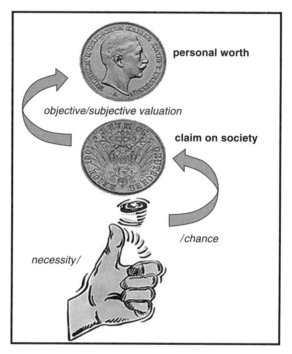

Figure 3 Money as a matter of necessity and chance

Kaiser König von Preussen' represents the ruling monarch as an image of imperial sovereignty who ensures that subjects and citizens have certain liberties, rights, and obligations in making use of the coin in everyday commerce. These flip sides – 'heads or tails' – thus represent the basic features of all currency in facilitating exchange, here expressed in terms of the complementary aspects of state power and national sovereignty on the one side versus market value and personal autonomy on the other (Hart 1986). The inscription on the side of this particular coin (not represented here), which reads '*Gott mit uns*' (God with us), may also suggest that this blend of superhuman necessity (divine and objective) and earthly contingency (human and subjective) defines the national currency and generates ordinary values in practical life. It seems that the coin toss and commercial trade share not just the same material substance but also a common philosophical and sociological foundation. Whether the coin is used as money or for some other purpose, the prior meaning and subsequent *interpretation* of each side of the coin (and of the coin itself) are a matter of both objective and subjective *valuation* (Zelizer 1994).

Later I elaborate on Simmel's discussion of how a person's worth and individual identity may be expressed in monetary terms, but first I want to consider his thesis in chapter 2 of the *Philosophy of Money* that money is a 'claim upon society' as a whole. By this he means that the value of money ultimately turns on the social functions it serves rather than on the materials that make it up: 'Money has value not on account of what it is, but on account of the ends that it serves' (PM: 201). As new and expanding spheres of interaction emerge from older and narrower transactions in the course of history, simple exchanges between two parties tend to be realized through a 'superindividual' third factor, such as the economic community as a whole or the government as its representative. When currency is minted by the state and trusted by members of the larger community, the significance of money extends beyond the direct line of contact between the parties of an exchange. To elaborate on this crucial point, Simmel refers to the common saying that money is 'a claim upon society [*eine Anweisung auf die Gesellschaft*]'. As he goes on to say, 'money appears, so to speak, as a bill of exchange from which the name of the drawee is lacking, or alternatively, which is guaranteed rather than accepted' (PM: 176; GSG 6: 213). His use of the German term *Anweisung* here is suggestive, since it implies that there is an analogy between the social function of money in general and the 'claim' someone makes for a debt or a reward, or the 'instruction' one gives to make a payment or redeem a remittance. By extension, the beneficiary of money transactions is not ultimately personal or easily identifiable but rather a collective and anonymous entity. Money is therefore an 'order' or a 'claim upon society' in the sense that the market or the state draws upon the anonymous trust of social members. Public and private institutions guarantee the credibility of money transactions even when the offer of exchange is not accepted by individuals or even completed in every instance.

From these observations, which connect the commonsense understanding of money with its technical uses, Simmel concludes that the value of money derives more from its *social function* than from its *material substance*. In a statement reminiscent of Marx (but developed in a different direction, as I show in the next chapter), he argues that money materializes social relations by making them appear as relations between things: 'money is the reified [or embodied: *verkörperte*] function of being exchanged; ... the reification [or materialization: *zur Substanz gewordene*] of the pure relationship between things as expressed in their economic motion' (PM: 175; GSG 6: 211). The philosophical significance of money consists in how it seems to transcend or even erase the presence of people by reducing the differences between them, along with the nuances, and peculiarities between things, to a common denominator. In theory, all goods and humans can be assigned a numerical value and then compared with one another or calculated and considered equivalent. In practice, Simmel observes, there is a trend against the use of hard cash in modern commerce, a tendency that is unavoidable because no amount of precious metals could ever keep up with the steady increase in the volume and velocity of transactions. When everything and everyone can be viewed in terms of abstract monetary values, the functions of money as the measure and means of exchange come to outweigh the material basis of money as a substance and store of value: 'The functional value [*Funktionswert*] of money exceeds its value as substance [*Substanzwert*] the more extensive and diversified are the services it performs and the more rapidly it circulates' (PM: 142; GSG 6: 158). To be sure, in order for the social functions of money to be fulfilled, some material substance is always necessary, if only in the form of a note on a piece of paper, a magnetic strip on a credit card, or a code programmed into a computer (as we now see with the new crypto-currencies). Nevertheless, in a modern money economy, the work of subjective and objective valuation – of weighing and balancing supplies or accumulating and transporting resources, and so on – increasingly depends upon *the symbolic processes of measuring, counting, and converting values.*

So how can one explain the many forms that money has taken throughout history and the materials that have been used as money in various cultures? Since Simmel's perspective is not empirical or economic but rather philosophical and sociological, he does not attempt to answer this question (Poggi 1993). Instead, he offers some speculations on how the functions of money follow from its material forms. For example, to the extent that precious metals and gemstones are assigned a certain value in particular social interactions, these materials have often been singled out to serve as the general medium and measure of exchange. The meaning and value they are assigned are therefore primarily social and relational rather than an intrinsic property of their substance: 'Exchange, as the purest sociological occurrence, the most complete form of interaction, finds its appropriate representation in the material of jewelry, the significance of which for its owner is only indirect, namely as relation to other people' (PM: 176–7). Following a similar logic, Simmel does not examine the plunder of South American silver and gold mines through conquest and colonization in any historical detail, nor does he treat these events as a political or moral dilemma. Instead, he examines them indirectly and implicitly as an intellectual and conceptual problem: 'One of the greatest advances made by humankind – the discovery of a new world out of the material of the old – is to establish a proportion between two quantities, not by direct comparison, but in terms of the fact that each of them relates to a third quantity and that these two relations are either equal or unequal' (PM: 144). Far from simply ignoring empirical or ethical questions, however, Simmel is interested in reflecting on their broader sociological, theoretical, and even metaphysical implications. He observes that metal recedes in significance when the speed, intensity, and widespread character of commercial transactions require new ways of safeguarding the general functions of money as a medium and measure of circulation rather than as a material for stockpiling or displaying wealth. Simmel often refers to this tendency in terms of the 'pure concept' of money, which consists in serving as a means of exchange, a standard of value, and a method of storing value quite apart from its practical application or actual accumulation. He notes that 'the coin used for calculation is deliberately set in opposition to the metal coin', in the sense that an intellectual operation takes precedence over its possible implementation (PM: 192). To recall my analogy with coin tossing, we could say that the prior ground rules, calculated probabilities, and imagined consequences of the act of tossing ultimately matter more than the material composition or intrinsic worth of the coin itself.

The cultural and philosophical implications of Simmel's argument are far-reaching and profound. One of the commentators who has elaborated on the implications of his thesis that 'money is a claim upon society' in an especially illuminating way is Nigel Dodd (2016, 2014, 2012). Dodd notes that the logic of money entails a claim upon 'varying modes of shared existence and experience', so that even apparently non-commercial interactions can indirectly take on a financial character (2014: 386). Not only do money transactions presuppose certain psychological habits of thought, relations of trust, and social institutions that guarantee their legitimacy, but money itself also has a social life of its own. Metal, paper, or even so-called electronic currencies – not to mention barter and virtual ways of recording and redeeming debts – tend to coexist with and even reinforce rather than replace each other. With particular attention to Simmel's discussion in chapter 2 of the *Philosophy of Money*, Dodd draws our attention to the agency money exercises beyond the actions or actors that make use of it. For instance, money exchanges are never completely bound to the places where they take place. There has never been a pure realm of territorially bounded currencies, since 'state currencies have intermingled with other monetary forms for as long as they have been in circulation' (ibid.: 212). For this reason, money often serves as an agent of deterritorialization and globalization by facilitating commerce and communication across national frontiers. At the same time, however, it can also be an instrument for creating and preserving local places within geographical borders, such as a town, a neighbourhood, an urban district, or a nation-state. Financial crises both in Simmel's day and in our own reveal this social life of money – that is, 'the complex and dynamic configuration of social, economic, and political relations on which money depends' (ibid.: 386). Such crises expose the positive functions of money in enabling the circulation and exchange of people and products, but at the same time they show us *what money is not*: 'that is to say, it is not an objective entity whose value is independent of social and political relations' (ibid.). Once again, the double aspect of money – its 'heads or tails' character – is a matter of both subjective and objective valuation, a process involving a mixture of chance and necessity, and a material medium facilitating social interactions that take on the form of a thing that seems to have a life of its own.

Money as a Measure of Personal Worth

The analytically distinct components of money – its social functions as opposed to the value it has as a material substance, the pure concept of money in exchange versus its uses in practice, and so on – can be approached from a more 'synthetic' perspective as elements that make up a sense of one's personal worth and individual identity. In chapter 5 of the *Philosophy of Money* Simmel considers the ways in which a price tag can be placed on people, so to speak, and he describes some examples such as prostitution (sex work) and mental labour (intellectual work). Today we might also think of how someone's earning power or credit rating somehow reflects his or her value in areas of life that go beyond the economic realm to include their social standing or cultural prestige in a community. The tendency to reduce human beings – or parts of their personal life – to the measure of money 'not only makes money the measure of man, but it also makes man the measure of money' (PM: 357–8). How does the money economy assign value or worth (both words translate the German *Wert*) to each one of us and how does value become an integral part of our individual identity and an expression of our self-worth?

A telling example of this tendency is the medieval practice in Anglo-Saxon and Germanic law of the *wergild* (from the old English 'man-payment'), a fee paid as compensation to the relatives or lord of a slain person which sets a price on taking a human life in accordance with the victim's rank. For instance, a fine might be set at 300 shillings for the killing of a nobleman and 100 shillings for a lower-status freeman. In later historical periods when a higher value was placed on the personal dignity of each individual, regardless of social rank, financial atonement for murder and fines for other serious crimes would become impossible or even unthinkable. Simmel begins his discussion of the value of the individual in the modern money economy with the example of *wergild* in order to emphasize the continuity of this practice with the price that is placed on personal worth. Today we might think of life insurance policies as a way of calculating the value of an individual's life for family members, employers, and the larger society. In Simmel's view, payment for services rendered for time worked represents only a difference in degree from the *wergild*. Wages, salaries, fines, premiums, and fees are largely a method of maintaining a peaceful society by upholding a standard of measurement through money exchanges. Since the eighteenth century, these practices have become integral not just to the money economy but also for guaranteeing the legal equality of all people, the personal dignity of each individual, and even the right to free expression (PM: 362).

Simmel first developed these points as a young scholar in a seminar which he was invited to present at Berlin University in 1889 by his mentor, the eminent economic historian Gustav Schmoller. Simmel's article 'On the Psychology of Money' discusses how financial transactions ideally unfold in a strictly objective way, and yet they also have personal meaning and subjective significance. In theory if not always in practice, monetary exchanges tend to exclude any hint of interpersonal pleasantness or violence, and so they are supposed to suppress all individual emotions and sense impressions – hence the saying 'money has no smell' (*non olet*) (SC: 240). In the *Philosophy of Money*, Simmel notes that even an act of bribery, where one person buys someone's compliance or influences others by paying them off in cash, simply highlights the features of secrecy, invisibility, and silence inherent in most monetary exchanges. If money transactions in their purest expression are essentially neutral and private, in their publicly sanctioned and social aspect – as fines and taxes, for instance – they are also ways of assigning prices to individual actions and imposing payments for personal services (PM: 400). On the one hand, the process of buying and selling has a levelling effect by bringing personal distinctions between people down to the common denominator of their value and price. On the other hand, people cultivate their own identities and find a sense of themselves in the world of commodities, which endows them with the vigour, stability, and inner unity that they otherwise lose through money exchanges: 'The constant selling and exchanging of things – often the mere fact that they are saleable – often means a selling and uprooting of personal values' (PM: 407).

One of Simmel's most memorable examples of how even intimate encounters can be made anonymous and impersonal through money is prostitution (PM: 378–82; also in ISF: 121–6). Prostitution epitomizes the principle that all distinctions between people of high rank and low social status can be rendered equivalent and shows us how qualitative differences can be reduced to numerical values. In the context of a permanent and developed capitalist economy, where money has become the standard for almost all values of life, people who engage in the world's 'oldest profession' lose their personal peculiarities and subjective idiosyncrasies and encounter one another first and foremost as types. In the exchange between the prostitute and the client (or john), personalities disappear behind their functions as each becomes a mere means for the other, something to be discarded as soon as its purpose is fulfilled. Since any desire can presumably be satisfied through purchase and consumption in the money economy, the sexual appetite is instantly awakened in the exchange between the prostitute and the client and just as quickly extinguished without any ongoing relationship or lasting commitment. Adopting the heterosexist conventions of his day, Simmel concludes that in the pact of prostitution the prostitute must objectify what is most private and personal, while the client can leave the encounter with his whole self intact: 'the woman gives her total self, with all its worth, whereas the man gives only a part of his personality in the exchange' (PM: 381). Crudely put, sex work involves only a minimum of the man's ego but a maximum of the woman's whole person.

In contrast to the cool character of these observations, Simmel takes up an explicitly moralizing tone as a liberal critic of modern prostitution in an anonymous editorial published in the early 1890s, 'Some Remarks on Prostitution in the Present and in Future' (SC: 262–70). Here he condemns the prevalence of poverty, helplessness, isolation, and lack of education among many prostitutes in Berlin, who are often humiliated into accepting degrading conditions in becoming merely 'an ejaculation mechanism' for men. He contrasts the refined and elegant form of prostitution conducted in high society with the impoverished practice of prostitution common in brothels and on street corners, where conditions are frequently unhealthy and demoralizing. In earlier periods of history where money exchanges were more intermittent and less all-embracing, he suggests, sex for money might not have been as humiliating and was often even socially accepted under certain circumstances. In a modern money economy, by contrast, a kind of 'moral syphilis' has infected both the prostitute and the client, each of whom is degraded and dehumanized in the course of their encounter. The modern money economy devalues private sexual relations by treating them as mere commercial transactions even while the existence or prevalence of prostitution is publicly disavowed. In a capitalist context, Simmel concludes, prostitution promotes a culture of denial, self-deception, and hypocrisy with respect to its own hidden sexual practices.

These remarks with respect to male privilege and women's subordinate position in a money economy, and on the relationship between the sexes in general, hit a note that Simmel will sound again and again in many ways throughout his career (as I discuss further in chapters 5, 9, and 10). All human relationships potentially reduce persons to mere means for one another, he points out, but the sex trade has an especially close affinity with 'the economy of means' understood in the strictest sense (PM: 379). In this regard, sexual commerce is only an extreme instance of a broader cultural phenomenon involving the role of money in the relationship between the sexes (PM: 372–87). Many common cultural practices reveal how gendered inequalities and power differences are facilitated and enhanced by the money economy, including the exchange of women as daughters- and sisters-in-law between men and families, the transfer of dowries from a bride's parents to a suitor, and marriage by purchase (which today we can see in the international market in brides). But sexual inequality may also be challenged when relations between women and men are mediated through money, such as when women gain power by controlling their own wage labour. At the same time, the gap between men's activities outside the home and women's domestic activities can become wider when financial transactions are involved: 'Money makes possible separate production for the market and for the household economy and this separation initiates a more rigorous division of labour between the sexes' (PM: 377). The social divide between public work for men and domestic work for women is often reflected in the realm of professional work outside the home, where different kinds of caring and emotional labour are expected of women in contrast to the manual and intellectual labour of men.

This last point suggests that not just the division of labour between the sexes but also the division of labour between manual and mental workers tends to be exacerbated when social life is saturated, subsumed, or claimed by the money economy. At the other end of the spectrum from sex work Simmel examines intellectual work as another illuminating example of how money measures personal worth. Against the socialist theory that only physical labour power possesses value, he argues that all human effort, encompassing both manual work and the expenditure of mental energy, entails the accumulation of competencies, skills, and tools passed on from past generations which then form the basis of present performances and future valuations (Howell 2016). In discussing the notion of 'labour money', in which the amount of time worked is considered the only just basis for compensation (an idea he mistakenly attributes to Marx), Simmel makes a number of original points about the valuation of intellectual work (PM: 409–32). Where physical effort is usually exerted immediately and all at once, mental exertion requires a more elaborate process that involves 'the whole complicated system of bodily-mental dispositions, impressions and impulses' which must be coordinated 'in a specific organization, tone and proportion of rest and movement' (PM: 423). Since the energy needed for thinking is ultimately just as calculable and monetizable as the energy expended for muscular exertion, he speculates, perhaps in the future all these activities might be seen as equivalent to one another: 'Mental labour would then be dealt with on the same footing as manual labour, and its products would enter into a merely quantitative balancing of value with those of the latter' (PM: 422). For example, we might think of academic work in this regard, where a researcher's worth is measured by the grants he or she is able to acquire. In short, intellectual work in the money economy – including the time and effort used to create art, write novels, manage accounts, engage in politics, and conduct scholarly investigations – can be subjected to both psycho-physical analysis and financial calculation.

With the rise of the industrial division of labour, physical work tends to become more refined and integrated into mental work at a higher level. This tendency is among the many manifestations of the broader natural and cultural development of modern capitalism that concerned Simmel and many of his contemporaries (see the 'Excursus on Cultural Capitalism', pp. 56–8). He sketches this larger framework in his first major book, *On Social Differentiation*, especially the last chapter, 'Differentiation and the Principle of Saving Energy'. There he discusses the evolutionary advantage that results from economizing means in order to attain ends more efficiently, often as a result of reducing friction in the work process and through the specialization of functions in all areas of life: 'All culture aspires not only to harness more and more natural energy to our ends, but also to achieve all such ends in ways that save more and more energy' (1976: 111). The economization of energy (which he assumes is a basic human phenomenon) and the monetization of personal worth (as we saw with the examples of sex work and intellectual work) go hand in hand and can be viewed as flip sides of the coin of competitive commerce: 'The differentiation of economic life in general is the origin of money, and for the individual its ownership is the opportunity for any economic differentiation' (1976: 136). On the one side, harnessing and saving energy in a money economy encourages the expansion and differentiation of social groups; on the other, the production and consumption of energy also propels each individual to cultivate his or her inner life in new ways (1976: 116, 119). The principle of saving energy thus creates the conditions for economic specialization, social differentiation, and personal distinction. Viewed from this perspective, class conflicts between employers and workers are just the latest stage in this human and cultural process of differentiation, where the objective structure of economic relationships becomes more and more separate from the subjective experiences of producers and consumers. Simmel suggests that the economy of natural and social energy expresses something new and significant about the capitalist money economy and the modern lifestyles that emerge from this economy, as I discuss in the next chapter.

Excursus on Cultural Capitalism: Simmel with Weber and Sombart

Although the word 'capitalism' in its modern sense appears only a couple of times in the last section of Simmel's *Philosophy of Money* (PM: 496, 512), the term seems to have been coined, or at least circulated and popularized, through the work of his colleagues Werner Sombart (1863–1941) and Max Weber (1864–1920) (Clarke 2005: 22). While Simmel makes no references to Sombart or Weber in his published writings, he shares their interest in examining the social conditions and cultural consequences of modern capitalism, and specifically in assessing the function and vocation of intellectual work (*geistige Arbeit*) in the modern world (Kemple 2014a). In contrast to Marx's focus on the accumulation of wealth and the conversion of *capital*, these three thinkers are concerned with tracing the genesis and structure of capital*ism*, along with its personal and cultural significance. That is, they conceive of capitalism less as an economic mode of production than as a range of social and cultural systems, each employing various techniques of rational accounting, wage labour, and private enterprise for profit.

Sombart in particular emphasizes the social and cultural significance of 'the capitalist spirit', not just in industry and trade but above all in the arts, sciences, and politics. In influential books such as *Modern Capitalism* (1902) and *The Bourgeois* (1913) he touches on topics that concern Simmel in the *Philosophy of Money* and elsewhere, including high fashion, luxury consumption, art markets, and romantic love, which he treats as expressions of the middle-class ethos of competition, commerce, and entrepreneurialism (Sombart 2001). Sombart's lecture on 'Technology and Culture' at the first meeting of the German Sociological Association in 1910 – which Simmel attended and which elicited lively commentary from Weber – offers a wide-ranging survey of the part played by industrial technologies in the emergence of modern cultural phenomena, such as the effect of the steam engine in transforming capitalist industry; the use of gunpowder in enhancing the military force of the industrial state; the importance of the press in spreading the message of the church; the influence of transportation systems on the communication of scientific ideas; the role of labour-saving devices in promoting women's emancipation; and the invention of musical instruments in the development of the modern orchestra (Sombart

2005). Many of these examples are also discussed by Simmel in the *Philosophy of Money*, where he focuses less on explaining the empirical meaning of these phenomena for economic history and more on their philosophical and sociological significance as symptoms and signs of an emerging modern worldview (Frisby 1985).

This lack of empirical specificity prompted Weber to criticize Simmel's account of the money economy for not adequately clarifying its distinctively *capitalist* character. At the same time he has high praise for Simmel's 'simply brilliant' outline of the spirit of capitalism in the *Philosophy of Money*, one of the first books Weber took up when recovering from his nervous breakdown in the years before writing his great work, *The Protestant Ethic and the Spirit of Capitalism* (Weber 2009: 209, 464; Scaff 1988: 3, 7). In defending his argument from critics, Weber cites Simmel's 'wonderful essay' on 'The Adventure' (discussed below in chapter 9) as a way of clarifying the contrast between earlier opportunistic forms of entrepreneurial capitalism and later more ascetic forms of the capitalist work ethic: 'the transformation of the capitalist "spirit" in my sense of the word could be understood in terms of the transformation of the *romanticism of economic adventurism into the economic rationalism of methodical life practices*' (Weber 2001: 119).

Weber was especially generous in expressing his appreciation for Simmel as a logician of the social sciences, even though Simmel was interested more in metaphysical questions of meaning than in empirical matters of fact. In writing about the 'logical problems of historical economics', Weber praises his colleague for developing a theory of interpretation or 'understanding' (*Verstand* in German) in the social sciences (here singling out the second edition of Simmel's *Problems of the Philosophy of History*). For both social theorists, 'interpretive sociology' is concerned with providing an understanding of subjective intentions, meanings, and motives, and each acknowledges that the 'infinitude and absolute irrationality of every concrete multiplicity' that makes up social reality cannot adequately be conceived or simply copied by the sociological observer (Weber 2012: 59–61, discussing 1977: 63–102). As Simmel states with a pun on Weber's name (perhaps unintentionally), 'regarding the web of social life it is especially true that the weaver [*der Weber*] does not know what he is weaving' (1977: 55; GSG 9: 252; also in 'The Tragedy of Culture', SC: 69; GSG 14: 407). In his view, meanings and motives emerge through reciprocal interactions, sometimes in unconscious ways, while Weber is focused more on how subjective intentions and understandings are attached to social actions, often in unintended ways (Pyyhtinen 2018: 131–4). Weber's interests are more analytical in the sense that he constructs 'ideal types' that do not just interpret and understand meanings and motives but also *explain* the causes and consequences of social action. Thus, Weber finds Simmel's concept of 'interaction' – *Wechselwirkung* in the sense of reciprocal cause and effect – too ambiguous, since it does not draw a sharp enough distinction between subjectively intended and objectively valid meanings (Weber 1978: 4; Lichtblau 1991). In an unpublished review of Simmel's work, for example, he criticizes Simmel's discussion of 'Domination and Subordination' in the book *Sociology* for implying that the exercise of power is always a kind of reciprocal relationship and can never entail the unilateral imposition of one will upon another (Weber 2012: 421).

Despite these reservations, Weber was certainly indebted to Simmel's subtle reflections on how the money economy has become an agent of cultural rationalization and how people understand power and authority or domination and subordination as 'legitimate'. While Weber evidently admired Simmel's work as 'a sociologist and theoretician of the money economy', he took a more critical stance to his rival *Sombart's* approach to the cultural history and political economy of modern capitalism. Nevertheless, he was careful to concede that even 'those who feel stimulated time and again by Sombart's studies to oppose his views strongly, and directly to reject some of his theses, are obliged to clarify their reasons for doing so explicitly' (Weber 2009: 468; see Kemple 2014a: 208–10). Above all, Weber credits Simmel for establishing 'interpretive understanding' as the central concern for sociology. Along with Weber and Sombart, Simmel sketches the outlines of a comprehensive social theory of cultural capitalism and the beginnings of a detailed interpretation of modern social life.

4

The Lifestyles of Fast Capitalism

Along with cynicism and pessimism (as I note in the previous two chapters), scepticism is among the most prevalent moods of the modern age and the money economy. The sceptical attitude is not just a feeling of uncertainty or despair over whether anything can be true but also a cultural worldview and a philosophy of life. Simmel points out that our experience of how the world is changing and in constant flux may lead us to believe that all knowledge is subjective and therefore only relatively true (PM: 102). People in the sciences, the arts, politics, and every field of culture may experience this temptation to adopt an attitude of radical doubt in their search for convincing truths: '*The subjectivism of modern times* has the same basic motive as art: to gain a more intimate and truer relationship to objects by dissociating ourselves from them and retreating into ourselves, or by consciously acknowledging the inevitable distance between ourselves and objects' (PM 480, emphasis added). Simmel notes that a more intense awareness of the distance between ourselves and others and between people and things often entails adopting a humble perspective on our place in the world and acknowledging our limited capacity to realize our ultimate ideals and most cherished values. By presenting each individual with only a glimpse of so many goals and possible plans that might never be achieved, he argues, the fast pace of life under capitalism gives rise to this 'subjectivism of modern times' with its deep anxieties and sceptical attitudes.

This chapter discusses how typical forms of conflict and competition, along with the personal moods and feelings that accompany them in the money economy, emerge from the fragmentation, polarization, and 'reification' of social relationships. Simmel approaches strife and rivalry between groups and individuals in a capitalist world less as the expression of a natural and biological drive than as a social and cultural force that is pacified through economic and other forms of competition. In highlighting the personal dimensions, metaphysical underpinnings, and tragic implications of money transactions, he tends to focus on the cultural and experiential dynamics of technological progress and class conflict. As I note in a digression, his approach offers an important alternative and corrective to some of the views of Marx and Engels, who emphasize the material consequences and unintended effects of capitalist competition over its subjective and personal dimensions. I begin by sketching Simmel's analysis in chapter 3 of the *Philosophy of Money* of how the function of money as a means of exchange becomes an end in itself. His examples of the miser and the spendthrift represent extreme cases in which money takes on an absolute quality over and above everything else. I then turn to the famous final chapter 6 on 'The Style of Life', which had such a profound influence on many of his contemporaries and which examines how a capitalist culture that requires the pursuit of 'infinite ends' leads to the rationalization and acceleration of everyday life. These are the themes that Simmel will explore in more depth and detail in his later writings on the metropolis and modernity.

The Teleological Series of Commodities and Cash

At the end of the last chapter I mentioned Simmel's argument about the tendency in capitalist society for people to generate and use more energy while at the same time finding new ways to economize and save energy. Historical progress is often measured in general terms by the capacity of humans to achieve goals that in turn become the means for setting new goals, which then become links in a chain that seems to extend to infinity. As he observes in the *Philosophy of Money*, the most direct route to something is not necessarily the most efficient and may often be the longest one: 'by adding tools we deliberately add a new link to the chain of purposive action, thus showing that the straight road is not always the shortest' (PM: 209). Money is both a material means and a mental tool in this 'teleological series' that links together intentions and outcomes. In other words, money is a link in a sequence of purposes that can prolong the achievement of aims that are close to us or shorten the distance between objectives that are remote from us. Money is the purest example of a tool, Simmel argues, since it materializes human independencies and at the same time emancipates individuals from being bound to their immediate will, natural instincts, and subjective desires (PM: 211).

Money does not just make labour power more exploitable or trade more efficient, as a Marxist or mercantilist theory might argue. In Simmel's view, the value that money adds to life comes from the power it offers people to choose freely between potentially innumerable objects and from the potentially unlimited ways it can be saved and spent. This 'surplus value' may take material form as property and wealth accumulated through profitable exchanges, or it may take non-monetary and apparently immaterial form (Spivak 1987). For example, something might acquire social cachet or symbolic distinction simply by appearing a certain way, as we saw earlier with the example of the display of goods at a trade exhibition, or today when we notice how things can appear more valuable or desirable in a shop window, in a consumer catalogue, or on television. We could say that the labour of looking, such as the way in which our attention is trained and programmed by advertisements and other media, itself produces value for consumption and exchange (Beller 2006: 243–6). Simmel goes so far as to argue that the capacity of values to be enhanced by being exchanged and exhibited, their 'exhibition value', and to reach beyond every actual or potential use, constitutes 'the metaphysical quality of money'. Because money is 'the ultimate means', its distinctive power is '*to realize the possibility of all values as the value of all possibilities*' (PM: 221, emphasis added). This striking formulation summarizes Simmel's simple observation that commercial exchanges do not need to take place in any particular physical location, and that consumer culture does not have to be materialized in any one thing or realize any specific set of aspirations, aims, or ideals.

Before illustrating this general point about the money economy with some examples from social life, it is worth reflecting for a moment on Simmel's remarkable characterization of money as the ultimate tool, the supreme energy-saver, and an extremely efficient means for generating and realizing desires. Money becomes *the quintessential technology* insofar as it tends to replace human beings with machines, often by transferring human capacities into machine power while also incorporating machines into humans. In a remark from the final chapter of the *Philosophy of Money*, Simmel states that 'the vending machine [*Warenautomat*] is the ultimate example of the technological character of the modern economy. By mechanical means, human relationships are completely eliminated, even in the retail trade where the exchange of commodities was long carried out between one person and another, and the money equivalent is now mechanically exchanged against the commodity' (PM: 460–1; GSG 6: 639). Figure 4 depicts how human relationships in consumer culture can be entirely eliminated or simply switched off (*ausgeschaltet*) as one would a machine. Commodities can be bought without the presence of a seller just as producers can be removed from the sight of consumers. Rather than taking place through face-to-face interactions between retailers and customers, or between companies and clients, transactions are increasingly accomplished through a three-stage operation that is mechanically mediated and operated by a consumer acting alone and following a standard sequence of generic instructions: 1) *insert* coin; 2) *choose* from an

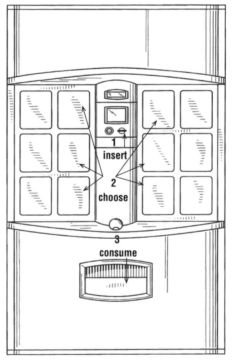

Figure 4 Consumer culture and the money economy

assortment of goods; 3) *consume* instantly, or save for later use. If we recall that Simmel's father owned a chocolate factory, and that the first vending machines manufactured at the end of the nineteenth century typically featured a selection of chocolates and other sweets, we can begin to imagine the personal, social, and historical significance that the automation (*Automat*) of money, machines, and commodities (*Waren*) must have had for him. In our own day, we might think of how consumer culture becomes *self-service culture* in supermarket check-out lines, fuel stations, and internet retailers.

I return to these points below, but for now we can consider some particular instances where money establishes this pattern in which 'the means become the ends' because, 'in the last analysis, ends are only means' (PM: 236). In a discussion of avarice and extravagance in chapter 3 of the *Philosophy of Money*, Simmel vividly contrasts the figures of the miser and the spendthrift (PM: 228–52; also in ISF: 179–86). Unlike the prostitute and the client, who become mere means for each other through the mediation of money, the miser and the spendthrift treat money as an absolute end in itself. Although these character types appear to be diametrically opposed, for each of them the material substance of money had been dissolved into a pure desire for its own sake (PM: 251). For the miser, the mere state of possession, the stable moment of having accumulated the symbol of value, becomes an enjoyable end in itself, and the stockpile of money alone is the greatest source of pleasure. For the spendthrift, by contrast, the process of spending and converting values into other forms is intrinsically pleasurable and the activities of acquiring particular goods or simply squandering money are themselves supremely enjoyable (PM: 248). While accumulation seems like an abstract and fixed state for the miser, expenditure appears to be a fluid and concrete process for the spendthrift. As Simmel observes in the essay 'On the Psychology of Money', spendthrifts 'are concerned only with the value of the *thing*, whereas misers are concerned only with the *value* of the thing' (SC: 236). Despite appearing to be polar opposites, each epitomizes the essentially impersonal and absolute qualities of money. Neither can accept that any measure of value should limit their desires or interrupt 'the sequence of purposes' mediated by cash, and neither is ever satisfied with the final consumption of commodities. The stingy old person and the dissolute young gambler are only extreme manifestations of the logic inherent in the money form when it is viewed as a symbol of unlimited desire and set apart from the most basic needs of life (PM: 251).

These exceptional cases only point to a more mundane and widespread pattern that is essential to the creation and expansion of the money economy. In chapter 3 of the *Philosophy of Maoney*, Simmel goes on to consider how money intensifies the abstract and colourless character of a capitalist culture that estranges people from things and from other people, a theme he introduces here and returns to throughout his career. Like the avaricious person who asks only 'how much' something costs and not 'what, why, or how' one thing comes to be worth more or less than something else, the merchant often has to maintain an impersonal distance from other people in seeing them more as customers and clients than as neighbours and familiars: 'not only is the trader a stranger, but the stranger is also disposed to become a trader' (PM: 225). In European history, he points out, Jews have often taken on this exemplary role as both moneylender and typical stranger and thus as both insider and outsider (PM: 224–7; Morris-Reich 2003). The overwhelming abundance of commodities leads to a blasé attitude in which the feeling for distinctions between people is lost and an appreciation for specific qualities of things is viewed with indifference (PM: 256–7). At the same time, the massive proliferation of goods, their appearance as 'a monstrous accumulation of commodities' (in the memorable opening lines of Marx's *Capital*), induces a perpetual quest for excitement and a never-ending pursuit of exaggerated differences (Marx 1977: 421; 1988: 49). Like the extravagant spendthrift, the crazed consumer driven by the latest bargains and fashions is constantly on the lookout for ways to spend and save or for opportunities to buy and give away. Today mass media and social media often take up this role of stimulating and satisfying desires and of frustrating and fuelling this bottomless craving for new stimulations and shocking impressions. As a cultural critic and commentator on the everyday experience of capitalism, Simmel tends to push the discussion of class conflict and social inequality into the background, even as he remains deeply concerned with the alienating dynamics that bring these disturbing phenomena into being for particular individuals (see the 'Excursus on Class Conflict', pp. 71–4).

Rationalization and Reification in the Modern Money Economy

The analysis of how means are turned into ends through the endless pursuit of merchandise and money provides the terms for Simmel's dazzling descriptions in the final chapter of the *Philosophy of Money*, 'The Style of Life' (PM: 433–518). Since Simmel returns to many of these themes in later writings, here I want only to highlight a few of the issues he is concerned with, especially how the general human capacities for competition, intellectualization, and objectification are transformed in becoming the core values of the modern money economy. Generally speaking, competition can be understood simply as a form of struggle between opponents, often for the benefit of another or by excluding a third party. In chapter 4 of *Sociology*, Simmel notes that competition can take the form of pacified conflict or antagonism, subdued strife or disagreement, and may even be considered a universal phenomenon: 'As the cosmos needs "love and hate", attractive and repulsive forces, in order to have a form, so society also needs some quantitative ratio of harmony and disharmony, association and competition, good will and ill will, in order to arrive at a specific formation' (S: 228). Competition can be thought of as an indirect form of conflict in which rivals strive for the same goal, which may result in some kind of subjective satisfaction or objective achievement (S: 260). While in the early stages of human history the stakes of competition may be brutal and personal, in modern capitalist societies competition often takes on an impersonal and civil character while its ruthless aspects are intensified as well as delayed and displaced (S: 272). As Simmel observes in the *Philosophy of Money*, 'the intensity of modern economic conflicts in which no mercy is shown is … unleashed by direct interest in money itself, … where the deadly antagonistic competitor of today is the cartel ally of tomorrow' (PM: 438). Capitalism tends to transform conflict into competition and to extend competition from the economic realm of industry and commerce into every aspect of modern life: in love and sport, education and the arts, the professions and play.

At a deeper and more personal level, the ferocity of modern forms of competition has its source in the effort to fill 'the lack of something at the centre of the soul', which can manifest itself 'as the tumult of the metropolis, as the mania for travelling, … and as the typically modern disloyalty with regard to taste, style, opinions and personal relationships' (PM: 490). Although competition is a kind of leitmotif throughout Simmel's discussion of the capitalist lifestyle, he begins by remarking on how the money economy actually heightens the intellectual, rational, and spiritual character of modern life. In a sense, he implicitly acknowledges that money creates both the material and the mental conditions that make his own philosophical investigation possible in the first place. Our everyday experiences foster a rudimentary awareness of the extended teleological series of means and ends that are essential to the money economy, but they also form the basis for a theoretical understanding of the web of personal and objective connections that constitute the capitalist lifestyle. Since modern times require considerable skills of weighing, measuring, and calculating, the intellect and the capacity to reason tend to prevail over feelings and the irrational will (PM: 448–50). Social interactions tend to unfold in more standard and logical ways and often without personal emotion or any reference to individual character, even when money transactions are ultimately driven by selfish interests: 'the elimination of all one-sided objectivity makes a clean sweep in favour of egoism' (PM: 445). To the extent that modern lifestyles are ruled by legal and financial systems, this rational ethos is increasingly indifferent to subjective and personal concerns. In the restless drive for rapid mobility, new sensations, intense impressions, and more contacts, people who get caught up in this lifestyle frequently resort to the intellectual attitudes of cynicism, pessimism, and scepticism, as I pointed out earlier.

The rationalization of everyday experience stems from the increase in material culture and the corresponding lag in individual culture that accompanies modern life. In describing this gap between personal (subjective) and material (objective) culture (PM: 453–73), Simmel identifies an underlying cultural logic that will preoccupy him into his final years. Here he defines culture (*Kultur*) broadly 'as the refinement, as the intellectualized forms of life, the accomplishment of mental and practical labour' (PM: 450; SC: 36). Just as a garden fruit displays its natural vitality when it is pruned and cared for, so a slab of marble manifests its potential as a work of art in being carved into a sculpture. In each instance, value is created and increased as it develops outwards into the objective world and then returns back to its human source in an enhanced form: 'by cultivating objects, that is, by increasing their performance beyond the performance of their natural constitution, we cultivate ourselves' (PM: 451). In other words, culture is a process of self-formation that also entails and extends the work of social education: '*the culture of things … is nothing but a culture of people*' (PM: 454; SC: 39, emphasis added). These general reflections are the basis for Simmel's unique understanding of the specific dynamic that characterizes the contemporary world. Just as commerce and trade overwhelm the consumer with more and more objects of consumption, so transportation and communication are crammed with signals and symbols that no single individual can ever fully make sense of or know how to use (PM: 453). The distance between the inner cultivation of the individual and the outward expansion of objectified achievements increases with the division of labour and the growth of the money economy.

Against the background of these general arguments, Simmel concludes with a dizzying series of observations in the final section of the *Philosophy of Money* that cannot fail to capture the imagination of any reader. With the expansion and intensification of trade, he argues, things that at first sight appear to be far away or too minuscule to be perceived are increasingly brought into the field of human experience and awareness. The disruption in everyday perceptions induced by the confusing bustle of money exchanges can have real and disturbing effects on the individual, such as the break-up of the family, the dissolution of the psyche, and hypersensitivity to every stimulus coming from the outside: 'The money economy reinforces and refines modern tendencies towards the increase and diminution of distance, the pathological symptoms of which are "agoraphobia": the fear of coming into too close a contact with objects, a consequence of hyperaesthesia, for which every direct and energetic disturbance causes pain' (PM: 480). At the global end of this process, commerce can have far-reaching effects on the integration of social, economic, and political life: 'only by means of money is it possible for a German capitalist and also a German worker to be actually involved in a ministerial change in Spain, in the profits of African gold mines, and in the outcome of a South American revolution' (PM: 482). As distances between people and places break down, remote relationships become more valuable and personal connections become less meaningful. Human life as a whole is increasingly alienated to its core and brought to an existential crisis of identity: 'The human being has thereby become distanced from itself; an insuperable barrier of media, technical inventions, abilities and enjoyments has been erected between humanity and its most distinctive and essential being' (PM: 489; GSG 6: 674). Overwhelmed by the experience of alienation, we may feel as if the meaning of our existence has become so remote that we are at risk of losing our sense of purpose altogether, or that we can only regain an appreciation for the genuine meaning of life through perpetual conflicts and ever more urgent struggles.

If money facilitates the conquest of space, Simmel argues, it does so by accelerating the tempo of life. As Marx writes in his *Grundrisse* notebooks, the tendency of capital is ultimately the conquest of space by time, and thus, 'in the final analysis, all economics can be reduced to an economics of time' (Marx 1977: 362). In Simmel's first publication on the philosophy of money, 'The Significance of Money for the Rhythm of Life', which he incorporated into the book's final pages (PM: 491–517), he argues that money transactions throw the spatial symmetries of social and personal relationships into disarray while at the same time upsetting the regular rhythms of ordinary life. The telegraph and the telephone have redefined our normal sense of the speed or slowness of communication, so that a message that once seemed to take an eternity now seems to arrive miraculously in an instant (or vice versa!). The pocket watch and the clock likewise alter our perception of duration by breaking down time into its components: 'Like the determination of abstract value by money, the determination of abstract time by clocks provides a system for the most detailed and definite arrangements and measurements that imparts an otherwise unattainable transparency and calculability to the contents of life, at least as regards their practical management' (PM: 450). The rhythm of domestic life and work life becomes tightly calculated and meticulously controlled in ways that were almost unknown or unnoticed in previous periods of history: 'The changing requirements of objective circumstances and the mood of the day ... already indicate how much the rhythm of mealtimes, and its opposite, corresponds to the rhythm of work' (PM: 495–6). As if to extend this analogy between capital time and work time, Simmel suggests that the roundness of the conventional clock and the cyclical motion of its hands matches the roundness of coins, which symbolizes how transactions can 'roll' at a certain pace and intensity or be 'rounded off' as the occasion requires, but always in the interests of a speedy conclusion (PM: 512–13). In short, 'there is no more striking symbol of the completely dynamic character of the world than that of money' (PM: 510). Not only does money seem to bring 'here' and 'there' into closer proximity, it also appears to make the 'here' disappear altogether. And not only does money accelerate the pace of modern life, it also defines time itself as absolute motion to the point where distinct sequences of time blur together or appear to occur simultaneously.

The *Philosophy of Money* may not have had the popular appeal or scholarly recognition that Simmel had envisioned, and for the most part it did not generate the innovative studies of modern culture among his contemporaries that he had hoped for. Nevertheless, the last chapter, 'The Style of Life', did have a significant influence on several of his students. Among them was the young Hungarian philosopher and literary theorist Georg Lukács (1885–1971), who attended Simmel's lectures and Sunday salons in Berlin before studying with Max Weber in Heidelberg. Lukács cites a key passage from this chapter in his classic essay 'Reification and the Consciousness of the Proletariat', in *History and Class Consciousness* (1922). In this passage Simmel is elaborating on the contradictory character of money as the 'reification' of the general form that all being has assumed in a capitalist world, and as the model for how things derive significance from their relationships to one another and even become incorporated into a person's innermost identity: 'These counter-tendencies, once started, may press forward to an ideal of completely pure separation in which all the material contents of life become increasingly objective and impersonal, so that the remainder that cannot be reified [*der nicht zu verdinglichende Rest*] becomes all the more personal, all the more the indisputable property of the self' (PM: 474; GSG 6: 652; quoted in Lukács 1971: 156–7). Here Simmel emphasizes how the impersonal and generic style of life promoted by the capitalist economy pushes the individual to resist being ground down into a 'thing among other things', in the hopes of preserving what is most intimate or personal to one's own authentic self.

Perhaps reflecting on the personal significance of his own scene of writing, Simmel goes on from here to remark on how the typewriter produces mechanically uniform letters and thus seems to convey the pure contents of writing more efficiently than handwritten manuscripts. Texts seem to allow us to avoid all personal, idiosyncratic, and creative elements of expression, which then become even more jealously guarded (PM: 474–5). Lukács takes this general point about the simultaneous loss and desperate search for authentic selfhood a step further by considering how the impersonal, objectified, and reified character of capitalist culture may itself be internalized in a way that gives a person's identity and worldview a sense of security and value. Lukács interprets the compulsion to reduce all personal and social relationships to the terms of standardized economic exchanges from the standpoint of the modern proletariat, for whom 'the unexplained and inexplicable facticity of bourgeois existence as it is here and now acquires the patina of an eternal law of nature or a cultural value enduring for all time' (Lukács 1971: 157). Writing from a Marxist perspective, he argues that theoretical critique and revolutionary practice are needed to rub away this illusory 'patina' of bourgeois self-identity, like removing the opaque film that has accumulated on the surface of a metal coin or the dust and rust that has gathered on an obsolete piece of machinery. Only when we acknowledge our own creative and critical capacities to reimagine and resist this ideological worldview will we understand that what appears to be an unchangeable natural fact or a perpetual value concerning our own place in the larger world is actually a cultural and historical process that we can change and control.

Simmel's reflections on how money mediates relations of power and wealth in the modern world do not just apply to the social and political realities that prevailed a century ago. They also shed light on the soft forms of stratification, surveillance, and social control that have become even more evident today. The cultural power of consumer advertising and financial markets in contemporary society consists largely in projecting a kind of 'virtual social life' that often does not need to be grounded in the lived practices or actual experiences of real people in order to be effective (Arvidsson 2016). Banks and marketing firms have become such lucrative machines of capital accumulation and financial speculation not just because of the goods and services they sell but also because they generate symbolic and material profits by predicting prices, influencing values, and promoting certain ways of thinking, being, and acting over others. In the journal Simmel kept in his final years he offers a summary of his book on money which can also serve as a précis of the worldview that we can now see radiating from this ultimate symbol of 'the inconceivable unity of being':

> Money is the only cultural formation that is *pure* power, that has fully eliminated material supports from itself, in that it is absolutely pure symbol. To this degree, it is the most characteristic among all the phenomena of our time, when dynamism has gained command of all theory and practice. The fact that it is *pure relationship* (and thus likewise characteristic of our time) without including any of the content of the relationship does not contradict this. For in reality, power is nothing but relationship. (VL: 186)

We might read this passage as a comment on our own times and observe that the money economy and its culture industries promote subtle forms of commodification and financialization that shape every relationship and define the very style and substance of modern life. Of course, money can never be completely free of all material supports (as we saw in the previous chapter), although it often projects an image of pure power by stamping all relationships with its own distinctly symbolic character. As Simmel notes elsewhere, 'style is always that type of artistic arrangement which … negates [an artwork's] quite individual nature and value, its uniqueness of meaning' (SC: 211). In a similar way, the capitalist lifestyle subjects everything that is singular about each person or cultural expression to the general law of economic, social, and aesthetic value, relieving all forms of life of their autonomy and transforming them into mere instances of a generic type, marking them as items with their own price tag, brand, or logo. Thus, the money economy intensifies the desperate subjectivism of modern times even as it finds its objective home in the hustle and bustle of mass society and the modern metropolis, as I discuss in the next part of this book.

Excursus on Class Conflict: Simmel beneath Marx and Engels

In the 'Preface' to the *Philosophy of Money*, Simmel states that his basic intention is to explore the 'upper and lower boundaries' that reach beyond the domain of economic facts (see my opening remarks to chapter 2). A few pages later he elaborates on this perspective by stating that his aim is to recover 'the ideal depths' beneath the economic base of practical and vital existence: 'The attempt is made to construct a new storey beneath historical materialism such that the explanatory value of the incorporation of economic life into the causes of intellectual culture is preserved, while these economic forms themselves are recognized as the result of more profound valuations and currents of psychological or even metaphysical preconditions' (PM: 54). In other words, Simmel does not dispute that material conditions give rise to intellectual culture, but he adds that these economic conditions are themselves shaped by deeper cognitive and even metaphysical relations. The implied reference to Marx here – although Marx himself did not use the phrase 'historical materialism' – gives us a helpful clue to understanding the originality of Simmel's project. Employing Marx's topographical imagery of base and superstructure, Simmel suggests that his philosophy of money digs beneath a political economy of capital in order to explore its deeper sources and to recover its contemporary relevance.

The differences between Marx and Simmel are perhaps a matter more of emphasis and style than of disciplinary approach or theoretical perspective. Where Marx stresses the primacy of production and class conflicts, Simmel addresses their effects on the circulation of money and commodities and on consumer culture generally. We could say that the focus for Marx is on the production of the worker and class relations while Simmel's is more on the seduction of the consumer and the metaphysics of money circulation (Leck 2000: 74, 107). In other words, where one highlights how labour is productive of value and how objectified value is alienated through work, the other shows how exchange generates value and how subjectified value is alienated in monetized desire (Pyyhtinen 2018: 71–3). Simmel would not have been aware of Marx's studies of the alienation of labour or his remarks on 'the universal prostitution' of the worker in the posthumously published *Economic and Philosophical Manuscripts of 1844* (Marx 1977: 78, 87). Nor could he have drawn upon the discussion in Marx's *Grundrisse* notebooks of 1857–8 of the dematerialization of monetary exchanges in the 'Chapter on Money' or his characterization of the 'automatic system of machinery [as] the last metamorphosis of labour' (Marx 1977: 373; Kemple 1995: 22–9). Despite the differences in political tone and empirical rigour of their writings, Simmel's philosophical and sociological treatment of these themes nevertheless complements rather than contradicts Marx's explicitly economic and activist concerns.

Like most German intellectuals of his day, Simmel would have read *The Communist Manifesto* and been struck by the memorable images of how bourgeois society acknowledges 'no other nexus ... than callous "cash payment"' and of how everything feudal and fixed evaporates so that 'all that is solid melts into air' (Marx 1977: 223, 225). He may also have found inspiration in chapter 1 of Marx's *Capital*, where exchange value is analysed as 'the necessary mode of appearance or form of expression of value', which is nevertheless independent of this form: 'the common substance that manifests itself [*das Gemeinsame, was sich ... darstellt*] in the exchange relation, or in the exchange value of commodities, is their value' (ibid.: 423; Marx 1988: 53). But rather than following Marx into the factory, where workers sell their labour power to produce commodities in exchange for a wage, Simmel explores the experience of buying and selling commodities for money in the marketplace. As he argues with a rare reference to the third volume of *Capital*, use-value, need, or labour-time alone do not provide an adequate standard of value apart from the circulation and exchange of money (PM: 430). In effect, Simmel aims to elaborate on what Marx calls 'the general formula of capital', M–C–M', but at the level of circulation: the transformation of money (M) into commodities (C) and back into more money (M'), or buying cheap in order to sell dear (Marx 1977: 445–6). Simmel's primary concern is not with the industrial side of this formula, where labour power – including sex work and intellectual work – becomes a commodity like any other. Rather, he is interested in unpacking the psychology and sociology of trade and commerce as well as the philosophy and metaphysics of shopping and consumption. These deeper cultural dynamics underlie the formula C–M–C': the transformation of commodities into money and the change of money back again into more or new commodities – or selling in order to buy something new, different, or more desirable. Marx's comment on the miser as a kind of productive consumer suggests an illuminating contrast to Simmel's reflections on the psychology of avarice as a dynamic of waste and excess: 'This boundless greed after riches, this passionate chase after exchange-value, is common to the capitalist and the miser; but while the miser is a capitalist gone mad, the capitalist is a rational miser' (ibid.: 449). In the last analysis, both theorists envision the monetary transformation of capital on the historical horizon through the promotion of investment and finance, which Marx expresses in the formula M–M', or money that magically seems to beget more money (and which might also be seen in the credit and debt economy, where C–C^1 expresses an apparently limitless buying spree or the obsessive hoarding of commodities).

While the play of sanity and irrationality in the age of commodity production is a common theme for both thinkers, Simmel characterizes this dynamic more generally as the very fate and inevitable tragedy of modern culture. His point of departure seems to be the statement in 'The Fetish-Character of the Commodity, and its Secret', which Marx added to the second edition of *Capital*: 'A commodity appears, at first sight, as a very trivial thing, and easily understood. Its analysis shows that it is, in reality, a very queer thing, abounding in metaphysical subtleties and theological niceties' (Marx 1977: 435). What might appear to be a flippant or a joking remark for Marx becomes a very serious problem for Simmel. For both, the exchange of commodities 'is a definite social relation between men that assumes, in their eyes, the fantastic form of a relation between things' (ibid.: 436). But

Simmel's emphasis is on how this process of *reification* – by which social relations are objectified and humans are reduced to things – follows 'an immanent developmental logic' within the whole of modern culture, and on how this process of reification is a relentless and even reckless tendency inherent in our way of life. As he argues later in 'The Tragedy of Culture' with reference to Marx (included in *Philosophical Culture*), the contents of culture are 'created by human subjects and are meant for human subjects but ... become alienated from both their origin and their purpose' (SC: 70).

In the end, Simmel follows Engels rather than Marx in examining the process by which cultural processes become alienated from physical necessities, including the need for sexual reproduction and personal intimacy. As Engels argues in a statement that profoundly influenced later generations of feminists, over time natural needs and culturally induced desires become the political and spiritual stakes in a process that gave rise to the first class conflicts and gender inequalities in human history: 'The overthrow of mother-right was the *world historic defeat of the female sex*. The man took command in the home also; the woman was degraded and reduced to servitude; she became the slave of his lust and a mere instrument for the production of children' (Engels 1972: 120–1). Engels's thesis concerning the gendered beginnings of class conflict in *The Origins of the Family, Private Property, and the State* may also have served as a provocation for Simmel's sociology of sex and philosophy of gender (as I note in chapters 3, 5, 9, and 10). In excavating the layers of the modern system of property and gender, Simmel hopes to find the metaphysics of capitalist exchange underneath and to recover the deeper sources and redemptive potential of female culture.

Part II

Sociology of Metropolises

The magnificent opening sentence of Simmel's celebrated essay on mental life in modern cities sounds the keynote that resonates throughout his sociological studies: 'The deepest problems of modern life flow from the claim of the individual to preserve the autonomy and particularity of his or her existence against the superior powers of society, of historical heritage, of external culture, and of the technique of life' (SC: 174–5; GSG 7: 116; also in ISF). Where primitive human beings once struggled for sheer bodily survival, modern individuals now strive to release their souls from social and historical constraints and to attain personal liberties through cultural and technological means. They demand *freedom from* restrictive religious, political, moral, and economic institutions (as pronounced in the slogans of the eighteenth-century revolutions), and they desire *freedom to* cultivate their own creative capacities to the fullest (as expressed in the nineteenth-century cultural and social movements). These struggles go beyond the experience of any particular individual and point to a deeper problem concerning what Simmel calls 'the soul of the cultural body'. As if to stress the asymmetry of this relationship, he juxtaposes the powers (plural) of modern life with the demand (singular) of the individual to maintain his or her autonomy. Thus the English title should more accurately be 'Metropolis*es* and Mental Life', just as the alliteration (also in the original German: '*Die Großstädte und das Geistesleben*') echoes the relentless repetition of the cultural challenges that cities pose to each individual's spiritual well-being. Socialism, liberalism, and other modern responses to the challenges of city life all stem from the resistance of the individual to the prospect of 'being leveled down and worn out by a social-technological mechanism' (SC: 175). The impulse driving individuals to assert their freedom and to express their uniqueness gives rise to the main problems of modern life and thus informs the fundamental questions of sociology.

Simmel's interest in justifying a scientific method for this new field of inquiry did not begin with his famous essay but stems from the very beginnings of his career. The psychological and socio-logical studies that make up his first book, *On Social Differentiation* (1890), announce many of the topics that would later preoccupy him, such as the intersection of social circles and the rise of indi-vidualism. His massive two-volume *Introduction to Moral Science* (1892–3), which examines a variety of views about altruism, guilt, happiness, obligation, and freedom, might be characterized as a kind of 'sociological ethics', along the lines of his essay 'Sociologi-cal Aesthetics' and his references to 'sociological metaphysics' and 'philosophical sociology' in later works (1968: 68–80; S: 660; 1950: 58; Harrington and Kemple 2012). In the years he was revising the *Philosophy of Money*, Simmel pursued his sociological investigations in tandem with epistemological and metaphysical inquiries, such as the *Problems in the Philosophy of History* (1905) and his lecture cycles *Kant* (1904) and *Schopenhauer and Nietzsche* (1907). (A third volume on Hegel was envisioned but never executed; GSG 22: 342–3.) Despite these interdisciplinary interests, his writings still tend to be selectively read, edited, and translated in ways that focus on his social scientific approach to modern cities while ignoring his broader philosophical concerns. The uneven reception of Sim-mel's work has created a blind spot in how we understand him as a classic, and also presents a misleading picture of what sociology and philosophy once were and might yet become (Goodstein 2017: 304; Kemple and Pyyhtinen 2016; see also Suggestions for Further Reading, pp. 189–9).

As Elizabeth Goodstein points out, Simmel considered his socio-logical interests to complement his philosophical writings, even though his colleagues often thought they represented conflicting disciplinary commitments. In a letter to Celestin Bouglé, a young scholar associated with the sociologist Emile Durkheim, he wrote about his frustration in establishing a clear professional identity for himself: 'It is altogether rather painful for me that abroad I am only known as a sociologist – whereas I am a philosopher, see my life's task in philosophy, and only pursue sociology on the side' (quoted in Goodstein 2016: 31; GSG 22: 342–4). Perhaps because of his eclectic intellectual interests, Simmel's popularity as a university lecturer began to grow among a wide variety of socially active students, including Robert Park (1864–1944), a journalist and advocate for technical training for Afro-Americans and one of the founders of urban sociology in the United States; Helene Stöcker (1869–1943), an activist for the rights of single mothers; and Kurt Hiller (1885–1972), a leader in the movement against the discrimination of homosexuals, although Simmel himself was not as politically engaged (Leck 2000: 207–65; Köhnke 1996; see chapter 9). Around the time when his application for a professorship in Heidelberg was rejected, his friend and colleague Max Weber wrote that, 'even when Simmel is on the wrong path, he fully deserves his reputation as one of [our] foremost thinkers and as one of the main inspirations for academic youth' (Weber 2012: 418). Many of these students were drawn into feminist, expressionist, activist, naturalist, and other cultural movements of the day and shared his interest in learning more about urban social problems. As Simmel told his son Hans, 'Berlin's emergence from metropolis to world city in the years around and after the turn of the century coincides with the period of my own strongest and broadest development .... Perhaps I could have pursued something just as worthy in another city, but the particular achievement that I accomplished during these decades is undoubtedly tied to the Berlin milieu' (quoted in H. Simmel 1958: 256).

Simmel's essay on modern metropolises does not stem directly from his lectures and seminars in Berlin, however; it derives from a talk he gave at the German Metropolitan Exhibition in the much smaller provincial city of Dresden in 1903. This unprecedented public exhibition was sponsored by the Gehe Foundation and featured urban planners, business leaders, and academics from Germany's major industrial cities (Frisby 2001: 131–9). In contrast to the other lectures in the series, which focused on the geography, politics, demographics, and scientific culture of particular cities in historical and comparative perspective, Simmel's talk addressed the lived experience and intellectual life of modern city dwellers in broad terms and with only passing references to Berlin, Paris, and London. Although examples of urban experience are scattered throughout his sociological writings, this famous essay represents his only concentrated discussion of the modern metropolis. Thus, in the following three chapters I weave together some of the most memorable descriptions and influential claims he makes in 'The Metropolis and Mental Life' (hereafter 'the metropolises essay') with key concepts from *Sociology* and with related ideas from his philosophical writings during this phase of his career.

In a rare footnote, Simmel acknowledges that the metropolises essay is less a discussion of the current literature on cities than an illustration and elaboration of the main cultural ideas he developed in the *Philosophy of Money* (SC: 185). At the same time, this short essay explicitly advances a theory of modernity and vividly illustrates what in *Sociology* he calls the 'forms of association' (*Vergesellschaftungsformen*). David Frisby identifies Simmel's primary themes in a thesis that I expand on here with reference to these broader sociological concerns: 'Whereas the metropolis is, as it were, the *concentration* of modernity, the mature money economy (which also has its focal point in the metropolis) is responsible for the *diffusion* of modernity throughout society' (Frisby 1992: 69). Simmel conceives these two 'sites of modernity' as complex webs of relationships and as intricate labyrinths of social interaction, with the money economy *extending* modern lifestyles on a global scale and the metropolis *intensifying* the modern experience of individual and social life. Although these tendencies are discussed throughout *Sociology*, I highlight the book's three middle chapters on the struggle for privacy and secrecy in mass societies (which I discuss in chapter 5), the tension between individual differentiation and social conformity (chapter 6), and the patterns of interaction and estrangement that characterize relations between the poor and the propertied (chapter 7). Each of these topics advances Simmel's general point about the dynamics of inclusion and exclusion among individuals and social groups (his second apriority of membership discussed in chapter 1). At the same time they pose philosophical questions about the refinement of feelings and fashions and the gaps between social classes and individuals in the big city. As I show in excurses on several of Simmel's contemporaries, these ideas resonate with prominent trends in the sociology of his day as well as in recent debates over gender roles, social networks, and global cities.

5

Privacy and Secrecy in Mass Society

Anyone who has visited a city for the first time, or discovered an unfamiliar part of their own native city, can recall the shock of taking in new impressions, the confusion in following its strange rhythms, and even the terror of simply crossing the street. In order to cope with 'the *intensification of nervous stimulation* that results from the swift and uninterrupted change of outer and inner stimuli', everyone in the city must find a way of adapting to 'the metropolitan type of individuality' (SC: 175). Each city has a certain sensory flow, a characteristic tempo that shapes every experience and directs the ceaseless movement of people and things. Life in the big city requires maintaining a certain intellectual distance from other people, learning to understand one's surroundings in a rational way, and remaining wary of the dangers and temptations that can threaten one's security or sanity at any moment: 'Thus the metropolitan type – which naturally plays out in a thousand individual variations – creates for itself a *protective organ* against the threatening currents and discrepancies of the external milieu that threaten to uproot it' (SC: 176, emphasis added). With every appeal and aggression from the world around us, we eventually become accustomed to approaching each encounter with the head rather than the heart. We learn to respond to every incident by reasoning things through instead of reacting out of the impulse of the moment. As our nerves wear down from overstimulation and excitement, the intellect takes over and a matter-of-fact attitude settles into our bodies and minds as we learn to accommodate to the fast pace and heightened energy of everyday life. Over time we become numb, and eventually we learn to adopt the apathetic stance of the blasé attitude.

In this chapter I consider Simmel's remarkable elaboration on the experience of life in the metropolis, with particular emphasis on his description of the techniques that city dwellers develop to protect themselves from its often overwhelming cultural, historical, technological, and social forces. The blasé attitude is familiar to anyone who has lived for some time in a city, but it is just one among many coping strategies. A sophisticated mind, a habit of mental reserve, a cautious way of presenting oneself, and a whole array of technological devices can also effectively serve as 'protective organs' and techniques of self-preservation. As Simmel states in the opening pages of the metropolises essay, 'the human is essentially a being that makes distinctions [*der Mensch ist ein Unterschiedswesen*]' (SC: 176; GSG 7: 116; see also 'Socialism and Pessimism', GSG 5: 554). The idea that humans are uniquely capable of distinguishing momentary impressions from one another and of filtering out 'regular and habitual contrasts' is one of the great themes of Simmel's sociology of cities. In order to explore his deeper thoughts on these matters, I turn to chapter 5 of *Sociology*, 'The Secret and the Secret Society', where he describes the human capacity deliberately to conceal things and consciously to deceive others not just as a common tactic of self-interest and self-expression but also as one of the highest achievements of modern civilization.

After the publication of the first edition of the *Philosophy of Money*, Simmel turned more and more to a sociological investigation of feelings, perceptions, and experiences specific to modern urban life. In a sense, his particular way of doing sociology relies less on philosophical speculation or scientific fact than on exploring sense data and personal experience. As I note in my Introduction, he focuses on forms of *association* (*Vergesellschaftung*), a term that includes but cannot quite be captured by the words 'socialization' (within the family or the state, for example), 'social construction' (the term used in the subtitle of the English edition of *Sociology*), or the technically awkward terms 'sociation' and 'societalization' (in contrast to 'communalization'). Unlike the term 'society', which implies a finished state or fixed substance, 'association' suggests an incomplete process and a set of ongoing relationships that we might choose or a series of relationships that might be unconsciously chosen for us. The 'forms of association' are the products or effects of all kinds of relationships and reciprocal interactions (*Wechselwirkungen*), and these *forms* are themselves the *content* of Simmel's social scientific investigations. Thus, in shifting topics from the money economy to the metropolis, Simmel does not really switch disciplinary commitments from philosophy to sociology. Rather, he refines his theoretical framework and narrows his scope of inquiry by turning his attention from the many ways in which everything connects with everything else through a particular symbol (money) to the many ways that human relationships in particular exhibit general social and individual forms, especially in the city.

The Mind Versus the Masses

In his programmatic essay 'The Problem of Sociology', Simmel does not attempt to define sociology, a science that did not yet exist as a distinct discipline in university departments or with its own scholarly societies. Rather, he considers the problem areas that sociology might address and suggests some ways of approaching them. Sociology is not the scientific study of some static object called 'society', he insists, but rather a method for investigating the forms of association and a certain way of studying how individuals interact with, exist for, and live beside one another (1994a: 33). In rewriting this essay as the opening chapter of *Sociology*, Simmel elaborates on dynamic processes, relationships, and interactions where social 'doings', 'moments', 'events', or 'happenings' are frequently fleeting and ungraspable but can nevertheless be observed and described. He describes how humans look at one another, become jealous, exchange letters, eat lunch, elicit sympathy, show gratitude and loyalty, ask directions, dress and adorn themselves, and so on, all as part of the warp and woof of the vast tapestry that is social life: 'such threads are woven at every moment, allowed to fall, are taken up again, substitute for others, and then interwoven with others' (S: 33). What he calls the 'problem of sociology' consists of 'overcoming the individualistic way of seeing', and, although such a perspective does not give this new science its own object of study, the sociological view of the world has itself become a subject of scientific knowledge as well as a general human concern: 'The insight that the human being may be defined in all its essence and appearances as living in interaction with other human beings must lead to a new mode of *observation* in all the so-called cultural sciences' (S: 20; GSG 11: 15). This 'phenomenology' of social and cultural life reflects an impulse and a sensibility that is only just emerging in recent times with the rise of a developed money economy, a mass society, and a metropolitan way of life (O'Neill 1973; Backhaus 1998; Goodstein 2002).

Figure 5 displays how these forms of association are presented in the ten chapters that make up Simmel's path-breaking *Sociology*. The book brings together and revises several dozen previously published essays from as far back as 1890, many of which were quickly translated into English, French, and other languages. Simmel acknowledges the incomplete and patchwork character of these investigations, conceding that each chapter can offer only 'examples with regard to method' and that second-hand historical materials really serve only as 'object lessons' rather than as factual proofs (S: ix, 32, 54). Although the book appears to be a haphazard collection of general concepts and discussions of disconnected topics, in figure 5 I suggest they might be loosely grouped into *basic social processes* that characterize all social life (chapters 2, 3, and 4) and *forms of association* that are more specific to the spiritual and mental life of social groups (chapters 5, 6, and 7) or that characterize cultural life

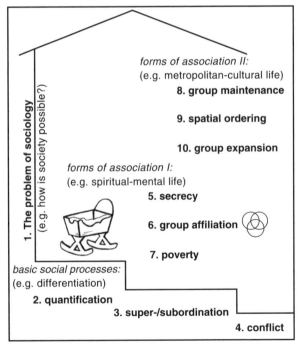

Figure 5 Outline of *Sociology*

in the city or mass society more broadly (chapters 8, 9, and 10). In any case, it is important to remember that Simmel formulates the key concepts in each of these chapters in general terms that may apply to many manifestations of social life, including but not limited to modern metropolises.

Simmel does not examine social processes and forms in abstraction from the contents of social life or as 'containers' separate from what they contain. Rather, social forms are interwoven with 'the stuff, so to speak, of interaction' – impulses, drives, motives, interests, purposes, predispositions, psychological states, and so on, which are shaped by and swept up into the dynamics of social life (S: 23). In this regard, he emphasizes processes and relationships that resemble the relativistic worldview of modern physics at the same time as he recovers an older tradition of thought. Rather than assuming that 'instrumental causality' is the only standard of scientific explanation, he also considers what Aristotle calls 'formal', 'substantial', and 'teleological' causality (Lichtblau 1991: 46–7). In other words, the bits and pieces of social life and the fragments of experience that sociology studies are not only treated in terms of how they fall within a sequence of 'efficient' causes and effects. Simmel is also interested in studying how the *substance* of social life is made up of individuals and groups as they interact, how they *form* reciprocal relationships, and how they pursue various *ends* or purposes with respect to one another.

Simmel's forms of association are presented here in the shape of a house as a way of emphasizing what he does not consider in the metropolises essay but often addresses in *Sociology*, namely, the role of the private sphere in preserving social order and a sense of self (see, for example, his discussion of the incest taboo, S: 579–83). Although in this book he does not elaborate on the arguments of his 1895 essay 'On the Sociology of the Family', he does discuss the home as the traditional domain of women (see the 'Excursus on Maternal Feminism', pp. 91–5). In his ground-breaking chapter 'Space and the Spatial Ordering of Society', he also remarks in general terms on how personal meanings are attached to the concentration and organization of particular places and locations: 'Social interaction among human beings is – apart from everything else it is – also experienced as a realization of space' (S: 545; GSG 11: 687; also in SC). When individuals enter into interaction, empty space is filled with social meaning and animated with personal significance. Any *spatial order* – from the room of a house to the street of a metropolis – is defined by the boundary that separates inside from outside, public life from private life. In general terms, a boundary is not so much 'a spatial fact with sociological effects, but a sociological reality that is formed spatially' (S: 552). The limits of the city and the walls of the home, for example, thus serve a sociological function insofar as they give clarity and security to a set of mutual relationships between oneself and the larger society.

Boundaries define who can be included and who must be excluded, what is revealed and what must remain hidden. Even a crowd gathered in the open air at night takes on a definite spatial form, combining the sense of being enclosed with the feeling of being exposed in a fantastically indefinite realm: 'Darkness gives the assembly actually a rather peculiar framework that brings together the significance of the narrow and wide into one of characteristic unity' (S: 556). Likewise, the individual in the city risks being absorbed and effaced by the crowd, but people may also find spaces of freedom and sites for self-cultivation in the city, such as a library, a garden, or a home. A house or an apartment may serve as a private refuge, but such spaces are also typically numbered rather than named and therefore marked as points in a larger network of relationships connecting them to other places both within and beyond the city (S: 614). While a family household solidifies kinship relations between generations and genders, the streets of the city extend social connections on a massive scale by locating residences within an abstract grid. Keeping these ideas in mind, we might reflect on the English translation of the German *Großstadt* (which simply means 'big city') with the word *metropolis*, from the Greek *mētēr* (mother) and *polis* (city or state). This word conveys the sense of how domestic and public worlds accommodate one another in urban space and also how mother cities (metropoles) can serve as a model (matrix) for generating other cities (symbolized by the cradle in figure 5).

Simmel asserts that the new science of sociology is specially tasked with 'the theoretical pursuit and reflection on the practical power that the masses have acquired in the nineteenth century against the interests of individuals' (S: 19). With the spread of industry and the concentration of people in urban centres, the nineteenth century witnessed an unprecedented growth in population and productivity coupled with the rise of an individualistic lifestyle (1950: 31–9; S: 58–60). These developments created unique conditions for leaders to appeal to the mass emotionality of crowds and for individuals to experience new forms of isolation. As Simmel points out in the metropolises essay, 'one nowhere feels as lonely and lost as in the metropolitan crowd' (SC: 181). In chapter 2 of *Sociology*, on 'The Quantitative Conditioning of the Group', he addresses this dilemma by posing an elementary question of 'social arithmetic': 'How many persons must one invite for it to be a "society", or simply a "gathering"?' (S: 73). In other words, what is the numerical threshold between 'a few', 'several', and 'many' beyond which a social group or informal occasion takes on an objective character independent of its individual members? Why do we say that three or more is a 'crowd'? And at what point do troops make up an army, how does a clique become a party, when is an assembly more like a multitude, and what makes a cultural community a nation? In the *Fundamental Questions of Sociology*, Simmel defines the branch of 'general sociology' as an approach to historical life that examines patterns over time at the levels of the social mass and the individual mind. In particular, general sociology is concerned with studying the recent tendency for refined and rare individuals to be pulled 'down' to the lowest common denominator and for great persons to be reduced to the base impulses of the majority. Echoing the crowd psychologists of the late nineteenth century, Simmel points out that 'a collective nervousness – a sensitivity, a passion, and an eccentricity' characterizes the crowd, which exerts a relentless force over every individual who is drawn into its centre of gravity (1950: 35). He calls the conflicts that emerge from this uneven development of personal intellect and mass emotionality 'the sociological tragedy', as if to suggest that history has reached a dramatic moment when the unruly vitality of individuals is under threat of being levelled by the impulsive dynamism of crowds (1950: 32; Borch 2010).

So where do we find sanctuary from the madding crowd and how can we protect ourselves from the relentless forces of city life? In the metropolises essay Simmel emphasizes the ways in which cities require a matter-of-fact attitude, a calculating mind-set, and a scrupulous attention to punctuality. As a consequence, some personalities are dragged down into a feeling of their own worthlessness in the face of the objective world while others are overvalued (SC: 179). The predominance of the intellect under these cultural and spiritual conditions has its source in the money economy, which finds its primary seat in the metropolis: 'London has never acted as England's heart but often as England's intellect and always as her moneybag!', Simmel points out (SC: 177; also PM: 504). The rational logic and impersonal calculations of money exchanges give rise to the blasé attitude as a strategy for warding off the overwhelming onrush of impressions and for filtering out 'the rapidly changing and closely compressed contrasting stimulations of the nerves' that threaten a person's sense of self, safety, and security. When 'an incapacity thus emerges to react to new sensations with the appropriate energy', Simmel observes, the result is a 'blunting of discrimination' in which everything appears 'in an evenly flat and gray tone' (SC: 178). He introduces this theme in the *Philosophy of Money*, where he notes that the endless exchanges of money and merchandise result in 'the loss of any feeling for value difference', to the point where nothing seems worth getting excited about, people are instantly satiated (and yet perpetually stimulated), and their appreciation for specific qualities is nullified (PM: 257–9). At the same time, this prevailing attitude of indifference compels the individual to guard their own sense of self: 'insofar as money is the symbol as well as the cause of making everything indifferent and externalizing everything that lends itself to such a process, it also becomes the gatekeeper of the most intimate sphere, which can then develop within its own limits' (PM: 475). In the metropolises essay, Simmel describes this mental strategy of self-preservation in the big city as an attitude of tact, discretion, and reserve, and even as an act of withdrawal into a concealed world marked off as private and secret.

Secrets in the City

Life in large cities entails not only the heightening of nervous and emotional life but also the need to gather a repertoire of techniques for managing this intensity with civility and circumspection, or with scepticism and suspicion. Anonymous exchanges and fleeting transactions between people – 'the touch and go elements of metropolitan life', as Simmel puts it – are carried on at all times and in all places; they often mean that neighbours may not know one another by sight, and that many encounters are approached with 'a slight aversion, a mutual strangeness and repulsion' (SC: 179). City dwellers protect themselves from hateful outbursts and violent conflicts by holding their antipathy in reserve and by keeping their social, psychological, or physical distance from the many people they see or meet on a daily basis. What appears to be a pattern of atomization and dissociation is at the same time a coping strategy, a habit learned through practice and repetition and therefore one of the 'elemental forms of socialization' (SC: 180). Generally speaking, city life is sustained not just through social and spatial remoteness but also by cultivating psychological relationships of participation and withdrawal and by maintaining a tactful balance between ignorance and knowledge of other people.

In the chapter of *Sociology* on 'The Secret and the Secret Society', Simmel elaborates on the degree to which people are included or excluded from social life according to whether they are aware of or oblivious to one another. He points out that human beings depend upon their knowledge of others, and thus upon relations of trust. At the same time, however, many relationships are based on error, deception, prejudice, and incomplete information about other people, or even about oneself: 'Someone who knows all need not *trust*, someone who knows nothing cannot reasonably trust at all' (S: 315). We can never know someone absolutely, and another person's thoughts, attitudes, and beliefs often remain partially or wholly inaccessible to us. Thus, we often need to exercise a certain sensitivity and self-control in curtailing our natural wish to inquire about other people while respecting their right to privacy, even in the most intimate relationships (S: 325). This need for discretion comes both from an awareness that one self should not violate another self and from a sense of duty that a person should abstain from knowing everything that another person does not freely reveal, such as not listening at closed doors or glancing at other people's letters. For this reason, our thoughts and actions about ourselves and others often proceed in 'zigzag movements' and through a 'confusing whirl' of images and ideas, or by making 'merely tentative combinations' and 'leaps' through an apparently irrational chaos (S: 310). We could say then that, in general, social life happens somewhere along this sliding scale of reciprocal knowledge and ignorance; it occurs at some point between truth-telling and lying; it emerges along the curved line that connects secrecy and publicity; and it takes place on a shifting ground of discretion and trust. The extreme ends of these fundamental characteristics of social interaction become most prominent in the cramped space and rapid pace of the city. Indifference towards neighbours and distrust of strangers are for the most part protective devices in this regard, 'without which a person in the metropolis would be mentally torn and shattered' (S: 569).

Simmel repeatedly stresses that the sociological and psychological pressure of the money economy both limits and facilitates these attitudes of indifference or evasion that are so prevalent in the metropolis: 'Money, more than any other form of value, makes possible the secrecy, invisibility and silence of exchange' (PM: 387).

Most of our everyday transactions are impersonal and anonymous in a way that relieves us from the need to make direct contact with things and with other people. These are the conditions under which modern individuals struggle to 'secure an island of subjectivity, a secret closed-off sphere of privacy' (PM: 474). Through money and other media, people learn to create an internal barrier between themselves and others which is indispensable for their mutual sanity and security: 'Since contemporary urban culture, with its commercial, professional and social intercourse, forces us to be physically close to an enormous number of people, sensitive and nervous modern people would sink completely into despair if the objectification of social relationships did not bring with it an inner boundary and reserve' (PM: 483). In a sense, then, the money economy spreads a kind of crypto-society of silence, just as the metropolis encourages people to create secret societies and clandestine subcultures within it. The massive scale of city life facilitates spaces where secrets can be kept and shared, and where individuals can refashion, conceal, or simply become themselves in private spaces that are parallel to and sealed off from the official world: 'the secret offers the possibility of a … second world next to the apparent one, and this is influenced by the former most strongly' (S: 325). The paradox of social life in the modern city consists in how matters of general concern become exposed to public scrutiny while those that interest the individual often remain hidden from view (S: 329). The business of governments, markets, and courts, for example, loses its secret and inaccessible character, while the individual citizen increasingly withdraws inwards: 'what is public becomes ever more public, the private ever more private' (S: 331). Far from being a regrettable or accidental effect of the rise of modern mass societies, however, this disconnect between secrecy and publicity is one of the greatest achievements of a mature civilization: 'contrary to the childish condition in which every idea is immediately spoken, every undertaking is open for all to see, an immense expansion of life is achieved with the secret because its various contents cannot make an appearance at all with complete publicity' (S: 325).

Simmel elaborates on several examples of these tendencies in ways that have implications for his reflections on cities. 'The Secret and the Secret Society' is interrupted by two digressions that at first glance seem to have little to do with his main topic. One discusses jewellery and adornment (both words translate the German *Schmuck*), and the other is about written communication or commerce (both words translate the German *Verkehr*, though his main focus is on letter writing). How do these examples illustrate the general problem of knowledge and ignorance in social interaction, and specifically the social form of the secret? And can jewellery and letters be considered protective devices or strategies of self-preservation in the city? Personal adornments such as jewellery, tattoos, make-up, perfume, and fashion accessories all have the effect of both drawing attention to the individual and creating distance from others. In a sense, they reveal something unique about a person while at the same time concealing his or her peculiar qualities under a veneer of impersonality (S: 332–6; also in SC: 206–11). The irony here is that 'one adorns oneself for one's self and can do that only while one adorns oneself for others' (S: 332). What seems to be something objective that anyone might possess – a piece of clothing, a ring, a haircut, and so on – is also a distinct feature of the personality itself. And what appears to be authentic, elegant, or unique also projects a stylized aura around a person. In other words, adornments are props on a stage for the performance of self. They play a part in the social masquerade of hide and seek and in the game of involvement and detachment where individuals reveal aspects of themselves while keeping other aspects hidden and stashed away.

Although Simmel seems to have intimate circles of acquaintances in mind, his general point can be expanded to account for certain features of mass society and to address both the secret and the spectacular dimensions of urban experience. In articles written for the feuilleton section of the *Frankfurter Zeitung* in the 1920s and early 1930s, Simmel's student Siegfried Kracauer (1889–1966), the philosopher, journalist, and cultural critic, proposes to analyse 'inconspicuous surface-level impressions' of the modern epoch. His focus is on how musical reviews, sporting events, military parades, and other mass spectacles conceal 'unheeded impulses' and deeper destructive trends. Along with the Marxist philosophers Georg Lukács and Ernst Bloch, Kracauer attended Simmel's lectures at Berlin University as well as seminars and salons at his Westend home. He writes of Simmel's importance both as a sociologist of the individual and society and as a philosopher of culture and the soul: 'With gentle fingers he carefully probes the soul, laying bare what was previously hidden, exposing the most secret impulses and untangling the tightly knit weave of our feelings, yearnings, and desires' (Kracauer 1995: 227). Elsewhere he argues that in mass society individuals are pressed together, counted, lined up, regulated, and rendered anonymous in collective 'ornamental' figures that both conceal their individual souls and display their objective function in abstract systems: 'The mass ornament is the aesthetic reflex of the rationality to which the prevailing economic system aspires' (ibid.: 79). Where Simmel emphasizes the double purpose of personal adornment in both guarding and exposing unique aspects of the self, Kracauer describes the mass ornament as a symptom of a system in which personal features of individuals in communities are concealed and effaced by the homogenizing patterns of mass society.

Simmel's remarks on the sociology of the letter also have implications for how we might understand certain aspects of mass society, in particular the function of written texts in intimate interactions as well as on a larger scale (S: 342–5). Even when sealed in an envelope (or transmitted privately on a mobile phone), a written message seems less likely to remain secret than an oral conversation between individuals. And yet in some ways writing can also be more durable and secure: 'The letter … directly links the objective revocation of all security of the secret to the subjective increase of this security' (S: 343). Within a close friendship or a secret society, and in the management of household finances or government bureaucracies, written communications require a measure of mutual trust and assurance, even as they also place each party under the risk of exposure. Since written texts must communicate without the sound of the voice, hand gestures, and facial expressions that are features of direct speech (note that emojis are only an imperfect substitute!), they are more open to multiple interpretations and misunderstandings. Writing may even raise questions about whether someone is telling the truth or not, as Simmel notes in this connection in his remarks on lying (S: 310–14). A lie is neither an exaggeration nor a blatant falsehood but, rather, a manifestation of the peculiar human capacity deliberately to deceive or consciously to conceal things from others. The lie projects a false impression about something to another person, not unlike a simple error or a misconception, but with the added element that 'what one [person] will accept about the inner opinion of the lying person is [in fact] a deception' (S: 311). Our ability to betray other people, to keep secrets (including 'open secrets'), to tell lies (including 'white lies'), and thus to distort something about our own true intentions in communicating with others is potentially at work in any social relation, Simmel argues. Our capacity deliberately to deceive and purposefully to hide parts of ourselves is often enhanced through written communication and may even provide a paradigm for the relationship between the individual and society more generally (Barbour 2012: 226).

In the course of interacting with and communicating in the social world, we create a private inner world for ourselves that can also be shared with others. With this paradox in mind, Simmel seems to be raising a question about our capacity for keeping parts of ourselves clandestine while at the same time affecting those around us. In 'The Maker of Lies', another of those odd 'Snapshots under the Aspect of Eternity' (*Momentbilder sub specie aeternitatis*) published under a pseudonym in the journal *Jugend* (like the one on money discussed in chapter 2), Simmel obliquely considers a related conundrum: can we ever truly deceive ourselves? (2012: 409–10). A narrator tells the fanciful story of a magician who gives a man the power to make others lie. With the zeal of a torturer, the man compels people to say things they know are not true, until one day he falls in love with a woman who is indifferent to him. He then uses his power to force her to declare her love for him but soon realizes that he cannot make her truly love him. Finally, he turns his power to produce lies on himself, hoping to deceive himself into thinking that he and the woman will love each other and live happily ever after. And indeed, we are told, 'everything was as good as it could be – or almost so' (2012: 410). Without explaining what this might mean, the story ends with the man puzzling over the magician's 'good intentions', perhaps suspecting that the magician himself had maliciously lied to him after all. In pondering Simmel's story (which he did not sign with his own name!), we might recall how written texts express a relationship of trust between a writer, who may be holding something back for later or leaving something in reserve for others to make use of as they please, and a reader, who may be misled or manipulated by certain deceptions and delusions, perhaps unconsciously or even willingly …

Excursus on Maternal Feminism: Simmel between Marianne Weber and Gilman

The classical tradition of sociology is not usually known for placing women's issues and questions of gender at the centre of concern. Although Marx and Engels consider the exploitation of women's work in the factory, Weber notes the regulation of women's sexuality within ascetic religious practices, and Durkheim traces the emancipation of women with the rise of divorce rates, these issues tend to be lost in their respective discussions of the large-scale historical dynamics of alienation, disenchantment, and anomie in the modern world. A notable exception is Simmel's career-long focus on the politics of the feminist movement, the psychology and sociology of women, and the philosophy of gender and sexuality. He develops these ideas in over a dozen essays written between 1890 and 1911 and in related discussions of prostitution, fashion, flirting, jewellery, and various other cultural and political topics. For example, in 'The Women's Congress and Social Democracy', an unsigned newspaper editorial (SC: 270–4), he reports on the antagonism in 1896 between the members of the Organization of Social Democratic Working Women and the middle-class leaders of the Berlin Women's Congress. While social democratic feminists are fighting for better working conditions, access to employment, and equal wages, bourgeois feminists participate in organizations for women's rights, female student unions, and movements advancing women's social and political interests. Each class of women is concerned with whether the household is a space of freedom or confinement: 'The present-day industrial mode of production, on the one hand, has torn the proletarian woman away from the household activity and, on the other, impoverished the domain of the bourgeois woman which is limited to that same sphere' (SC: 273). As Simmel puts this point in *Sociology*, 'one class of women wants back in the house, the other wants out of the house' (S: 400). Despite the issues that divide these classes of women, a consideration of the 'sociological evolution of the concept of "woman"' reveals their common experiences and shared structural position. In particular, the domestic sphere isolates each class of women from other women and separates all of them from merchants, labourers, businessmen, and other cultural workers who occupy a public sphere that is dominated by men (S: 398–401).

Simmel's writings on women combine sociological observation with philosophical speculation in ways that often make his arguments appear contradictory, surprising, confusing, or simply wrong. In 'The Relative and Absolute Problem of the Sexes' and in 'Female Culture' (from the essay collection *Philosophical Culture*), he develops a feminist critique of certain naturalized assumptions that arise from idealized versions of womanhood which have effectively kept women from contributing fully to 'objective culture': 'With the exception of a very few areas, our objective culture is thoroughly male. It is men who have created art and industry, science and commerce, the state and religion' (1984: 67). Male energies, emotions, and modes of reasoning have monopolized the spheres of art, scholarship, politics, economics, and law, while women's sphere of activity has historically been limited to the home. At the same time, Simmel also makes a metaphysical claim that men and women represent essentially different modes of being, with different rhythms and outlooks. Each sex is structured according to 'a completely autonomous rule', and each has its own 'metaphysical nature' and 'sociological locus' (1984: 72, 107). Where the masculine world separates subjective from objective culture through the pursuit of specialized tasks, the feminine nature is 'intrinsically sexual' and centred on a 'state of serene, self-contained completeness, ... [where] all the lines of the cosmos of culture conspire in an inner unity that is concrete and continuous' (1984: 94). With this argument in mind, Simmel concludes that 'the ideal of the women's movement cannot be an "independent humanity" ... but rather an "independent femininity"' (1984: 98). Women may reform or revolutionize a male-dominated public sphere by contributing uniquely feminine values to cultural tasks that are best suited to them, such as developing a feminine sense of justice, an intuitive approach to historical scholarship, the acting skills needed to excel in the dramatic arts, and the compassion required in the medical professions. Although Simmel calls for a cultural revolution guided by essentially feminine universal values, he cannot envision a future humanist social order or trans-sexual objective culture that men and women might contribute to equally.

Not surprisingly, Simmel's peculiar blend of avant-garde radicalism and social conservatism occasionally generated both controversy among students active in the women's and homosexual rights movements and confusion in his personal relations and intellectual exchanges with the strong, independent, and cosmopolitan women in his life (Leck 2000: 131–61). His wife, Gertrud, an accomplished painter and philosopher, probably contributed as much to his open-minded intellectual views and aesthetic insights as he did to the development of her ideas. His lover Gertrud Kantorowicz (1876–1945), who bore him an illegitimate daughter whom he never publicly acknowledged, was a distinguished art historian, poet, and scholar who wrote an extensive introduction to a collection of Simmel's posthumous papers, as did a close friend, the prominent writer and intellectual Margarete Susman (1872–1966). Significantly, Simmel also maintained a friendship with Marianne Weber (1870–1954), despite their intellectual differences, and dedicated his monograph *Goethe* to her (see the epigraph to this book). A member of the German Democratic Party, a delegate to the Baden parliament, and chair of the League of German Women Associations, she also published essays and books that both complement and depart from the writings of her famous husband, Max Weber, and of Simmel.

In her 1907 book *Wife and Mother in the Development of Law* (*Ehefrau und Mutter in Rechtsentwicklung*), and in other works, she focuses on marriage as both an institution for the subordination of women (coerced or voluntary) and a potential basis for women's autonomy. The Puritan ideal of a 'soul relationship' between free and equal partners expressed this potential for the first time: 'Freedom of conscience, the mother of all personal rights of the individual, stood ... at the cradle of women's rights', she writes (Marianne Weber 1998: 216–17). In 'Women and Objective Culture' and 'Women's Special Cultural Tasks', she advances a forceful critique of Simmel's feminist writings (both essays are included in her 1919 collection *Reflections on Women and Women's Issues*). In her view, Simmel confuses factual observations with value-judgements and mixes up metaphysical ideals with sociological facts. Everyone has the capacity to be a full human being, she argues, and men and women are not so much different life-forms based on sex (*Geschlecht*) as they are overlapping circles belonging to the same genus (also *Geschlecht*): 'Men and women both belong to the genus of humanity, which through physical and spiritual characteristics distinguishes them from all other species' (Marianne Weber, in Leck 2000: 157; van Vucht Tijssen 1991: 210). Women experience a conflict between life and thought not only because they lack opportunities to realize their intellectual powers, but also because they are forced to choose between their calling or profession and their roles in marriage or motherhood. Between the separation of objective and personal culture, which men and women experience differently, lies 'the middle ground ... of immediate existence', where the individual soul is formed through 'companionship, friendship, love, marriage and family' (Marianne Weber 1998: 225). This everyday world of living falls to women in the first instance, since their cultural task is to transform a house into a home for the recovery, restoration, and renewal of all its members.

Despite their differences, Marianne Weber and Georg Simmel embrace an ethic of what might be called *material feminism*, the view that a woman's cultural tasks as wives and mothers in the home are distinct from and yet make an essential contribution to the male-dominated public world. A more radical version of this maternal ethic is advanced by their contemporary Charlotte Perkins Gilman (1860–1935), the American sociologist, fiction writer, and public intellectual. Marianne Weber approvingly cites Gilman as 'our comrade-in-arms' for pointing out that wage work may free women from many of the responsibilities of housework and child care, although paid labour does not necessarily purchase women's economic autonomy (Marianne Weber 1998: 221). Gilman's classic work *Women and Economics*, published in 1898, introduces the idea that housework should be valued as a professional activity on a par with men's work outside the home, but then goes further than either Marianne Weber or Simmel to ground this argument in evolutionary biology: 'Economic production is the natural expression of human energy – not sex-energy at all, but race-energy – the unconscious functioning of the social organism. Socially organized human beings tend to produce, as a gland to secrete' (Gilman 1989: 163). In her mature sociological work, especially *The Man-Made World: Our Androcentric Culture*, from 1911, she seems to echo Simmel in arguing that industry is essentially a feminine function and that the 'surplus energy' of woman's work is naturally expressed in productive industry: 'Because of her mother-power she became the first inventor and laborer; being in truth *the mother of industry as well as all people*' (ibid.: 212, emphasis added). On the basis of this 'gynaecocentric theory of life', she advocates not for the feminization of androcentric culture but, rather, for the humanization of women on the biological assumption that the 'female is the race-type, the man the variant' (ibid.: 237). In this regard, Gilman's position appears to be even more essentialist or 'naturalist' than that of Simmel, who nevertheless agrees with her that 'the woman represents the universal fundament that comprehends the sexes substantially or genetically ... because she is the mother' (1984: 127–8). In Simmel's view, by contrast, the belief that there is some purely human culture beyond the differences between men and women is itself the product of an androcentric culture that naively identifies the 'human' with 'man' (1984: 67).

We could say, then, that Georg Simmel's metaphysical version of maternal feminism lies somewhere between the social-cultural ethic of motherhood advocated by Marianne Weber and the natural-evolutionary theory of mother-power developed in the writings of Charlotte Perkins Gilman.

6

The Cosmopolitan Worldview and Urban Fashion

Life in the big city does not just grind us down, wear us out, and exhaust all our spiritual resources, forcing us to find a refuge where we can recover and revive ourselves. Many of us are also lifted up by its exhilarating pace, drawn into its restless rhythms, and energized by its tantalizing attractions. We often forget about others or lose ourselves in the crush of the crowd, but we also encounter enticing strangers and find our inner selves in the hunt for extreme impressions, in the pursuit of speed and change, and in the quest for excitement. As Simmel observes in the *Philosophy of Money*, we look for a release from the weariness and boredom of everyday life by seeking out the next distraction, another entertaining spectacle, or an additional piece of information, but usually 'without thinking it important for us to find out why these stimulate us' (PM: 258). Citing recent research in physiology, he speculates that, just as electric shock treatment turns the initial result into its opposite – a dull indifference and numbness – so also can repeated and relentless nervous stimulation from the urban milieu compel us to search for ever new dangers, more extravagant risks, and outrageous displays for attention (PM: 262, 266). Generally speaking, the heightened tension of everyday life in the city can inspire us both to expand our spatial and temporal horizons outwardly and to refine our sense of personal style by cultivating new ways of expressing our inner selves.

Contemporary urban ways of living are often characterized by their fleeting and ephemeral qualities. These experiences are epitomized by the shopper at a trade exhibition, the aimless wanderer out for a stroll (the *flâneur*), or, as we might add today, the internet surfer endlessly scrolling through webpages. Far from being merely frivolous, excessive, or superficial, experiences like these are symptoms of deeper social and historical forces emerging from the expansion of capitalism and the intensification of urban life. Modern metropolises and money economies shape the inner perceptions of individuals (centripetally) while extending their reach outwards through multiple networks (centrifugally). Perhaps inspired by Simmel, Max Weber also describes the unprecedented aesthetic sensibilities and cultural forms that are created by the modern metropolis, 'with its railways, subways, electric and other lights, shop windows, concert and catering halls, cafes, smokestacks, and piles of stone, the whole wild dance of sound and colour impressions that affect sexual fantasy and the experiences of variations in the soul's constitution that lead to a hungry brooding over all kinds of seemingly inexhaustible possibilities for the conduct of life and happiness' (Weber 2005: 29). City dwellers are often forced to adapt to or flee from the realities of urban life, sometimes by protesting against the old ways and at other times by inventing new ways of surviving and thriving.

In what follows, I elaborate on Simmel's influential ideas concerning how cities become sites for the spread of cosmopolitan worldviews and metropolitan lifestyles, typically by turning their backs on the narrower perspectives of the ancient city, the medieval town, or the rural village. He is interested in understanding how the lives of people in the modern metropolis become detached from one another and at the same time intersect within multiple social circles, a theme he examines in *Sociology* in terms of the expansion of social networks and the intensification of group affiliations. These general arguments are vividly illustrated in his writings from the second decade of his career (after 1900) on modern fashion, playful social gatherings, flirting, art exhibitions, and other forms of sociability fostered by the unique conditions of the modern metropolis. Rather than view urban experience from any one perspective, Simmel considers multiple viewpoints – from the subjective interests and desires of world citizens and city dwellers to the objectifying forces that create social displacement and cultural disorientation. As I note in an excursus, his interest in the collective and personal dimensions of social life resonates with the sociological perspective of his Hungarian student Karl Mannheim and in the writings of the French philosopher Henri Bergson. Despite the general sweep of Simmel's sociology of cities, his ideas continue to speak forcefully to us today about the prospects of developing a civil society and the potential for cultivating a cosmopolitan outlook in an increasingly urbanized world.

The City as Site of Cosmopolitan Attitudes

When someone who has grown up in a large city enters a rural village, or imagines what it might be like to live in an ancient polis like Athens or a small city like Weimar in the early nineteenth century, he or she might feel stifled by the parochial restrictions that seem to be placed on the thoughts and actions of everyone. 'City air makes one free (*Stadtluft macht frei*)', as a common expression puts it, and so the metropolitan visitor to a small town may even feel unable to breathe (SC: 180). The spatial horizon of the city extends outwards both materially and virtually as populations and communication networks expand into the hinterland, as if by 'a geometrical progression': 'A city consists of its total effects which extend beyond its immediate confines, [and] the range of the person [is] constituted by the sum of effects emanating spatially and temporally beyond the limits of a person's body or sphere of activity' (SC: 182). In the chapter in *Sociology* on 'The Intersection of Social Circles', Simmel elaborates on the idea that social differentiation and cultural frictions create new conflicts and tensions between individuals, ultimately expanding their horizons and opening their minds to new perspectives: 'People who are in themselves strongly differentiated and variously educated and occupied are more inclined towards cosmopolitan feelings and opinions than those one-dimensional natures … [who] are unable to put themselves in the shoes of other personalities and thus penetrate the experience of what is common to all' (S: 397; also in 1964). For residents of London, Paris, and Berlin (to mention only the big cities named by Simmel in the metropolises essay), the whole world seems to have become their own home and habitat: 'it is … in transcending this visible expanse that any given city becomes the seat of cosmopolitanism' (SC: 181).

Living in close-knit families and kinship relationships, the inhabitants of a village tend to view the opinions and lifestyles of outsiders from their own narrow standpoint, either banning them altogether or drawing them into their 'insular spell [*Bann*]' (S: 401). By contrast, the citizens of an ancient city or medieval town often participate in a variety of social groups without becoming alienated from their membership in the original one. The Stoics offer the classic model of a cosmopolitan worldview in which the local ties of the ancient city were encircled by the larger social circle of the empire. They imagined that reason could transcend all national boundaries and social exclusivity by embracing a common bond of human equality and solidarity. In a similar way, the members of a medieval knighthood accepted that some of them might occupy a higher status than others, although each should foster the development of everyone on an equal footing. The cosmopolitan impulses of liberal-minded aristocrats during the Middle Ages, and the liberal views of open-minded scholars with an interest in seeking out relations with people in practical trades, could sometimes come into conflict with the imperial ambitions of nobles fighting to impose the values and symbols of their fiefdoms on other domains (S: 381). In the modern city, liberal attitudes are fostered on a grand scale where individuals often find an outlet for their many inclinations and where their personal liberties are enhanced by mutual obligations. By definition, a social group is composed of individuals, but, as Simmel adds, an individualistic way of life results from the pluralistic worldview of 'a cosmopolitan disposition'. As he suggests in a striking aphorism, 'society arises from individuals, the individual arises from soci*eties*' (S: 387, emphasis added). In the modern era, the most widely conceivable social circles have expanded across the globe so that the idea of 'humankind' can become more important than national integration, and yet the rights of the individual can take precedence over 'human rights'.

Many of these ideas are presented in a dramatic and condensed way in the metropolises essay. Figure 6 displays how the outline of this essay is structured around Simmel's opening statement about the tension between the forces of the external culture and technique of life, on the one hand, and the struggle of the individual to ensure his or her autonomy, on the other (SC: 174–6; note the original German essay is organized into ten long paragraphs; GSG 7: 116–31). His main argument is that individuals respond to the cultural and social power of the money economy by adopting a blasé attitude to life in the city (SC: 176–80). This discussion is followed by an account of how the large-scale division of labour in the metropolis lays the social and economic foundations of the money economy while also propelling individuals to find new ways of expressing their uniqueness by distinguishing themselves more sharply from one another (SC: 180–3). This observation leads him to conclude that the external or 'objective' culture of the money economy and the division of

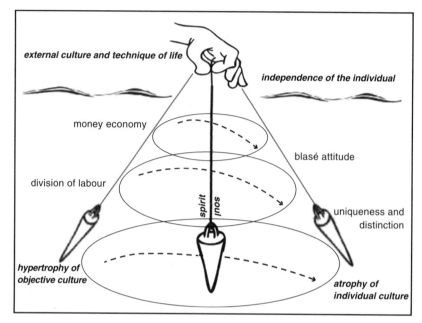

Figure 6 The metropolis and mental life

labour in the metropolis has now grown out of proportion to the capacity of individuals to preserve and cultivate their inner lives, and that even the remnants of this personal culture now seem to be wasting away (SC: 183–5). In short, Simmel wants to show how social circles intersect, group affiliations expand, and cultural spheres overlap in the big city in ways that threaten the independence of everyone and push each person to accentuate his or her selfhood.

In the closing pages of the metropolises essay, Simmel asserts that his great theme is to describe the 'rank order of the modern metropolis in the world history of the spirit' (SC: 184). The emergence of big cities since the beginning of the modern age is the latest and perhaps greatest manifestation of the power of the human intellect to control and enhance every aspect of life. A few pages into the metropolises essay Simmel draws an analogy between how a plumbline is used to check the depth of a body of water and his own method of tacking back and forth between particular observations and broader concerns: 'But here too this entire task of these observations becomes obvious, namely, that from each point on the surface of existence – however closely attached to the surface alone – one may drop a plumbline into the depth of the soul so that all the most banal externalities of life finally are connected with the ultimate decisions concerning the meaning and style of life' (SC: 177; ISF 328; GSG 7: 120). The image of the plumbline or lead sounding (*Senkblei* in German) – a device used to measure distances between surfaces and depths – suggests to Simmel a way of picturing the connection between the outward appearances and the inner workings of the metropolis. Since he uses this analogy in several strategic places elsewhere, it seems to offer a key to understanding the approach he takes in his philosophical, sociological, and aesthetic writings as a whole (for example, see his 1901 summary of the *Philosophy of Money* and the 1916 Preface to his monograph *Rembrandt*; GSG 6: 719; 2005a: 3).

Where other sociologists of his day, including Weber and Durkheim, were suspicious or dismissive about the use of symbolic imagery or literary language in scholarly writing, Simmel freely employs analogies and other tropes as a way of bringing concepts alive and rendering ideas more vivid. His former student Siegfried Kracauer, discussed in the previous chapter, makes a useful distinction between how Simmel studies 'relations of essential congruence or belonging together', on the one hand, and his use of analogies to depict 'relations of affinity and similarity between things', on the other (Kracauer 1995: 251). Kracauer suggests further that analogies show a relationship between objects, while metaphors represent a relationship between objects and subjects insofar as things have a significance for, make an impression on, or are conceived by some person. Simmel's analogies are not simply 'witticizing deviations from the goal of the particular investigation, they are to a large extent themselves this goal' (ibid.: 257). In other words, the use of figurative language is not a decorative flourish but rather his method for identifying nodal points and passageways into expansive complexes and elusive connections in reality. Like lights illuminating hidden caverns, his use of imagery, metaphors, and analogies shows how 'the entirety of his thought is basically only a grasping of objects by looking at them' and reveals the sense in which concepts are always grounded in perceptual experience (ibid.).

Simmel's 'plumbline method' involves descending from the surface phenomena of city life into the murky depths of the individual soul and the collective spirit. He proceeds by following the back-and-forth movement between general social and economic processes and the experiences of particular individuals – or, in other words, by tracking the pendulum swing between the objective and subjective aspects of culture. For example, with the historical shift from small-scale established communities – including families, clans, and churches – to larger and more mobile group affiliations – as in movements of young people, workers, and migrants – individual lives are shaped by the expansion and intersection of social circles in ways that are increasingly complex and more precise: 'The groups to which the individual belongs form, as it were, a system of coordinates in such a way that each additional one defines the individual more exactly and unambiguously' (S: 372). With reference to this 'social geometry', Simmel argues that the more groups an individual belongs to the less likely these groups will converge at any single point and the more latitude is given to the development of the individual (S: 373). When the knight is transformed into the soldier with the shift from medieval to early modern society, for example, or when the craftsman becomes a factory worker, the bonds of community and kinship become looser and social connections take on a more mechanical and soulless character. At the same time, individuals are given more space to cultivate their own personal style and to develop a sense of themselves, as I show in the following section.

Simmel makes a few passing comments that vividly illustrate these broader concerns. He asks us to consider how mechanical time-pieces have become indispensable and pervasive, for instance, so that punctuality, reliability, and calculability now regulate every aspect of professional and personal life in the city: 'If all clocks and watches in Berlin were suddenly to go wrong in different ways, even if only for one hour, all economic life and communication in the city would be disrupted for a long time' (SC: 177; also see PM: 450). As anyone running late to school or work knows, even the smallest deviations from a schedule can throw the whole day out of order. Exact calculations to the minute and strictly coordinated timetables are essential to the effective organization and maintenance of social life in the city. They are also a clear indication of how 'cities are, first of all, seats of the highest division of labour' (SC: 182). To illustrate this point, Simmel mentions the custom of the so-called *quatorzième* among the Parisian upper classes: 'persons who identify themselves by signs on their residences ... [indicate that they] are ready at the dinner hour in correct attire, so that they can be quickly called upon if a dinner party should consist of thirteen persons' (SC: 182). Although this superstitious practice might strike us as bizarre, it should remind us of the role of extras on a movie set or when wealthy people pay others to wait in long lines to purchase the latest

electronic device. To be sure, Simmel ignores the ethical and economic implications of the *quatorzième*, where a class of rich people
(hosting a lavish meal) has the privilege and the money to command
the disposable time of a lower class of people (who are supposedly
well mannered yet eager or needy enough to be on call for an invitation). In any case, his larger point is that the business of everyday life
in the city entails a well-regulated division of labour, a refined sense
of one's social position, and a carefully calculated understanding
of time as ways of differentiating and coordinating the activities of
social groups (a point he also expands on in *Sociology* with reference
to the classification of railway workers; S: 395). In short, Simmel's
anecdotes about pocket watches in Berlin and dinner parties in Paris
demonstrate how even apparently trivial phenomena have deeper
sources in the precise calculations of the money economy and in the
specialized functions of the social division of labour.

Fashion as a Site of Metropolitan Sociability

Simmel's philosophical-sociological method consists of exploring
how apparently insignificant incidents and superficial phenomena
from everyday life are rooted in profoundly antagonistic forces and
unresolved tensions. These relationships cut to the core of what it
means to be a social or individual being, and at the same time they
speak to the ordinary experience of living in a modern metropolis.
The second of his 'sociological apriorities' (discussed in my Introduction) describes the fundamental experience of being excluded
from and set apart from others as a condition of belonging to a
group. Simmel develops this idea in explicitly sociological terms in
the last chapter of *Sociology*, 'The Expansion of the Group and the
Development of Individuality', where he notes that, especially in
modern societies, individuals are internally divided in their relations with others while parts of themselves are also outwardly
distributed across many situations: 'We lead, so to speak, a double
or ... halved existence: one time as an individual inside the social
circle, with a perceptible separation from its other members, but
then also as a member of this circle, in disengagement from what
does not belong to it' (S: 627). He goes on to point out that fashion
is among the most vivid illustrations of the fundamental experience
that individuals have of showing how they are members of a social
circle while at the same time distinguishing and separating themselves from others (S: 628–30).

Simmel published several pieces on fashion from 1895 to 1908, culminating in an expanded essay included in the collection *Philosophical Culture* in 1911 (SC: 187–206; also in ISF: 294–323). His inspiration may well have been the poet Charles Baudelaire's description of fashion as a recurring mode of 'the eternal present' which is paradoxically also 'transient, fleeting, and contingent' (Baudelaire 1964: 13; here I draw on Pyyhtinen 2018: 51–60; and Frisby 1986: 95–102; 1992: 70–1). Simmel's discussion goes beyond simply providing cultural commentary on passing trends and recurring patterns insofar as his larger aim is to examine 'the vital conditions of fashion as a universal phenomenon in the history of our species' (SC: 188). In his view, fashion is not simply an expression of frivolity, eccentricity, or capricious impulses but also a symptom of a deep desire and a contradictory compulsion to adapt to social groups while at the same time remaining elevated and apart from them. In a modern money economy and a capitalist consumer culture, fashion tends to display the new as the ever-same, an insight later developed by the philosopher and cultural critic Walter Benjamin (1892–1940) in his monumental studies of the prehistory of modernity in nineteenth-century Paris (Benjamin 1978). For Simmel as for Benjamin, the flash of the now and the shock of the new, which have ironically become such normal features of modern fashion, are symptoms of a primary phenomenon and a profound current that run deep into the very sources of human culture and illuminate essential features of contemporary existence as a whole (Frisby 1986: 210; Mičko 2010: 235–79).

In the metropolitan milieu, changes in fashion are largely a way for the modern city dweller to manage the dilemma of having to choose between conformism and rebellion. Fashion reflects how individuals strive to satisfy both the need for acceptance and the desire for attention. As social and physical distances between people decrease in the city and as spaces become more densely populated, individuals tend to exaggerate their differences and accentuate their peculiarities (Kracauer 1995: 247). In the metropolises essay, Simmel notes how people in the city are induced to display 'the specifically metropolitan extravagances of mannerism, caprice, and preciousness' (SC: 183). Everyone seems to want to stand out, to be different, to make an impression. Since most encounters in the city tend to be brief and rare, individuals often strive to magnify their eccentricities and amplify their unique qualities. The individual summons 'the utmost uniqueness and particularization, in order to preserve his or her most personal core, which one has to exaggerate in order to remain audible even to oneself' (SC: 184). In the city we can hardly even hear ourselves since everyone wants to stand out and be heard.

In the essay on fashion, Simmel stresses how trends in clothing, jewellery, and speech, for example, are frequently (though not always) bound to class relations. The lower classes of his day are often slow to take up new fashions while the upper strata tend to be conservative or even archaic in their tastes, at times discarding fashionable items as soon as the lower classes adopt them. For this reason, the middle classes tend to set the overall pace of cultural trends by demanding constant change, in part because fashions have become less expensive for low-income groups and less a mark of status distinctions among upper social strata (SC: 202–3). In the *Philosophy of Money*, Simmel remarks on how rich people may even view overly ostentatious displays of wealth and sophistication as a sign of a person's *lack* of distinction (PM: 480). As 'machinery has become so much more sophisticated than the worker', modes of linguistic expression, transportation, scientific investigation, and artistic expression among the professional classes also become more subtle, refined, and inaccessible (PM: 453). The difference between a highly specialized dress store marketed to a mass of consumers and a tailor plying his craft at a customer's house highlights this growing social and economic gap between consumers and producers in the money economy (PM: 462). At the same time, changing fashions in books, the arts, furniture, and clothing styles are also evidence of how class barriers are becoming weaker while upward social mobility for many groups is increasing (PM: 463). In short, in an age where mass production and consumption are dominated by major manufacturing and urban centres, the impulse to equality at the social level often encourages the impulse to exaggerate distinctions on a personal level.

Although fashions seem to exist in a rarefied, specialized, and superficial world, they might also serve as another name (a metonym) for modernity itself. Fashion offers a repertoire of urbane cultural styles and worldly social types that populate what might be called the ethos of metropolitanism. Viewed from the cosmopolitan perspective of the metropolis, the smaller world of fashion appears to combine the transitoriness and speed at which things change with the promise that they will exist for eternity: 'The fact that change itself does not change endows each of the objects it affects with a psychological shimmer of permanency' (SC: 204). In an early essay, 'Sociological Aesthetics' (1896), Simmel develops this point in terms of how current modes of aesthetic expression, contemplation, and evaluation tend to reduce phenomena to what is most fundamental, important, and eternal: 'What is unique emphasizes what is typical, what is accidental appears as normal, and the superficial and fleeting stands for what is essential and basic' (1968: 69). In modern art, in fashion, and in everyday life, the classic charm and rational power of symmetry grows with the erasure of personal particularities and the disappearance of the individual in mass culture. As a consequence, 'exhausted nerves which are drifting between hypersensitivity and lack of sensitivity can be excited only by the most opaque forms and rudely accurate details, or by the most tender and *starkest* stimuli' (1968: 80). The modernist aesthetics of fashion are as much an index of this underlying culture and pervasive experience as a form of communication between groups and a symbolic system for expressing some values and meanings over others (Barthes 2005: 26, 53). In other words, the consuming passion for novelty and difference in today's world is in some ways a reaction to the democratizing demand of modern societies for collective imitation and mechanical reproduction (SC: 195). Where the slave to fashion displays a willingness to go along with the crowd, and where the person who clings to retro styles acknowledges the prevailing social trends in the very act of rejecting them, the 'fashion hero' tries to strike a delicate balance between these socializing and individualizing impulses.

Cultural phenomena like these can be observed in a simple way by thinking of a fashionable party or some other exclusive social gathering (perhaps like the one in the illustration on p. x). In the essay on 'Sociability', Simmel describes how configurations of conversation and patterns of interaction at events like these usually follow certain codes of etiquette for entering and exiting social groups, or they imply rules for closing or opening social circles to others (see the translations in SC, ISF, and 1950). Participants in improvised gatherings and intimate social settings typically suspend ordinary expectations about dress that prevail in the outside world, often in ways that allow people to display the latest styles or to express themselves in extraordinary ways. For example, 'a lady would not want to appear in … extreme *décolletage* [a low-cut evening gown] in a really personal, intimately friendly situation with one or two men as she would in a large company without any embarrassment' (SC: 123). As in this example, sociable gatherings frequently inspire games of light-hearted teasing and erotic seduction, as Simmel notes in an essay on flirting in *Philosophical Culture*. The sidelong glance with the head half-turned, the swinging hips, the strutting walk, and the carefully placed hand are all ways of making visible an invitation that is also partly a refusal, a seduction that stops short of submission, a 'perhaps' that stands above a 'no' but beneath a 'yes' (1984: 143). In short, even flirting has its own fashions, just as fashion can also involve a kind of flirting. Each is a body technique and a form of sociability in which we show how we are a part of a relationship in the very act of standing apart from it.

Simmel refers to such revealing moments of sociability as 'the play form of association', here drawing a comparison with how games and art-forms likewise suspend certain serious features of reality in a spirit of fun, pleasure, and light-hearted rivalry. 'The impulse to sociability distills ... out of the realities of social life the pure essence of association' and promotes association as a value to be pursued for its own sake (SC: 121). In such a formally ideal world, my pleasure is contingent on your pleasure, and each of us enjoys the serious play of conversation, disagreement, and embarrassment, or simply the game of making sense together. Such scenes project a miniature model of social life that Simmel calls 'the freedom of bondage', a kind of voluntary subordination in which free expression is tied to strictly held rules of interaction (SC: 128). Realities from outside the social circle mark off upper and lower 'thresholds of sociability': above a certain limit interactions become abstract, impersonal, or formulaic, and below a certain limit they become too personal, coarse, or even rude. Each of us can recall how a light conversation falls apart or becomes artificial when the participants become all too real, embarrassingly intimate, or deadly serious. An incident on the news or problems at home can interrupt the flow of the interaction when one person holds court or no one knows what else to say. When we note that Simmel's essay on sociability was originally delivered as the keynote lecture for the first meeting of the German Sociological Society in Frankfurt in 1910, we might reflect on how professional and academic gatherings follow certain codes of sociable conduct and protocols of rational and playful discussion as well (Kemple 2014a: 208–10).

Although examples like these obviously speak to issues that are not limited to social life in big cities, the particular forms they take are often unique to the urban context. In an essay from 1890, Simmel characterizes the spectacle of art exhibitions in major metropolises like Berlin as 'the inevitable extension and outcome of modern specialization in art', and thus as symptomatic of a culture experiencing transition, uncertainty, and decline (2015: 88). The serial display of so many artworks in one place incites in the viewer a desire to taste the widest variety of styles, ideas, and sensations imaginable. Such exhibitions tend to evoke a whole gamut of responses, 'from attraction to repulsion, indifference to enthusiasm and back, in rapid succession'. Such a range of emotions does not foster an appreciation for great deeds or informed judgements about creative personalities, however; rather, it encourages reactive opinions and even a blasé attitude. Writing a few years later in a similar vein in a short piece called *'Infelices Possidentes!'* (roughly, 'Unhappy are Those Who Own Things!'), Simmel remarks on how the urban culture of distraction and boredom is intensified in the entertainment establishments of Berlin, where 'titillation of the senses and intoxication of the nerves' predominate over any kind of serious reflection (SC: 259). Recreation halls, gambling casinos, and mass spectacles, for example, transform work into play and leisure into labour, as if to submit everyone to the same dreary command: 'just amuse yourself!' (SC: 261). As Siegfried Kracauer writes a couple of decades later (but before the era of television), the sheer necessity of keeping four million inhabitants of 1920s Berlin in circulation 'transforms the life of the street into the ineluctable street of life, giving rise to configurations that invade even domestic space' (Kracauer 1995: 325). By breaking down the barrier between private and public life, these shrines of distraction fuse the surface effects of commodity and artistic culture into a cult for worshipping the city itself as a kind of total work of art (*Gesamtkunswerk*).

In the essay on fashion, Simmel admits that not just artworks and consumer goods but also 'religiosity, scholarly interests, even socialism and individualism have ... become fashion items' (SC: 190). The seduction of the new and the now and the charm of the fast and the fleeting often extend beyond the external appearances of dress to absorb aesthetic tastes, political opinions, moral convictions, and intellectual ideas (SC: 193). Even a 'classic' literary or academic work, which may seem removed from and alien to the whims of fashion, may be subject to the frivolous manias of the moment. In the metropolises essay, Simmel refers three times to Friedrich Nietzsche as a philosopher who has recently become popular and fashionable, a cultural icon who is passionately loved and even worshipped by people in the metropolis (SC: 174, 178, 184). Many see him as a saviour and prophet of a future world where the irrational and instinctive impulses of the sovereign individual are no longer threatened or suppressed. The irony here is that Nietzsche and other intellectual iconoclasts of the time epitomized the most extreme individualism while vehemently expressing their bitter scorn for the urban culture of exactness, calculability, and punctuality: 'From the source of this hatred of the metropolis surged their hatred of the money economy and of the intellectualism of modern existence' (SC: 179).

Simmel himself can be counted among a small group of European intellectuals, including the influential sociologist Ferdinand Tönnies (1855–1936), who brought Nietzsche's eccentric writings to public attention while at the same time developing their own original philosophies of modernity and sociologies of city life. Simmel's lecture cycle *Schopenhauer and Nietzsche*, published in 1907, a few years after the metropolises essay and just a year before *Sociology*, concludes with some reflections on Nietzsche's view that modern life exhausts the vitality of individuals. Fearing the oversocialized, hyperobjectified, and dehumanizing character of contemporary conditions, Nietzsche hopes to cultivate a kind of 'pathos of distance' among free thinkers who are committed to realizing 'the ideal of evolution for power, … beauty, freedom, and security' within a life lived to the fullest and apart from the common herd (1986: 148). He calls for a new morality of nobility, elegance, and distinction (*Vornehmheit*) that would place a supreme value on personal qualities rather than submit to the stupefying powers of the crowd. Although generally sympathetic to Nietzsche's critical views, Simmel also points out that modern individuals cannot be completely self-sufficient but have developed new needs and make ever more demands that can often only be satisfied by cooperating with other people and within a metropolitan way of life. In contrast to Simmel, Nietzsche advances a kind of antisociology that privileges the will of the superior person over social connections created out of the hub of everyday life, and he even opposes the vision of a common humanity (Lichtblau 2011: 97–124; Partyga 2016). Where Nietzsche concedes that each of us must cultivate a sense of responsibility, if only to ourselves, Simmel goes further to argue that there is no substitute for a sociological understanding of the human interdependencies that nourish, sustain, and enhance the full development of both singular and social life (see the 'Excursus on Sociological Vitalism' below).

Excursus on Sociological Vitalism: Simmel through Bergson and Mannheim

Sociologists often talk about 'social life' without saying much about what they mean by *life*. Simmel is rare among classical thinkers in describing the social world as a form of living, conceiving social forms as forms of life, and imagining sociological thought itself as alive. When we emphasize the term *social* then stable structures and well-defined systems tend to be highlighted, but when *life* is stressed then transformations and movements become more prominent. Because Simmel addresses the realities covered by both terms throughout his sociological and philosophical writings, commentators tend to characterize him either as a modernist impressionist and idler (*flâneur*), with a meticulous yet roving sense of form, or as a postmodern improviser (*bricoleur*), endlessly tinkering with the formless shards of modern existence. 'There is no essential Simmel', it has been argued, 'only different Simmels read through the various positions in contemporary discourse formations' (Weinstein and Weinstein 1993: 153; Frisby 1992). Where one Simmel seems distant and disengaged, carefully sorting through and methodically ordering the fragments of modernity, the other makes do with whatever is at hand, tracing affinities and noting ruptures that make up the postmodern condition. A systematic Simmel who methodically attends to stable social forms seems to contradict a shape-shifting Simmel who drifts along with amorphous social processes.

Simmel's own evolving conception of social life is partly the source of these conflicting ways of reading his work. Around 1908 or so, and thus at the time he was completing his *Sociology*, he began a serious study of the writings of the philosopher Henri Bergson (1859–1941), who was becoming *en vogue* among European intellectuals in the early twentieth century. Bergson's *Matière et mémoire* (*Matter and Memory*) had been published in 1896 (the German translation in 1908), and *L'Evolution créatrice* (*Creative Evolution*) appeared in 1907 (Fitzi 2002). Where Bergson embraces a cosmic view of life as a dynamic of fluxes and flows, Simmel cleaves more closely to the facts of social life and the details of individual experience while also conceiving life itself as a cosmic fact (Loiskandl et al., in Simmel 1986: li). Simmel was inspired by Bergson's ideas on life as an alternating current passing through the medium of organic bodies and as a vital impetus (*élan vital*) pulsing through and endlessly transforming the whole of existence: 'to exist is to change' (Bergson 1998: 7). Like Bergson, Simmel is interested in how life is manifested in duration (*durée*) and unceasing change, and how thought is enlivened through a constant process of association and dissociation. As Simmel writes in the journals he kept in his final years, 'Bergson's difficulty – how can the intellect conceive of life, given that it is an emanation of life – is solved through the fact that this retrospectiveness, this understanding of itself, is the essence of living consciousness' (VL: 162). In other words, by folding back on itself through reflection, the intellect, mind, or spirit (*Geist* in German and *esprit* in French) comes to understand itself as alive and creative. For Bergson (1998: 31), conceptual systems are only 'partial views of the whole', an idea to which Simmel seems to allude in the title of his last work, *View of Life* (*Lebensanschauung*), which also echoes his colleague Wilhelm Dilthey's notion of *worldview* (*Weltanschauung*). Simmel and Bergson share a concept of *form as creation* rather than as containment and an idea of *change as an interactive process* rather than as an undifferentiated flow: 'adapting is not repeating but replying' (Bergson 1998: 58). Anticipating his later writings on the philosophy of life, Simmel concludes the metropolises essay by noting that the life forces of the city 'have grown into the roots and the crown of the whole of historical life', where each individual has merely a fleeting existence 'as a cell' within a larger organism (SC: 185).

The crux of the matter for Simmel is not whether life becomes social but, rather, how dynamic fluxes and flows are taken up and transformed through structured processes and forms of association (*Vergesellschaftung*). In an important essay from 1912, 'On Some Contemporary Problems in Philosophy', Simmel singles out the work of Bergson and Edmund Husserl, whose *Logical Investigations* was published in 1900–1, for emancipating philosophy from Kantian presuppositions, a feat which even Schopenhauer and Nietzsche were unable to achieve with their ideas on the metaphysics of the will and morality (Pyyhtinen 2018: 106–11). For Bergson and Husserl, life-philosophy is not a kind of moral preaching or a reflection on the typical contents of life but, rather, 'the physical-metaphysical fundamental emergence of the world process' that reaches both upwards with the human spirit and downwards toward mechanical materiality (GSG 12: 383–5). Simmel extends this philosophical approach to what we might call a *life-sociology* – that is, a concern with how social life both creates singularities and reproduces itself as a whole (Lash 2005, 2010). Broadly speaking, he is interested in how contemporary societies manage the tension between the ceaseless invention of relationships and the establishment of social forms (Fitzi 2016: 60). In the chapter in *Sociology* on 'The Self-Preservation of the Group', he notes that this basic duality characterizes the life of all forms of association: 'a relationship, which is a fluctuating, constantly developing life process, nevertheless maintains a relatively stable external form' (ISF: 351; S: 522; GSG 11: 659). Later, in the chapter on 'philosophical sociology' in *Fundamental Questions of Sociology*, he contrasts eighteenth- and nineteenth-century views of individual life with respect to 'the claims and commands of "society"', which 'develops its own vehicles and organs' (1950: 58). Rejecting Bergson's cosmic vision of life in which living beings seem to maintain and regenerate themselves endlessly, Simmel ultimately embraces a tragic view of social and individual life-forms as they develop, decay, and die from their own internal forces.

Simmel's sociological vitalism seems to lie at some distance from the writings of his young Hungarian student Karl Mannheim (1893–1947), who is often reproached for holding an oversocialized conception of human life in which individual differences are ultimately levelled by mass culture. A participant in the intellectual salons of Budapest, Berlin, and Heidelberg centred on Georg Lukács, Simmel, and Max Weber, respectively, Mannheim is also criticized for conceiving sociology as a form of a disengaged reflection and ungrounded observation. Like the image of Simmel the city dweller on a casual stroll, or the stranger who arrives today and stays tomorrow simply to observe without fully engaging in social life, Mannheim seems to take up the role of the supercilious scholar hovering in a vacuum. This impression comes in part from his influential notion of an 'oscillating intelligence' (*freischwebende Intelligenz*), a free-floating stratum of educated people that he discusses in his classic book *Ideology and Utopia*: 'Participation in a common educational heritage progressively tends to suppress differences of birth, status, profession, and wealth, and to unite the individual educated people on the basis of the education they have received' (Mannheim 1936: 155). Insofar as intellectuals are existentially connected but not bound to the particular interests, conflicts, and commitments of the age in which they live, they are able to cultivate skills of critical reasoning rather than simply reproduce strategic or instrumental ways of thinking (Kemple 2014b). For Mannheim, modern knowledge is not a kind of formless drifting, however, but rather a method of engaging in reflection from a relatively stable position which is loosely yet firmly connected to both the standpoint of the thinker and the situation of knowing (Mannheim 1936: 57). As he argues in a 1917 lecture on 'Soul and Culture' that was heavily influenced by Simmel, a generation of educated people bound together by common interests and a shared view of life might be able to bridge the gap between an increasingly mechanized culture and the vital forces of the individual soul (2012: 287). In later writings he formulates this argument in vitalist terms with the concept of 'generational location' understood as the actualization of a certain style of life, the realization of a living potential, and the unfolding of a life force or *entelechy* (see, for example, his path-breaking 1927 essay 'The Problem of Generations'; Mannheim 1952: 309).

Viewed as engaged life-sociologists rather than as free-floating intellectuals, Simmel and Mannheim follow the radical middle path of liberal humanism and cosmopolitanism by navigating between the extremes of ideological conservatism (especially its romantic and fascist variants) and utopian communism (including its anarchistic and socialist versions). In contrast to Bergson's cosmic vision, they believe that social antagonisms and cultural conflicts should be approached by appealing to cosmopolitan principles of justice and freedom, and they warn intellectuals who believe they have no attachments to economic, social, and political pressures against drifting into elitism and isolation (Harrington 2016: 271–99). At the same time, Simmel and Mannheim embrace certain features of scientific and political vitalism by resisting the mechanistic character of modern social arrangements and embracing a vision of social growth, cultural ripening, and personal self-actualization. Neither can imagine escaping from social restraints into intimacy or fleeing from social forms into the inner *durée* of unbounded life flows.

In any event, problems of duration (Bergson) and generation (Mannheim) certainly run *through* Simmel's ideas about social life, even though they are not entirely resolved – or dissolved – in the solutions he imagined.

7

The Propertied and the Poor Person in the Big City

In bringing so many people together in new ways, big cities can threaten the autonomy of the individual and challenge a person's sense of self. Modern living arrangements force us to mix in and interact with many people who appear to be nothing like us – people from different ethnic communities, with strange religious beliefs, and with all kinds of skills and levels of education, not to mention rich and poor people. If we are to maintain social order and personal civility and ensure that everyone is fed, clothed, and sheltered, then buildings must be constructed, amenities have to be provided, and municipal institutions must maintain order. In 'The Metropolis and Mental Life', Simmel largely leaves such practical considerations aside, focusing instead on the impact of the money economy and the division of labour on the spiritual and mental life of the individual. He does not discuss government, housing, and policing in any detail and alludes only vaguely to transportation, architecture, and the built environment. Instead, he emphasizes the struggle of the individual to survive as an independent being and to become something more than a mere cog in the machineries of power and wealth: 'Here in buildings and educational institutions, in the wonders and comforts of space-conquering technology, in the formations of community life, and in the visible institutions of the state, is offered such an overwhelming fullness of crystallized and impersonalized spirit that the personality, so to speak, cannot maintain itself under its impact' (SC: 184). Simmel's sociology of cities is a theory of stress and a philosophy of suffering, but it is not a complete account of the conditions that give rise to and the consequences that follow from these experiences.

In the closing paragraphs of the metropolises essay, Simmel hits a high note (already introduced in the final section of the *Philosophy of Money*) that he will take up again in various ways in the final decade of his life. The fundamental conflict of modern culture lies in 'the preponderance of what one may call the "objective spirit" over the "subjective spirit"', which he describes as 'the atrophy of individual culture through the hypertrophy of objective culture' (SC: 184–5). The paradox of living in large cities is that the surrounding social and cultural world grows ever more impressive and overwhelming as the inner life of each person weakens and wastes away, like an organ that has been exhausted or rendered useless. Simmel's concern here is not with the gap between rich people and poor people but, rather, with how the abundance of material wealth is accompanied by the poverty of spirit within each individual.

Elsewhere in his sociological and philosophical writings Simmel does turn his attention to the increasing distance between social classes and the unequal power relations between dominant and subordinate groups. As people come more frequently into contact, he observes, they make comparisons between themselves and others more readily and are more inclined to agitate for revolution or call for egalitarian social reforms (PM: 270). The present chapter considers Simmel's interest in the dynamics of inclusion and exclusion, in particular how the moral obligations of wealthy individuals towards the poor give rise to distinct forms of social interaction in the metropolis, which has become the locale of 'personal inner and outer freedom' (SC: 181). Simmel's sociology of wealth and poverty is challenging for today's readers because he emphasizes the *liberty* of individual members of social classes and the *solidarity* between groups over questions of social *equality*. His approach to class conflicts highlights the possibility of mutual recognition between rich and poor rather than the uneven distribution of wealth and resources. Nevertheless, his sociological approach is interesting for the way he considers how people perceive strangeness and otherness through their interactions with others. I elaborate on this perspective with reference to everyday encounters between propertied and poor people that are the focus of Simmel's discussion of private charity and social welfare. I also illustrate his argument in a digression on race relations, strangers, and marginalized people in the work of two important American sociologists, W. E. B. Du Bois, who studied in Berlin when Simmel was a student, and Robert Park, who attended Simmel's lectures and introduced his work to urban sociology.

The Solidarity of the Propertied and the Poor

While the conflict between the citizen and the masses has provided sociology with its two core concepts of individual and society, the tensions between rich and poor present sociology with a pressing practical problem (Helle 2015: 81–92). As Simmel acknowledges in the opening paragraph of *Sociology*, 'the concept of "society" hardly conveys the import and concern that the lower classes have caused the upper classes' (S: 19). One of the main tasks of classical and contemporary sociology has been to describe the perceptions that each social class has of the others and the social distance between them, despite the ways in which rich and poor are bound together in mediated social networks and through direct interactions. Simmel calls the chapter where he addresses these issues 'The Poor Person', rather than 'Poverty' or simply 'The Poor' (in the plural), as a way of drawing attention to a paradox at the heart of these relationships. An individual may be considered the product of social conditions, a member of a certain group, or a social type, and simultaneously as a unique individual in his or her own right and a particular moral concern for others. The poor person thus exemplifies one of the many ways in which people are social and non-social beings at the same time, insofar as they are in some sense both included as members and excluded as outsiders (as formulated in the second of Simmel's sociological apriorities discussed in my Introduction): 'The poor person is admittedly put outside the group, but this being-outside is only a particular kind of interaction with it that weaves one into a union with the whole in this widest sense' (S: 417; also in ISF). The poor person is not just another social problem or practical challenge for others who are not poor; rather, a person *becomes* poor through a certain perception of oneself and *in interaction with others*. Here Simmel makes an important distinction between poverty (*die Armut* in German), understood as a social condition defined by institutions of social welfare and treated as a specifically modern and metropolitan concern, on the one hand, and the poor person (*der Arme*), who is defined through his or her inter-individual interactions and through charitable relationships, on the other: 'The state comes to help poverty; private charity comes to help the poor person' (S: 431; GSG 11: 543). Where government agencies aim to alleviate impoverished conditions, to provide social support, and thus to create independent and economically valuable individuals, private charities hope to relieve the distress of the poor person by providing assistance as a moral end in itself. In short, welfare expresses 'the solidarity of humanity in general' while philanthropy forges a moral bond between persons from different social worlds (S: 411).

These institutional and individual relationships between propertied and poor people are the effect of a reciprocal network of obligations and rights. (Note that Simmel is being descriptive rather than prescriptive here, in the sense that he examines what these duties and entitlements *are*, not what he thinks they *should* be). The public and the prosperous have a duty to support the poor and the destitute as a class, and this duty corresponds to a claim on the part of poor people for help in improving their circumstances or for compensation in times of emergency or loss: 'The right to support belongs to the same category as the right to work and the right to one's existence' (S: 411). The bonds between rich and poor typically consist of social networks and group affiliations forged both within and between social classes: 'State, municipal, community, parish, professional organization, friendship circles, and families may have … exceedingly different relationships with their members; still, each of these relationships seems to contain an element that is actualized as a right for support in cases of pauperization' (S: 411). Social welfare can therefore be viewed as a public arrangement that benefits all citizens and affects everyone, not just the poor: 'Care of the poor is part of the organization of the *whole* to which both the poor and the propertied classes belong' (S: 419). Welfare provisions thus resemble the construction of a dam to prevent future floods, just as funding 'the military and the police, school and roads, court and church, parliament and research' promotes the common good (S: 413, 415–16; see his comments on social medicine for another use of this analogy; 1998).

Neither private philanthropy nor public welfare should be thought of as advancing a communist or socialist policy of social equality: 'while [each] takes from the prosperous and gives to the poor, [doing so] still in no way approaches an equalization of these individual positions and … will not at all overcome the *tendency* for the differentiation of society into rich and poor' (S: 413). In a similar way, assistance to the beggar, the homeless person, or the pauper also sets these individuals apart from and outside the group that cares for them but does not fully integrate them into the larger society. By acknowledging that poor relief and welfare provisions tend to reproduce inequalities rather than diminish class divisions, Simmel's point at first appears ethically conservative or politically regressive. But from a sociological perspective his argument highlights the *relative* character of what it means to be poor, both subjectively as a moral relationship between individuals and within oneself, and objectively as a social standard of wealth and well-being. In other words, each of us may be 'poor' compared to others – destitute in certain ways and deprived at different times in our life – just as the measure or indicator of 'poverty' for a society varies by historical period and cultural context.

Simmel's core thesis is that the social and ethical difficulties of caring for the poor as outsiders are 'mirrored' in their interactions with others who are considered insiders and full members of the social whole (S: 417). These contrasting points of view can be pictured as *relations of asymmetrical yet mutual recognition*. Figure 7 depicts how one can see both oneself and others as either 'propertied' or 'poor', depending on one's perspective and who is looking at whom. One can look in the face of the poor person and see a version of oneself as relatively propertied and even prosperous, or,

Figure 7 The mutual recognition of the propertied and the poor person

conversely, one can look into the face of a person of property and recognize oneself as fairly poor by comparison. Depending on whether 'poor' and 'rich' are understood in material-economic or spiritual-cultural terms, one might also see one's own poverty one way (such as not owning a house) and one's wealth in another (such as being well educated).

In a long and complex sentence, Simmel tries to spell out these alternating perspectives between what someone perceives on *the surface of social life*, such as the economic and cultural conditions that give rise to poverty as a social fact, and *the deeper qualities of the individual*, such as the characteristics of a poor person whose circumstances cannot be attributed simply to weakness, discrimination, or bad luck:

> Here, as in many other respects, the general public, its conditions, interests, and actions encompasses … individual determinations: on the one hand, it represents *an immediate surface on which the members perceive their appearance, the results of their own lives*; on the other hand, it is *the broad underground where each individual life develops* – but in a way that, from its unity, *the differences of individual predispositions and circumstances* give that surface of the whole a conspicuous colorfulness of individual phenomena. (GSG 11: 543–4, emphasis added; S: 433)

This passage is challenging not just because of its difficult grammar, but also because Simmel is attempting to convey the effect of 'infinite mirroring' potentially involved in all social interactions. The propertied see themselves in the poor just as the poor see themselves in the propertied; or they see themselves as others see them; or they see others as they see themselves, or at least as parts of and as potential future or past selves, and so on (O'Neill 2001: 85). In any case, Simmel's point is ultimately a simple one: in order to be social beings we must see ourselves as both part of and apart from a group or even the public at large (*Allgemeinheit* in German), sometimes as relatively included and at other times as relatively excluded, in some circumstances at the centre of things and at others on the margins. He argues that what we see on the surface of collective life – our particular achievements or failures in all their 'conspicuous colorfulness' – only becomes apparent from a 'broad underground' of opportunities and fates affecting each one of us differently. The unique situation of the poor person is such that his or her position as an outsider is emphasized in an extreme way, but also partly as a condition of his or her membership in the society as a whole.

Recall how these relationships play out in everyday life. In an 'Excursus on the Sociology of the Senses' included in the chapter of *Sociology* entitled 'Space and the Spatial Ordering of Society', Simmel remarks that city life transforms how, and how often, we see other people. The metropolis 'manifests an immeasurable predominance of seeing over the hearing of others ... Before the development of buses, trains, and streetcars in the nineteenth century, people were not at all in a position to be able or to have to view one another for minutes or hours at a time without speaking to one another' (S: 573; also in SC). This simple observation, which we often forget about or leave aside as trivial, offers a glimpse into the deep structure of everyday life in the city. The constant flow of traffic and people means that in order to make our way around the city our gaze is often fixed on people's faces, and our interactions tend to be more visual than verbal. Simmel points out that, 'as an organ of expression, the face does not act like the hand, the foot, or the whole body; it does not convey the internal activity of the person, but it certainly speaks of it' (S: 572). When we look into the face of others we do not truly or intimately know them (in the sense of cognition or *kennen* in German), although we may at least recognize or acknowledge them (*erkennen*) from their outward appearance. For example, we recognize many people as fellow bus riders, workers, high-society people, paupers, strangers, and so on, but we hardly know them as unique individuals. We are inclined to bring certain features into the foreground of our perception – their character as 'propertied' or 'poor', for instance – while minimizing or marginalizing other features, such as their inner struggles and their complicated personal histories. Simmel's insight about streetcars and street scenes reminds us how these relationships and sense impressions are literally built into the infrastructure of urban life, and how the surface appearances of individual selves are mirrored in one another.

In the closing pages of *Sociology*, Simmel makes an important distinction between different kinds of relationships in a way that places these insights into broader perspective. *Individual* and *social* relations are the main topics of sociology, of course, but these are not identical with *human* relationships, and nor are they completely separate from natural, material, or *objective* relations (S: 671–5; also in ISF: 36–40). Just as the individual cannot be completely reduced to his or her social existence, so social relations are not always or entirely human, and humans cannot be adequately understood simply as objective things or as mere matter. Olli Pyyhtinen has explored the radical and far-reaching implications of these distinctions by elaborating on what he calls Simmel's 'relational sociology' (see Pyyhtinen 2010: 110–32, 2015: 63–85, 2016, and 2018: 30–49, among other works). For example, he takes up Simmel's brief remarks on the sociology of the gift as it overlaps with the sociology of poverty (S: 437–9; I consider Marcel Mauss's influential sociology of the gift in the following chapter). Following Simmel's argument that 'one is poor in a social sense only if receiving some support' and within a context of social interactions (S: 439), Pyyhtinen notes that 'poverty is relational, a relative state of affairs' (Pyyhtinen 2014: 103). The 'gift' is an object that imposes obligations at the same time as it grants rights, whether as alms from a private charity to a poor person or as transfer payments from a welfare office to an impoverished class of people. On multiple scales, and not just on social (macro) and individual (micro) levels, both the charitable gift to the poor and institutional support to alleviate poverty are things that tie people together, at once attaching them to one another and marking off the differences and distances between them. These exchanges include some people as members of the social whole while excluding others as outsiders, and they sanction some kinds of relationships while placing others out of bounds. The gift is therefore a human bond that is not-only-human, a relationship that is partly other-than-social and yet not-entirely-individual, and thus an object that embodies multiple layers of reality on several scales. The same can be said of relationships involving the poor person, the stranger, or anyone immersed in situations where objects and things determine how he or she is included in or excluded from the life of the society.

The Freedom of the Poor Person

Like the digression on the sociology of the senses, Simmel's famous 'Excursus on the Stranger' is also part of the chapter on social space and brings sociology to the limits of its imagination (S: 601; also in ISF: 143–9). He notes with some irony that the stranger and the poor person are each located outside the majority and may even confront the dominant group as 'inner enemies'. Of course, poor people are not always strangers and strangers are not always poor, although both 'face the social circle as partner or as object, as an opposite subject to which they nevertheless belong' (S: 435). The stranger 'comes today and stays tomorrow' (S: 601; ISF: 143), while the poor person does not typically experience the same degree of social and spatial mobility, whether forced or freely chosen. Like the poor, strangers may be perceived as having 'certain more general characteristics in common' than differences dividing them, and so they tend to be viewed more as social types than as unique individuals. Strangers and poor people often experience 'repulsion and distance' from other people in various ways, and each may feel detached from or involved in social groups at different times in their lives and in particular places (ISF: 144). In Simmel's view, sociology must account for how actions and actors of all kinds interact with and are transformed or even taken over by *others*, whether as opposites (as conveyed in the Greek *hetero*), as the same (*homo*), as simply themselves (*auto*), or as something altogether different (*allo*) (Kemple 2007). Marked off as Others and as Objects (represented in figure 7 by the concentric and overlapping ovals), the poor person and the stranger occupy the outer edges and even the ultimate boundaries of social life (see the 'Excursus on Race Relations, Strangers, and Other Marginals', pp. 126–31).

'Where does the poor person belong?' (S: 420). Simmel's answer to this question is that, in being offered assistance and accepting support, the poor person plays a specific social role while both claiming and being granted a particular social status. In this regard, the poor person serves a 'membership function' within the existing society and therefore belongs organically to a historical reality (S: 440). At the same time, the suprapersonal unity of social life stands above poor people, just as in some ways the social whole seems to have a reality that exists apart from other citizens, such as the government with respect to the taxpayer, the education system with respect to the teacher, the law in relation to the official, or the market in relation to the merchant. And yet the poor seem to inhabit a space all their own, typically on the margins of everyday social life or apart from the mainstream. In the big city they may occupy a street corner, a homeless shelter, or a food line, and they may also be relegated to an entire urban district with its own virtual or physical social boundaries. These areas – already prominent features of the modern cityscape of Simmel's time – include slums for concentrating people in deprived living quarters; ghettos for containing people deemed dangerous or undesirable, often as a result of ethnic or racial discrimination; or so-called skid rows, where people and places considered derelict and dejected are abandoned and ignored (Huey and Kemple 2007). These urban spaces erase the unique identity of the poor person while ensuring that he or she remains both unsettled and fixed somewhere. Such spaces are often considered 'no-go zones' for propertied city dwellers or as empty spaces marking the distance between poor and rich, foreigners and familiars, criminals and law-abiding citizens. As Simmel points out, designating an area as 'empty land' (*terra nullius* in legal terms) potentially leaves it open for others to settle or colonize, to purchase and develop according to their own interests rather than to protect and hold in common as public property (*quaeque terrae vacuae, eas publicas esse*; S: 615–20). When the poor are neglected and ignored, or confined to some areas and barred from others, they are effectively assigned an identity that paradoxically leaves them both inside and outside the spatial and moral limits of the city.

These observations highlight how relationships between the propertied and the poor are based not only on relative wealth and deprivation but also on domination and subordination, as well as privilege and exclusion. Although Simmel does not directly address these power dynamics in his discussion of the poor person, elsewhere in *Sociology* he emphasizes how modern social conditions can open up new spaces of *freedom* to all social classes. In the chapter 'Domination and Subordination' in *Sociology*, he argues that 'even in the most oppressive and cruel relations of subjugation there always yet remains a substantial measure of personal freedom' (S: 130; also in ISF). Even when an authority is experienced as oppressive or as a force of one-sided coercion, he argues, there is usually some acknowledgement, however minimal, that a person could somehow choose to give up or assert one's autonomy. (As I note in chapter 3, Max Weber criticizes Simmel on this point and later developed his own concepts of 'legitimate domination'.) Simmel examines a variety of power relationships, including interactions between privileged and underprivileged people and the domination of a population under a single sovereign, a ruling class, or a governing authority. In each case, he contends that superordination is always realized with a certain degree of consent and spontaneity on the part of those who are deemed subordinate. Along the same lines, he assumes that, in some sense, the poor person voluntarily submits to the impersonal principle of social welfare, consents to the regime of private property, or accepts charity from someone who is more powerful and prosperous by freely claiming the right to attain a certain standard of living.

Consider, for example, the working woman who in some sense is forced to leave home to find employment, and is thus in some sense 'liberated' from the oppressive social roles of wife and mother: 'The proletarian woman has too much, not too little, social freedom

– no matter how poor her individual freedom may be', as Simmel argues in a newspaper article on the Berlin Women's Congress of 1896 (SC: 202). The poor woman in the city, like any modern individual, enjoys an unprecedented degree of freedom insofar as she is 'emancipated' from political, religious, and other traditional impositions and is also potentially recognized as a distinct person in her own right. The opposite seems to hold for the middle-class woman insofar as she has been stripped of her domestic authority but without other spheres of activity opening up to her. Nevertheless, her relatively more prosperous material and cultural conditions present her with more opportunities to develop her inner life and personal talents. In the metropolises essay, Simmel discusses these two forms of individual liberty in broadly historical terms: one form originates in eighteenth-century struggles against the traditional and unnatural bonds of church, agrarian community, and guild; the other is rooted in the nineteenth-century desire for each person to express his or her qualitative uniqueness and irreplaceability (SC: 175, 184–5; also 1950: 64–84). These negative and positive visions of freedom are largely fought out in ways that often contradict the social and political ideal of equality, and they rest to a great extent on cultural and economic foundations of free competition and the division of labour that often undermine the equitable distribution of resources. In short, the culture of metropolitan life opens up new spaces of freedom for all while allowing a select few to benefit from expanding relations of power and unequal systems of control.

Just as modern forms of power give rise to new kinds of liberty, so too does leisure become the inextricable flip side of labour, and free time is increasingly tied to work time for rich and poor alike. With easier access to inexpensive and rapid transportation, more people are able to enjoy the beauty of nature regardless of what social class they belong to, as Simmel points out in a short article on alpine journeys (SC: 219–21). Working people and middle-class professionals alike can experience the excitement and emotional high that comes from struggling with the forces of nature or the moral and spiritual uplift that results from the vigorous exertion of their willpower and courage. However, the class differences that underlie these experiences often become immediately evident in these new forms of adventure tourism, such as when an affluent hiker places the life of a hired guide in danger (SC: 121).

Simmel's tone turns bitter when discussing some of these cultural and ethical implications of leisure culture and free time in an anonymous article written a few years earlier on Berlin's 'amuse-ment industry'. The proletarian viewing these 'pleasure palaces' from the outside might feel a bit like the resentful poor people of ancient and medieval times who believed that the propertied are indeed happy and blessed (*beati possidentes*). 'Yet if he could see deeper', Simmel objects, 'then he would recognize that the more sparkling, noisy and intoxicating is the hubbub inside, the more wretched is the exhaustion and the more tormenting is the obses-sion to lose oneself that brought it into existence' (SC: 261). Poverty and pain often force the masses to find joy in a bottle of liquor, he notes, or solace in a morphine syringe, hope in a gambling hall, and happiness in the many public spectacles on offer in the big city. As his student Siegfried Kracauer notes in his 1927 study of the salaried masses (*die Angestellte*), the rising middle classes and modestly paid employees concentrated in city centres are offered the promise of false freedoms through the pursuit of uniform pastimes. Among the many 'exemplary instances of reality' that Kracauer describes in his study, he mentions a young working girl who is employed in the filing room of a factory and dreams of the splendours of a bourgeois life, and who cannot help singing along to every popular hit she hears in a dance hall or in her local suburban café. 'But it is not she who knows every hit', he laments; 'rather the hits know her, steal up behind her and gently lay her low' (Kracauer 1998: 70). This newfangled brand of 'free time busyness' has an addictive quality, since it can fill up everyone's time without actually being fulfill-ing and keep everyone in a heightened state of 'permanent recep-tivity', much like our experience of social media today (Kracauer 1995: 332). Writing a few decades earlier than Kracauer, Simmel seems to have similar experiences in mind when he criticizes the 'temples of licentious pleasures' and concludes that these establish-ments should post a health warning over their doors to anyone who approaches, like a notice on the gates of hell: 'unhappy are those with possessions! (*infelices possidentes!*)' (SC: 262).

The solution to the social problem of poverty and the answer to the moral plea of the poor person cannot lie simply in the call for everyone to lead a simpler life. Rejecting the money economy is unrealistic for almost everyone and retreating from the metropolis is for the most part possible only for a privileged few (see PM: 252–5 on ascetic poverty). Very special conditions are required for one to attain the blessed state of the medieval Franciscans who 'found security, love and freedom in *poverty*, in their character as *nihil habentes, omnia possidentes*' – a community of the pious who own nothing and therefore possess everything (PM: 254). Likewise, only a few of us have the spiritual energy and material resources to lead a pure and divine life without desire, and thus to follow the Buddhist maxim: 'We who do not want anything live in an ecstasy of happiness' (PM: 255). In modern societies, Simmel argues, the poor and the propertied are each members of a status group where they inhabit a distinctive social position in their own right. Even bums, hobos, and homeless people (*Penner* in German) seem to mirror the social organization of the mainstream society when they invent their own precarious hierarchies and enforce their own laws among themselves (S: 440–1). As I have pointed out, Simmel stops short of examining socialist schemes for the equitable distribution of wealth and instead focuses on the moral bonds of solidarity and the practices of freedom that connect rich and poor people in the city. Like Nietzsche, he suspects that a trace of self-love may motivate the love of one's neighbour and that resentment may drive the weak to revolt, but he does not assume that the compassion of superior individuals simply affirms the misery or mediocrity of the masses (1984: 150). He notes a certain pettiness and egoism in the refusal among some members of the bourgeoisie to donate to charity simply on the grounds that it costs money, but he also acknowledges that what makes poor people poor is not their personal deficiencies but rather the individuals and associations that support them, however well intentioned (PM: 260; S: 442). Observing a world characterized by growing gaps between rich and poor, Simmel concludes that the challenge for the sociologist cannot be to condemn or condone these intricate relationships but rather to comprehend them, as he declares in the final line of the metropolises essay: 'it is not our task either to accuse or to pardon, but only to understand' (SC: 185). In contrast to the social critic and the advocate for change, the sociologist of cities can express only reasoned arguments, compelling interpretations, and well-formulated insights concerning the collective and singular circumstances of modern life.

Excursus on Race Relations, Strangers, and Other Marginals: Simmel behind Park and Du Bois

Major cities are obviously not the only places where different racial and ethnic groups come into contact, where strangers meet and interact, or where marginalized people are pushed aside and forgotten. In the metropolis, however, these complex and conflicting relationships reach an unprecedented scale and are intensified to an extreme degree. In a digression in the chapter of *Sociology* on the poor person, Simmel considers these general issues in terms of what he calls 'the negativity of collective modes of behaviour' (S: 425–9; also in 1950). His thesis is that, for collective life to be possible, one action often presupposes or gives rise to its opposite: what is permitted implies what is prohibited; the assertion of a right suggests the possibility of revoking it; every rule may potentially be broken; and so on. Neglecting to observe simple etiquette in a small gathering, for instance, may be permitted and forgiven, but it may also be a sign of a deeper antagonism: 'The greeting on the street does not necessarily give evidence of respect; its omission, however, very strongly indicates the opposite' (S: 428). A silent snub may reveal a profound gulf between individuals who otherwise do not interact at all. On a larger scale, the basic rights to food, clothing, and shelter are the flip side of the deprivation, vulnerability, and insecurity that some groups in the city experience more than others.

Simmel's discussion of the stranger is perhaps the paradigmatic social type of this negative dimension of collective behaviour. Strangers tend to be 'strangers of a certain type', grouped together in ways that efface or negate their individuality: 'what is stressed is nothing individual, but of alien origin, a quality which the stranger has, or could have, in common with many other strangers' (S: 605; ISF: 149). For this reason, strangers are typically excluded from the dominant social group while at the same time they serve a particular social function within it. (In other words, they embody all three of Simmel's apriorities, as discussed in my Introduction.) Simmel notes that 'the classic example' of the stranger as an integral yet excluded member of society 'is the history of the European Jew' (ISF: 144). He mentions how Jews were taxed in the Middle Ages as an ethnic and racial group rather than as individuals, and how they occupied the margins or interstices of European society in their role as merchants rather than a central place as producers or landowners (ISF: 144, 149). Although he does not explicitly develop a sociology of race relations, his account of the historical and spatial dynamics that give rise to the stranger as a social type, and specifically to the social space of the Jews in Europe, nevertheless suggests the outlines for such a theory (Morris-Reich 2003).

Among the most influential contemporaries and important successors of Simmel to expand on these insights in the context of the modern city was Robert Park (1864–1944), one of the founders of the so-called Chicago School that pioneered urban sociology in the United States. After completing a master's degree in philosophy at Harvard in 1899 and taking up a career in journalism, Park later continued his studies in Germany, where in the 1899–1900 academic term he attended Simmel's lectures in ethics, nineteenth-century philosophy, and sociology (see Pyyhtinen 2018: 147–54; Levine, in ISF: xlix–lvi; Levine 1985: 112–18). Simmel's sociology lectures, which he gave in the Philosophy Department, highlighted such themes as 'the self-preservation of the group' and 'super- and subordination, with special consideration of state forms' (Park's class notes are included in GSG 21: 281–355). Later Park was hired at the University of Chicago by the then head of the Sociology Department, Albion Small, the founder and first editor of the *American Journal of Sociology*, who translated and published many of Simmel's early essays. Simmel himself might have remained a marginal figure in both American and European sociology if Park and Ernest Burgess had not incorporated his ideas into their monumental textbook *Introduction to the Science of Sociology*, published in 1921, which included ten essays by Simmel (more than any other thinker), beginning with the piece on 'the stranger'. In their canonical book *The City*, published in 1925, they approach the city from a distinctly Simmelian perspective as 'a state of mind' – that is, as a body of attitudes, sentiments, customs, traditions, and spiritual dispositions and not just as a particular physical arrangement and institutional configuration (Park et al. 1967: 1). Park's contributions to the book characterize the city as 'the product of human nature' and 'the natural habitat of civilized man'. The city can thus be treated as a 'laboratory and clinic' for the study of marginalized groups such as youth gangs, the solitary hobo, and the ethnic ghetto at the level of the neighbourhood, the segregated area, and other urban zones. In the extensive 'Bibliography of the Urban Community' appended to the book, Park's younger colleague Louis Wirth describes Simmel's metropolises essay as 'the most important single article on the city from the sociological standpoint' (ibid.: 219). In short, the standard narrative of the early history of urban sociology in the United States can be understood to pivot on Park's influential writings and against the background of his reception of Simmel's ideas (Jaworski 1997).

One of Park's most cited and influential studies is the programmatic article 'Human Migration and the Marginal Man', first published in 1928 in the *American Journal of Sociology*. There he applies Simmel's general discussion of the stranger to how race relations emerge from historical patterns of migration. He characterizes the marginal man as 'living and sharing intimately in the cultural life and traditions of two distinct peoples, never quite willing to break, even if he were permitted to do so, with his past and his traditions, and not quite accepted, because of racial prejudice, in the new society in which he now sought to find a place' (Park 1950: 354). On the same page he cites Simmel's example of the stranger as his inspiration for this concept: 'The emancipated Jew was, and is, historically and typically the marginal man, the first cosmopolite and citizen of the world.' Despite his emphasis on the role racial prejudice plays in the making of 'the marginal man', however, Park refrains from mentioning the most accomplished empirical sociologist of race relations of the time, the African-American sociologist W. E. B. Du Bois (1868–1963) (see Morris 2015: 119–48).

Du Bois studied at Harvard under many of the same prominent philosophers as Park did and completed his doctorate in 1895, the first African-American there to do so. And, like Park, Du Bois also studied in Berlin, where he attended the lectures of Simmel's mentor, the economic historian Gustav Schmoller, among others, though apparently not with Simmel. He was unquestionably the most knowledgeable sociologist of race relations in the United States in the early decades of the twentieth century, publishing sociological studies from his 'laboratory' in Atlanta University and, in 1899, the first major empirical work in urban sociology, *The Philadelphia Negro*. Nevertheless, Park refers only briefly to some of these works in the *Introduction to the Science of Sociology* and mentions them hardly at all in his other writings. As Aldon Morris explains, 'the intellectual networks and ideas of the Du Bois–Atlanta school can be conceptualized as insurgent because they developed outside mainstream sociological networks and provided counteranalyses to those of the mainstream' (Morris 2015: 144). Although both Park and Du Bois approached sociology as an empirical and experimental science, they disagreed on whether social science can contribute to social change through gradual evolution (as Park maintained) or political agitation (as Du Bois argued). In light of Park's sociological focus on marginalized people, it is ironic that, in mainstreaming Simmel, he marginalizes Du Bois.

In *The Souls of Black Folk*, published in 1903, Du Bois famously criticizes the educational programme of economic submission and social segregation for African-Americans proposed by Booker T. Washington at the Tuskegee Institute, where Park worked as press secretary in the years after completing his doctorate and before joining the Sociology Department at Chicago. In that book, Du Bois describes the historical, social, and psychological experiences of inequality and exploitation among African-Americans in ways that contrast sharply with the ideas of Washington and Park. Nevertheless, Du Bois's lyrically moving and conceptually precise account of 'double-consciousness' may well have exerted a 'subterranean influence' on Park when he was formulating his ideas on the marginal man: 'It is a peculiar sensation, this double-consciousness, this sense of always looking at one's self through the eyes of others, of measuring one's soul by the tape of a world that looks on in amused contempt and pity' (Du Bois 1999: 11; see Morris 2015: 144–8). In Du Bois's view, the African-American is a stranger and outsider 'in a world which yields him no true self-consciousness, but only lets him see himself through the revelation of the other world.' Like Simmel's remarks on the stranger and the poor, but in language that is more poetic and philosophical than Park's, Du Bois describes how African-Americans live on the edges of society, perceiving themselves as if through a distorted mirror that reflects only the scorn or compassion of others.

In an article on 'The Negro Problem in the United States', Du Bois offers his sober assessment of the distribution of farmland, population growth, literacy rates, and different occupations among African-Americans while at the same time describing the spatial segregation of living conditions in a way that Simmel would have appreciated: 'In terms of *living together* it is possible in almost every Southern community to draw a color line on the map which separates the homes of the whites from those of the blacks' (Du Bois 2006: 265). In contrast to Simmel and Park, Du Bois believes that an important task of the sociologist is to criticize, to advocate, and even to prophesy in the interests of social change: 'the day of the colored races dawns. It is insanity to delay this development; it is wisdom to promote what it promises us in light and hope for the future' (Du Bois 1999: 287). Du Bois's paper appears in a 1906 issue of the *Archiv für Socialwissenschaft und Socialpolitik* (*Archive for Social Science and Social Policy*), edited by Max Weber, immediately after Simmel's lead article 'On the Sociology of Poverty', an early version of the chapter 'The Poor Person' in *Sociology* (GSG 8: 440; Du Bois 1999: 290). Simmel and Du Bois (and perhaps Mannheim, discussed in the previous chapter) might be called sociologists of the soul (Leck 2000: 58–9). However, these two 'soulciologists' do not seem to have met in Berlin in 1892 when Simmel was teaching and Du Bois was a student there; they may never have read each other's work in the journal where their essays appear together; and they may not even have been aware of their contribution in 1911 to the First Universal Races Congress in London, where Du Bois presented and Simmel is listed as a member of the General Committee (though it is not clear if he attended; see Gilroy 1993: 144, 214).

Despite the differences between them, Simmel thinks of marginalized people in modern metropolises in ways that often seem to be lurking behind how Park and Du Bois approach the modern industrial city, namely, as a laboratory for studying contemporary social problems and as a clinic for diagnosing the cultural and spiritual malaise of modern times.

Part III

Cultures of Modernity

What is distinctively *modern* about the world and the age we now live in? Many classic thinkers over the last few hundred years have asked some version of this question, and each seems to have come up with more questions than answers. Is the term 'modern' another way of referring to progress in the expansion of personal freedoms, the advance of more efficient technologies, or the growing surplus of material wealth? Does modernity express something 'new' about how people live, think, and feel about their relationships with other people, the natural and cultural worlds they inhabit, or themselves? Perhaps modernity is another name for all these aspects of contemporary life, and so this one word actually covers a plurality of realities, experiences, and transformations. David Frisby summarizes what is distinctive about Simmel's approach to modernity as both a new *culture* and a novel *experience*: 'The experience of modernity is viewed by Simmel as discontinuous experience of *time* as transitory, in which both the fleeting moment and the sense of presentness converge; *space* as the dialectic of distance and proximity (associated with social distance as boundary maintenance and the removal of boundaries ...); and *causality* as contingent, arbitrary and fortuitous' (Frisby 1992: 163–4). Simmel considers many such experiences from the perspective of everyday life in the modern world, such as how fashions express the transitory and present character of city life; how the rapid pace of money transactions both connects and divides people, places, and things across large distances; and how the accidental or unpredictable character of everyday life disrupts our traditional assumptions about historical necessity.

In a magisterial lecture Simmel gave towards the end of his life, 'The Conflict of Modern Culture', he diagnoses these phenomena as signs of a new phase of an age-old *cultural* struggle. Previous periods of Western history have interpreted the world according to one essential idea: the idea of *Being* among the Ancients; of *God* in the Christian Middle Ages; of *Nature* beginning with the Renaissance; and of *Society* in the nineteenth century. In the twentieth century, these philosophical, religious, and scientific worldviews came to converge on a single point: 'the idea of *Life* emerged at the centre where reality and values – metaphysical or psychological, moral or artistic – both originate and intersect' (SC: 79). Simmel argues that the latest conflict of culture has now reached such an unprecedented level of intensity that life struggles not just against old cultural forms that constrain or threaten it but also 'against form itself, against the very principle of form' (SC: 77). In the last decade of his life his main preoccupation was with *the conflict of life against form* and with the new experiences, feelings, and cultural expressions that emerge from this conflict.

Simmel's career cannot be neatly divided into phases with clear breaks and turning points – an early social-evolutionary period culminating in the *Philosophy of Money*, for example, followed by a formalist-sociological middle period highlighted by the publication of *Sociology*, and ending with a vitalist-metaphysical phase where these previous concerns are supposedly left behind. Nor can his writings be viewed simply as a random collection of impressionistic pieces, distinct from one another but not holding together in any consistent way (Weingartner 1960). Rather than working out a single idea from the beginning to the end of his career, Simmel takes up a variety of themes, returns to many of them in light of new examples, and then reworks them with different emphases (Levine 2012: 42). His writings in the last decade of his career on the cultures of modernity refocus and offer fresh perspectives on themes arising from his earlier studies of the philosophy of the money economy and the sociology of modern metropolises. He asks many of the same questions that have been raised by other thinkers over millennia – on the relationship between nature and culture, life and death, self and other – but argues that these questions often call for different answers.

Along with his ideas on interaction (*Wechselwirkung*) and association (*Vergesellschaftung*) discussed in the previous two parts of this book, the concept of culture (*Kultur*) emerges as the main motif guiding Simmel's later writings. Towards the end of the *Philosophy of Money* he notes that 'the culture of things is … nothing but a culture of people' (PM: 454), and in the concluding remarks of 'The Metropolis and Mental Life' he diagnoses what ails the modern age, namely, 'the atrophy of individual culture through the hypertrophy of objective culture' (SC: 185). Using the terms of the third apriority of commitment (which I discuss in my Introduction), he notes a cultural tension between the functions or causes that keep systems alive and the purposes or inclinations that sustain the life of the individual components of such systems. These arguments are refined and developed in his later writings on how cultural forms – especially in the realms of art, science, and religion – emerge from the life process itself. In other words, culture is not the opposite of nature but, rather, each is a way of looking at the same reality, either as a bundle of physiological energies or as a complex of human activities (SC: 41). Culture refers to the cultivation (*Kultivierung* or *Bildung* in German) of all forms of life – non-human and human, individual and social – through care or compulsion, through planning, technical intervention, or deliberate development, or simply through haphazard growth (SC: 45; Pyyhtinen 2018: 118–20). The process of culture can never be complete or fixed once and for all but, to some extent, is undermined by its own internal dynamics. Simmel repeatedly emphasizes that human culture is therefore inherently a *tragic* undertaking, although not necessarily a doomed or a sorrowful affair.

Although Simmel worked out his general concept of culture and many specific ideas about the cultures of modernity well before the First World War was declared in early August 1914, this military conflict marked a high point in the crisis of culture. As he told his son Hans, his patriotic enthusiasm was at its peak in the early weeks of the war: 'Germany must fight for its existence to the end … The teutonic furor has been released and also rages in me' (quoted in H. Simmel 1958: 267). In the wartime articles he published in 1917 under the title *The War and Our Spiritual Decisions* (*Der Krieg und unsere Geistige Entscheidungen*) he describes this conflict as a moment of national and personal self-reckoning, an ultimate test and an 'absolute situation' for Germans to become what they truly are but are not yet in actuality (see the translations in 2007b, 1976, and SC: 90–101). However, Simmel soon became disillusioned with the chauvinistic views of his fellow citizens and bitterly condemned the 'blindness and criminal frivolity of the handful of Europeans' who started the war in the first place: 'the spiritual unity that we used to call "Europe" is shattered, and no prospect of its restoration is in sight' (1976: 268). This change of tone came too late for pacifist and communist students such as Georg Lukács (discussed in chapter 4) and Ernst Bloch (discussed below in chapter 9), however, who denounced their teacher and only grudgingly acknowledged their debt to him in later years (Leck 2000: 284–312).

Simmel's output in the last decade of his career was remarkable, with the publication of seven major monographs and two revised editions of early books along with countless articles and unpublished essays. This level of productivity is all the more impressive in light of his continued frustrations in finding a permanent position in the university. Finally, in the spring of 1914 he was called to a professorship in philosophy and pedagogy at the Kaiser-Wilhelm University in Strasbourg, and with considerable resignation he and his wife Gertrud made the move to this provincial town at the border of Germany and France. As he wrote to his Berlin neighbours Ignaz and Anna Jastrow: 'The city is lacking a level of culture like that of Heidelberg, and the university is a pile of educated atoms without any unity, community or superindividual spirit of the whole' (GSG 23: 349). To convey a sense of what is most interesting and significant about Simmel's later writings, in what follows I select from the most intriguing essays collected in *Philosophical Culture* (*Philosophische Kultur*), published in 1911, especially his fascinating discussions of the ruin, the adventure, and the tragedy of culture. These pieces offer a useful point of entry into themes Simmel takes up in other essays, and in his studies of Goethe, Rembrandt, and his last book, the *View of Life*. Nowhere does Simmel offer a focused or comprehensive theory of contemporary life, although these works provide a glimpse into his theory of what is distinctive about *modern* culture. In discussing his metaphysical, aesthetic, and ethical writings, I insert a few digressions on how they relate to the sociological and philosophical ideas of his predecessors, contemporaries, and successors in Europe and America. Throughout his career Simmel acknowledges the inherently fragmentary character of life while tirelessly searching for his own unique ideal of unity and wholeness within the diversity, ambivalence, and conflict of modern experience.

8

The Ruin and Renewal of Life

It would be misleading to characterize Simmel as an unapologetic urbanist or as a naive enthusiast of modernism. His view of Berlin does not focus on industrial factories, social inequalities, and transportation networks but, rather, on the cultural institutions, intellectual circles, and entertainment districts that offer some distance from and perspective on the modern experience. His daily life was spent largely in the affluent and tranquil districts of Charlottenburg and the Westend, in the Tiergarten, the lecture halls of the university, and artistic salons (Podoksik 2012: 118). Simmel is less a classic modernist than what might be called a modern classicist. He looks for traces of movement within classical forms and for signs of permanence in the transience of modern life. His passion for the metropolitan splendours of London, Paris, and Berlin is often tempered by his fascination with the Italian cities that flourished at the birth of the modern age, which he treats as a kind of refuge from the chaos of modernity. In a trilogy of short articles published between 1896 and 1907, he portrays Rome as the eternal city of ruins, Venice as the classical city of adventure, and Florence as the Renaissance city of self-cultivation (see the translations in 2007b). His interest in the sources of European modernity is already evident from his early studies of the poetry of Dante and Michelangelo and from his repeated readings of Goethe's popular account of his Italian journey. Rome in particular captured Simmel's imagination as the birthplace of modern European culture and as a model for finding a precarious resolution to the tension between the weight of historical heritage and the relentless demands of the present. Viewed from the standpoint of a foreign visitor, the ruins of Rome seem to epitomize the balance between the preservation of diverse fragments of history and the fortuitous development of modern progress (2007b: 33). The Roman cityscape displays the dynamism that emerges over time from the process of integrating older buildings into newer ones. Rome thus offers a glimpse into how the image of an entire city can be formed out of the variety of its parts, and how the peculiar charm of ruins is not always a result of human neglect but often lies in the awesome work of nature to endow these fragments with new life.

Simmel's expansive *philosophy of life* is at the same time a *metaphysics of culture*. This multidimensional project is illustrated in poignant ways through his episodic remarks on the *cultures of modernity* and their historical sources. Nowhere is this unique combination of philosophical speculation, sociological observation, and cultural analysis more evident than in the eclectic collection of essays *Philosophical Culture* (no English version of this book exists yet, although translations are scattered over several volumes; see my Suggestions for Further Reading). In the 'Introduction' Simmel acknowledges that such a bewildering range of topics – from flirtation to fashion, from sculpture to the Swiss Alps, and from the personality of God to the politics of feminism – may seem arbitrary and incoherent. 'The results of the effort may be fragmentary', he admits, 'but the effort itself is not' (SC: 36). The guiding thread connecting these studies consists in tracing 'a fundamental turn ... from metaphysics as dogma to *metaphysics as life or function*' (SC: 35; GSG 14: 165, emphasis added). In other words, 'philosophical culture' refers not to an academic search for a single meaning of life but, rather, to a consistent intellectual and spiritual attitude to the whole of existence that underlies the particular manifestations, functions, and symptoms of a culture (Habermas 1996).

In this chapter I begin by discussing Simmel's essay 'The Ruin' in connection with related essays on mealtimes, the aesthetics of nature, and the artistic personalities of the sculptors Michelangelo and Auguste Rodin. These diverse topics exemplify his method of 'delving into things from the surface of life, excavating the respective succeeding strata of ideas under each of its phenomena', as he says in the 'Introduction' to *Philosophical Culture* (SC: 36). They are also given an explicitly metaphysical twist in the *View of Life*, where he describes the essence of life as a process of displacing and transcending boundaries and defines human life in particular as paradoxically 'bounded in every direction, and ... bounded in no direction' (VL: 2). As I note in a digression, Simmel's contemporaries Marcel Mauss in France and Thorstein Veblen in the United States worked on similar issues from a sociological perspective in their respective discussions of symbolic exchange and conspicuous consumption. In short, we could say that Simmel's 'archeological' approach reveals the deeper sources of modern culture in the cosmic cycle of the ruin and renewal of life, and in the process of living within and beyond the fragments of existence.

Beyond Subsistence and Self-Preservation

All living things are destined to die, and all life falls to pieces at some time or another. What Simmel calls 'the fragmentary character of life' in an essay published in 1916 in *Logos*, the international journal of the philosophy of culture that he helped establish in 1910, is exemplified in his vivid description of ruins in *Philosophical Culture* (translated in 2012 and 1959, respectively). His focus in this latter piece is on how the ruin resolves the tension between nature and culture not by synthesizing them, but by preserving and enhancing their multiplicity, ultimately in favour of nature. The new unity that is embodied in the ruin conveys a distinctive spiritual appeal and its own aesthetic charm: 'Nature has transformed the work of art into material for her own expression, as she had previously served as material for art' (1959: 262). Decay may be described as nature's revenge on the human achievement of constructing buildings and monuments, and yet these mindless natural forces of destruction also give rise to a new whole with a different meaning and a special beauty that often leaves us awestruck. Simmel himself was almost speechless when viewing the ruined castle across from the villa of his colleague Max Weber along the Neckar River in Heidelberg for the first time: 'This is *too* beautiful. One can't live with it' (quoted in Marianne Weber 1988: 453). The gravity of inert matter reverses the upward striving of the spirit materialized in the crumbling building: 'what has led the building upwards is human will; what gives it its present appearance is the brute downward-dragging, corroding, crumbling power of nature' (1959: 261). Simmel insists that this process of natural corrosion is tragic, although not necessarily sad or senseless, since it arises from a necessary tendency that is at work in the deepest layers of existence. For this reason, the unfinished and formless quality of a ruin often exudes a quiet peacefulness, as if the past has been preserved in the present instead of the present being constructed out of the remnants of the past. Ruins like those in Heidelberg or in Rome and its far-flung empire often attract a certain morbid fascination, prompting us to wonder about the power that nature has over humans and how humans bring about decadence and decay through passive neglect or their own destructive actions.

The counterforce to the internal tendency towards dissolution and ruination is the process of renewal and regeneration. Simmel begins his essay on the ruin by describing architecture as the art in which 'the great struggle between the will of the spirit and the necessity of nature enters into real peace' and where matter and mind find an inner balance (1959: 259). We can expand on this idea by thinking of architecture as a cultural technology for assembling and maintaining groups, individuals, and human bodies. In the chapter of *Sociology* entitled 'The Self-Preservation of the Group', Simmel elaborates on the collective, personal, and physical dimensions of self-preservation and group maintenance in terms of three overlapping planes of existence, namely 1) the psychological life of the individual; 2) the physiological processes of the organism; and 3) the sociological structures of the group. In this account, the capacities of individuals, organisms, and groups to sustain themselves in space and over time are shaped through 'uninterrupted processes … of peril and preservation, repulsion and reengagement among members' (S: 443). In the specific context of modernity, the overlapping struggles for self-preservation, natural regeneration, and social renewal ultimately converge in a life-and-death conflict between vital processes and cultural forms.

An ordinary meal offers a simple illustration of the universal dynamics of social sustenance and self-maintenance. Viewed from a broad perspective, a meal embodies both the natural economy of reproduction, growth, and consumption and the cultural economy of exchange, interaction, and conversation. As Simmel notes in 'The Sociology of the Meal', published in 1910, mealtimes can also be seen from a small-scale perspective in the way that they link 'the exclusive selfishness of eating with a frequency of being together' (SC: 130). The enjoyment we experience in satisfying individual biological needs animates and gives substance to the cultural forms of custom, convention, and ritual, a theme on which several of Simmel's contemporaries elaborated as well (see the 'Excursus on Sustainability and Surplus', pp. 149–52). Celebratory feasts, everyday table manners, and even the table-setting itself are occasions for elevating the lowest physiological functions to the level of the highest symbolic processes. Unlike a work of art, which remains self-sufficient, distant, and untouchable within its frame, the dinner table is an open space that is destined to be desecrated. In the end its harmonious appearance must succumb to the ravages of 'meal-time' (*Mahlzeit*): 'the refinement of the table is such that its beauty must in fact invite us to invade it' (SC: 133). Any of us can recall the hard work of cooking and serving dishes, followed by the effort of clearing away and cleaning up the mess after a sumptuous feast. We might say then that the dinner table is always a kind of ruin in the making.

In figure 8 I show how these macro- and micro-aspects of the dinner table can help us understand the outlines of Simmel's two great books *Philosophical Culture* and *View of Life*. Although *Philosophical Culture* covers a wide range of topics and themes, these essays can be loosely organized according to the three classic branches of philosophical thought: the *ethics* of psychological and sexual behaviour (which I address below in chapter 9), the *aesthetics* of natural phenomena and artistic personalities (my focus in this

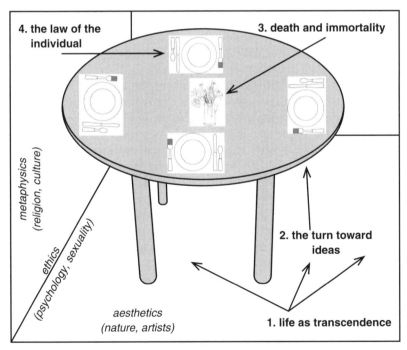

Figure 8 Outline of *Philosophical Culture* and *View of Life*

chapter), and *metaphysical* questions concerning religion and culture (discussed in my concluding chapter). I depict these philosophical approaches in terms of the interactions that take place along the three spatial 'dimensions' of the horizontal plane (aesthetics), the diagonal plane (ethics), and the vertical plane (metaphysics) of the dining room. Just as we could say that there is an ethics of table manners with respect to what one should and should not do or say while eating, so too is there an aesthetics of place-settings that reflect personal tastes and social customs, and even a metaphysics of mealtimes that transcends our biological needs and expresses a social and even spiritual meaning. These philosophical perspectives are informed by the psychological, physiological, and sociological significance of the act of eating together. Further, when a stranger is invited to share a meal with us (represented here by marking one table-setting with an X) we are often reminded how much we take for granted familiar habits such as seasoning, personal space, and sociable conversation. As Simmel points out, 'persons who in no way share any special interest can gather together in the common meal' (SC: 130).

Metaphysical questions are the special focus of Simmel's last book, *View of Life*. As he indicates in a footnote (VL: 19), the first chapter of this work presents his main thesis concerning 'life as transcendence' – his argument that all life strives to reach beyond its limits – which he elaborates in the three main chapters that follow. The focus of these latter chapters can also be illustrated with the example of the dinner table. We might imagine how a table serves particular purposes on many occasions, but often in ways that go beyond the 'idea' of those who designed and constructed it. We can also think of how mealtimes do not meet simply our physical needs, insofar as they also celebrate the 'temporary yet perpetual' character of social life (symbolized here with a vase of flowers that will eventually die and be discarded afterwards). Finally, at least in a Western context, there is usually just one table-setting or plate for each person as a way of acknowledging how 'the individual' is simultaneously both a part of and apart from the communal act of eating. Briefly put, we can imagine how even ordinary mealtimes embody 'metaphysical' questions concerning the essential relationships that make up the whole of existence, including the tension between the ideal versus the material, the living versus the dead, and the individual versus the social.

Although Simmel's essay on the meal is not included in *Philosophical Culture*, he does describe another homely example under the theme of 'aesthetics' in a way that fits well into this discussion.

In 'The Handle', he explicitly considers the handle of the flower vase and the eating utensil. Generally speaking, we can say that when an object has a handle, in a sense the self-contained sovereign realm of the work of culture is extended into the world of nature. The handle has a kind of dual reality since it inhabits the two worlds of aesthetic form and practical function. In other words, the handle connects a cultural artefact with a segment of reality beyond it, 'for it is held in the hand and drawn into the movement of practical life' (1959: 267). These apparently self-sufficient domains of nature and culture are connected by the hand, Simmel points out, which in turn is an extension of the will or the soul of the person: 'in effect, just as the hand is a tool of the soul, so too the tool is a hand of the soul' (1959: 269). In less mysterious terms, we could also say that the handle must be useful and yet it aspires to be beautiful. Unlike a piece of furniture, which makes contact with us and directly intervenes in our practical life even when it is also beautiful, or a picture frame which is predominantly functional in containing a work of art while separating it from the world outside, the vase and the utensil have a distinctively double existence as both aesthetic artefacts and useful objects (1994b: 14). When the handle is part of a flower vase or an eating utensil, it exemplifies how everyday things have both form and function and how things can embody the unity of human culture and non-human nature (De la Fuente 2016a: 172–7).

Under the heading 'artistic personalities', Simmel turns his attention from the mundane world of ordinary objects to the sublime domain of great artworks and the talented individuals who create them. His primary focus is on modern sculpture from the Renaissance to the present, with a particular concern for how the medium of stone poses a special challenge for aesthetically depicting the dynamism and movement of life. He argues that the work of aesthetic creation offers a glimpse not just into the soul or psyche of the modern artist but also into the experience of modern life as a whole. He formulates this argument in a passage that may be his most precise definition of modernity anywhere in his work: 'The essence of modernity as such is psychologism, the experience and interpretation of the world through inner reactions and indeed *as an inner world; the dissolution of firm contents in the soul's fluid element*, so that its forms are *forms of movement purged of all substance*' (forthcoming; also Frisby 1986: 46, 1992: 66; GSG 14: 346, emphasis added).

Two essays in *Philosophical Culture* elaborate on this key thesis concerning the link between modern art and the modern attitude of 'psychologism' – one examines the work of Michelangelo

(1475–1564) and the other (where the passage above appears) discusses Auguste Rodin (1840–1917).

To a significant extent, Michelangelo continues the tradition of classical sculpture by depicting human figures caught in fateful ordeals and mighty deeds that seem to take place in a sphere beyond the flux of time. We might think of his famous statue of David in this regard: gazing upwards with knitted brow and standing calmly and slightly off-centre (*contraposto*), this heroic figure almost seems to move ever so slightly in anticipation of his battle with Goliath. Even Michelangelo's paintings, such as the figures on the ceiling of the Sistine Chapel depicting the creation of the world, have a certain sculptural quality in the formal definition of their fleshy bodies and the solitude they exude within their own ideal space. By contrast, the Rondadini Pietà seems almost to sink into earthly life as the figures appear to move downwards from the sorrowful gaze of the seated Madonna to the dead body of Christ laid out before her: 'The soul, here freed from bodily weight, has not run its lap of victory into the transcendent but collapsed at its threshold' (forthcoming; GSG 14: 321). Simmel even suggests that Michelangelo himself may have encountered the limits of his own soulful struggles in this work, insofar as his artistic aspirations were unable fully to overcome his material medium.

Simmel's essay on Rodin, whom he personally met during a visit to the artist's studio in Paris, elaborates further on the theme of what is distinctive about aesthetic modernity. The essay is prefaced with a note on the Belgian sculptor Constantin Meunier (1831–1905), whose depictions of labourers, farmers, miners, and dockers are iconic of modern life: 'In their artistic perfection, with their lifting, pulling, rolling and rowing, Meunier's figures show us the powers that working people invest in materials and see returning to them' (forthcoming; GSG 14: 331). In finding a new subject matter for art in the movements of the worker, however, Meunier did not create a new stylistic principle for the artistic perspective on life. Only Rodin has been able to invent a novel way of transforming sculpture into the medium of movement and a 'mirror of mobility', and thus only he can be considered a truly modern artist in the sense defined above. In contrast to the upward movement of the soul depicted in medieval Christian and Renaissance art, Rodin's figures emphasize the body in motion, and indeed they become a 'monument' to becoming. Even when a particular work is left incomplete (whether on purpose or not), the sculptured body is not so much cut free from the block of stone (as Michelangelo famously describes his technique) as much as it emerges and unfolds outwards towards the viewer: 'it leaves in our imagination's activity of finishing the unfinished for itself, thereby displacing into ourselves the productive movement that flows from the work itself to its final effect' (forthcoming; GSG 14: 337). By taking the shape of figures that seem to follow their own laws of gravity and will, Rodin's sculptures embody the unity of being and becoming, the perpetual process of matter unfolding through movement, and the paradox of solidity dissolved into fluidity. Although occasionally these figures seem to convey the timeless image of a fleeting moment fixed in mute stone, they always evoke what Simmel calls the 'psychologism' of modern life, the experience and interpretation of the world as a flow of inner reactions that are dissolved into a fluid form of movement (a theme Simmel introduces in the *Philosophy of Money* in terms of the attitude of 'subjectivism', as I note in chapter 2).

Beyond Being and Beauty

The characteristics of flow, flux, and fluidity are elemental to the aesthetic culture of modernity, and at a deeper, more expansive level they are also integral to cosmic cycles of ruin and renewal. Ordinary objects and great artworks are among the many examples of 'philosophical culture' that Simmel examines in detail, but he also expands on the lessons from these particular studies by developing a general philosophy or 'metaphysics' of life. In the first chapter of the *View of Life*, he outlines his thesis that the basic impulse, tendency, and direction of life is transcendence: 'transcendence is immanent in life' (VL: 10). By this he means that the very essence of life is to reach beyond itself, to confront limitations, to attempt to overcome them, and to strive perpetually for something *more*. In Simmel's view, the general life process is always part of a sequence of events and a movement of time: 'Time is real only for life alone' (VL: 8). From a temporal perspective, the course of life may be viewed apart from its contents, separately from the moment where it exists in the present, and thus as flowing out of a past and in the direction of a future. It can never be just *mere-life*. He elaborates on this argument in terms of what he calls two mutually complementary definitions of life, which he formulates in very simple terms: 'it is *more-life*, and it is *more-than-life*' (VL: 13). We can imagine the former – *more-life* – to include metabolic processes of generation and reproduction, for example, or of birth, growth, and

maturation. Every living thing – from a single cell to a highly differentiated organism such as a plant or an animal – has the capacity
to change by becoming more of what it already is, and by evolving
and transforming itself on the way to ensure its own self-preservation,
perpetuation, or expansion. At the same time as living things bear
fruit and multiply, they also have the potential to become something *other* or *more than* themselves – that is, to be *more-than-life*.
Again, we can think of the metabolic process by which living things
reach out beyond themselves and incorporate what is foreign to
them; how they assimilate what is different from them and also
become something else in the course of their existence; and how
they decay, perish, and die through the very process of becoming
more-life and more-than-life.

   Although it is easy enough to imagine how organic life fits into
this picture of life-forms reaching out for 'more' and becoming
'more than' themselves, Simmel's metaphysical reflections also
account for non-organic beings, and indeed they aim to describe the
whole of existence as a form of life. Since this aspect of his argument
is hard to grasp without an example, it is helpful to consider another
of his aesthetic studies from *Philosophical Culture*. 'The Alps' appears
immediately after 'The Ruin', and considered together these essays
address the aesthetics of inorganic nature, which Simmel describes
not as inert matter but, rather, as a dynamic form of life itself. He
imagines how ruins are subject to organic processes and at the same
time are subject to the forces of gravity and erosion, just as the
alpine landscape is essentially a dynamic geological phenomenon
that also follows the cycles of nature (Gross 2001). The Alps are
formed through the pressure of folds and collisions that force the
snow-capped peaks to surge upwards, while ice, rain, and melting
snow pull the rocks, soil, and vegetation on the surface of the mountain downwards. Simmel suggests that the dynamic and sublime
character of these peaks is not just in the eye of the beholder but
also in some sense inherent in the alpine landscape itself. On the
one hand, he describes how powerful emotions are evoked from
spectacular mountain views: 'in the cliffs *we still feel* traces of down-
wardly directed forces: matter rolling, rinsing and crumbling away,
as well as matter pushing and rising up' (forthcoming; GSG 14: 300,
emphasis added). On the other hand, he describes in symbolic
terms how the distinctive granular snow on the alpine mountain-
side which has not been compressed into ice (called firn) somehow
has a life of its own, reaching beyond itself into a realm that is
'more-than-life': *'The firn landscape assumes* a timeless immunity

from the flux of things, … an absolute highness void of all relative depth' (forthcoming; GSG 14: 300, emphasis added). The alpine landscape can therefore serve as an icon for how life may redeem itself at its highest point of intensity while at the same time transcending and standing over and against life. The Alps exist on a scale that is ultimately unfathomable for human perception and therefore cannot be adequately grasped through either aesthetic or scientific representation. At most, their unique form of life and mode of existence can be imagined only through an analogy with the experience of the soul. In a sense, the Alps do not just evoke a feeling of the sublime for the person who beholds them; they are also inherently transcendent in their own right.

As I point out above, the remaining three chapters of the *View of Life* offer illustrations, variations, and elaborations on this general thesis concerning the transcendent character of life. The second chapter, 'The Turn toward Ideas', describes what Simmel calls an 'axial turn' towards the core ideas, symbolic systems, and 'great spiritual categories' that channel human life into objective forms, structures, and institutions: 'only when that axial rotation of life occurs around them do they become truly productive' (VL: 25). Especially in the modern era, this axial turn tends to transform the means into ends in themselves, as we saw in Part I with the example of the spiritual and rational meanings of money. In this context Simmel privileges the spheres of science, religion, and art, which he describes as efforts to unify and control the fragmentary character of life through the invention of forms that are more-than-life, each viewed as objective, significant, and valid worlds in themselves. As he writes in the closing sentence of his preparatory study for this chapter published a few years earlier: 'Where life and worlds intersect, they create fragments – fragments of life, fragments of worlds' (2012: 247).

Once again, we can consider the process of aesthetic perception and artistic creation in order to illustrate this challenging argument concerning the 'turn toward ideas'. In 'The Philosophy of Landscape', published in 1913 (and thus not included in *Philosophical Culture*), Simmel suggests that any human being might be considered partly as a proto-artist or as a kind of 'embryonic' painter. By this he does not mean that each of us has some latent artistic talent waiting to be tapped; he simply wants to remind us that both art and ordinary experience entail a capacity to piece together elements of reality into a perceptual whole and to assemble them in the imagination. As suggested by the suffix of the German word for landscape, 'Land-*schaft*', each of us in our everyday life in some sense *creates* (*schafft*) a coherent image out of certain aspects of the land by highlighting some features over others, such as a rolling meadow, a fish in a stream, a magnificent mountain peak, or the soft glow of the moonlight. Landscape painting 'capitalizes' on this ability to separate oneself from the objective world and thus to create wholeness and unity over and above the component elements of nature (2007b: 22). In the essay on Rodin, Simmel argues that 'the specifically modern achievement in painting is the landscape, which is an *état d'âme*, with its character more as colour and selection than as the firm logical structure of the body or of figural composition' (forthcoming; GSG 14: 346). In other words, landscape painting captures a 'spiritual state', an atmosphere or mood not just of the viewer but also of the land itself. Moods and emotions – 'cheerful or serious, heroic or monotone, exciting or melancholic' – are in a certain sense inherent qualities or inner dimensions of the landscape that are intertwined with and inseparable from how such a setting may be imagined in the mind of the artist and represented in a work of art (2007b: 28).

Of course, different people look at landscapes in different ways: the painter's artful gaze contrasts with the perspective of 'the causally thinking scholar, the religious sentiments of a worshipper of nature, the teleologically oriented tiller of the soil, or a strategist of war' (2007b: 26). Each person gathers meaning and feeling *from* the landscape rather than simply projecting or attaching such internal states *onto* the environment. Both the subject and the object of perception make up what we might call an 'aesthetic ecology of things' and provide the focus of what Simmel means by a 'sociological metaphysics' of culture (de la Fuente 2016a: 177–81, 2016b; Harrington and Kemple 2012). A particular aesthetic sensibility is not ultimately the property of any particular time, place, or person but, rather, 'radiates from every single point', as Simmel argues in his programmatic essay 'Sociological Aesthetics', written in 1896 (1968: 69). A year later, he published a short piece under a pseudonym in the avant-garde *art nouveau* journal *Jugend* called 'Beyond Beauty' (2012: 266–9). I mention it here as a way of highlighting yet another aspect of Simmel's writings on the aesthetics of modernity and to indicate once again his own creative talent for working in genres other than philosophy and sociology. Here he leaves aside the sober tone of his scholarly writings and assumes the wry voice of a critic proposing something like an 'anti-aesthetic of ugliness' as a way of compensating for the human costs of our impossible standards of beauty. His point seems to be that, even when we reflect on how our subjective views may be contradicted and made to appear relative, there are still some objective truths that remain from this process of radical reflection.

The piece begins with the internal dialogue of an anonymous narrator, who is musing over how people nowadays are often called witty simply because they say the opposite of what other people take for granted: if the majority believes the earth circles around the sun then a minority will assert that the reverse is true, and if most people say civilization and knowledge are the highest values then some others will reply that nature and lack of wisdom are even more important, and so on and so forth. But what about the ideal of beauty?, our narrator wonders. Isn't that the one remaining absolute value in an age where all values are relative and the only eternal ideal left in a world where every positive can be contradicted by a negative? At this point the voice of the narrator takes a contrarian turn of its own: perhaps if we could only embrace the absolute ideal of ugliness then ultimately there would be less suffering in the world. Maybe such an ideal would also be more realistic and more conducive to happiness and to 'the natural development of human beings and things' than all those impossible visions of beauty have turned out to be (2012: 269). Perhaps by adopting ugliness as 'a norm and measure of all things' we might finally be able to overcome the 'irreconcilable tragedy of the demand for beauty, and make way for the organic adaptation of souls to their world, and bring joy on this earth and pleasure for human beings' (2012: 269). Like many of the other pieces Simmel published in *Jugend*, this one also ends on a note of comic irony that reflects back on reader and writer alike: 'our friend' the unnamed narrator is moved to bear witness to this new-found gospel of ugliness by taking a look at himself in the mirror!

Excursus on Sustainability and Surplus: Simmel alongside Veblen and Mauss

The sources of what today we call 'sustainability' – the idea that the needs of the present can be met without compromising future generations – can be found in nineteenth- and early twentieth-century debates about the capacity of biological and cultural systems to persist and evolve through time. Simmel's contribution to these early discussions consists in reinterpreting the Darwinian and Spencerian ideas about survival, selection, adaptability, and fitness in broader social-cultural terms as group maintenance and self-preservation (*Selbsterhaltung*) (see my Introduction). In chapter 8 of *Sociology* he considers how the reproduction and sustainability (*Nachhaltung* in contemporary German) of the individual, the organism, and the group involve symbolic and material exchanges that bind them together. In order for these interactions to persist over time and in space they need to be secured with a bond of 'social faith'. In an excursus inserted into this chapter, Simmel examines how exchanges among intimates, friends, and strangers require symbolic ties of fidelity and gratitude: 'The factors that support the preservation of society – individual interests of the members, suggestion, force, idealism, mechanical habit, sense of duty, love, inertia – would not be able to protect it from breaking up if all of them were not complemented by the factor of fidelity' (S: 518; also in 1950). Along with fidelity, gratitude draws upon 'a definite capital of feelings', a fund of emotions and beliefs that can never be completely exhausted: 'Gratitude appears here as something gratuitous, the bond of interactions, of engendering, receiving and giving of reciprocal work, where no external force guarantees it' (S: 523). Together fidelity and gratitude express the emotional bonds of personal, cultural, and even biophysical life while sustaining them across generations and maintaining them through time as relatively stable states ('second order forms') in social space (Cantó-Milà 2013).

The argument that groups persist across generations and in social space is expanded upon in rich empirical detail and in interesting theoretical ways in the classic writings of the American Thorstein Veblen (1857–1929) and the Frenchman Marcel Mauss (1872–1950). Although these social scientists were Simmel's contemporaries, none of them appear to have read or met each other. Nevertheless, Simmel's account of how status symbols and return gifts serve as techniques of self-preservation and group maintenance (S: 480, 555) resonates remarkably well with Veblen's cultural sociology of conspicuous consumption and Mauss's social anthropology of gift exchanges. Veblen's 1899 book, *The Theory of the Leisure Class*, famously argues that the economic codes of work and wealth overlap in significant ways with the cultural codes of leisure and status: 'Possession of wealth confers honours: it is an invidious distinction' (Veblen 1953: 35). He provides an abundance of anecdotal evidence in support of this thesis, often in playful and satirical ways. For example, he describes the consumption of intoxicating beverages, smoking, women's fashions, book manufacturing, and other everyday practices as evidence of a competitive culture of conformism and distinction: 'high bred manners and ways of living are items of conformity to the norm of conspicuous leisure and conspicuous consumption' (ibid.: 179). A rich man is happy to spend ten dollars on a rare hand-crafted silver spoon, for example, while a worker is satisfied with the latest machine-made aluminium spoon that he can buy for ten cents. Each utensil is perfectly serviceable, of course, but only the silver spoon 'masquerades' under the time-honoured guise of beauty, refinement, and delicacy (ibid.: 94–5). Veblen's larger point is that the prestige of leisure, taste, and waste form a *cultural economy* that is grounded in the practical world of work, production, and consumption (Varul 2016).

If Veblen is the classic sociologist of cultural divisions and class loyalties, Mauss is the classic cultural theorist of symbolic exchanges and rituals of gratitude (Kemple 2013). In contrast to Veblen's creative blend of comic examples and critical insights, Mauss's *Essay on the Gift*, published in 1923–4, offers a more sober mix of ethnographic and historical materials interpreted through his systematic theory of generosity and obligation. The *kula* ring in which goods are exchanged between Melanesian tribes and the *nexum* bond between households and fields among the ancient Romans, for example, illustrate how the acts of giving, receiving, and returning gifts involve 'the whole group in its total behaviour' (Mauss 1967: 77–9). Just as Simmel acknowledges the deeper cultural, social, and even metaphysical relations that are at work under the surfaces of the modern money economy, so Mauss argues against the common assumption that barter and sale drive the exchange of cash and credit throughout economic history (Papilloud 2002). Rather, at a deeper level, 'barter arose from the system of gifts given and received on credit, simplified by drawing together the moments of time which had previously been distinct' (Mauss 1967: 35). Mauss's aim is not simply to document his historical and anthropological thesis about gift exchange but also to draw 'conclusions of a moral nature about some of the problems confronting us in our present crisis' (ibid.: 2, 63–81). These lessons include his call to revive certain codes of courtesy and civility in everyday life, as well as his more dramatic demand that modern industrial societies 'return to a group morality' and 'humanize the liberal professions'.

Mauss acknowledges that renewing an ethic of gift exchange might reproduce certain relations of domination and subordination and hierarchies of superiority and inferiority, such as when generous support for the poor makes them indebted to the rich (Pyyhtinen 2014; see chapter 7 above). Alternatively, gift exchanges can create reciprocal relations and promote mutually beneficial interactions between equals in the interests of promoting peace and prosperity. By way of conclusion, Mauss cites the mythical story of King Arthur and his Cornish carpenter, who built 'the miraculous Round Table at which his knights would never come to blows' (1967: 81). Since there was no 'head of the table', and 'none need be excluded', the happiness and prosperity of each guest depends upon the health and wealth of all. Mauss reads this fantastic tale of mutual respect and reciprocal generosity as a model for nations that today are 'strong, rich, good, and happy' (ibid.: 375). The round table of mutual recognition, material redistribution, and inclusive participation may therefore serve as a symbol of political renewal and cultural sustainability in the fragmented world of modern societies.

Although Mauss, Veblen, and Simmel probably never met or even read each other's work, their common interests in the social dynamics of fidelity and gratitude and in the cultural economies of sustainability and surplus might inspire us to imagine them sitting alongside one another at a simple round table, each observing certain scholarly codes of chivalry and civility while exchanging ideas in a spirit of intellectual fellowship and international friendship.

9

Adventures in Space and Time

There are many compelling ways of imagining modernity. One might say that the modern world is built on the *ruins* of the past and is itself experienced in fragments, as discussed in the previous chapter. Or modernity could be called a controlled *experiment* on nature and even on ourselves, but an experiment that now seems to be out of control. Simmel often seems to suggest that modernity might best be pictured as a kind of *adventure*, a leap out of the customs, habits, and patterns of previous periods of history and into a risky world that seems enticing and exciting, unprecedented and unknown. From colonial expeditions to commercial enterprises and from foreign travel to love affairs, the cultures of modernity seem to expand the range and intensity of adventures that anyone might have, whether by choice or by force. Simmel's model for this aspect of contemporary experience seems to be Venice, which he calls 'the classic city of adventure' in a short piece from 1907 which forms part of his trilogy on Italian cities (2007b: 46; see my comments on Rome in the previous chapter and on Florence in the Conclusion). His characterization of Venice refers not just to the late medieval financial centre and port for world trade but also to the modern-day destination of mass tourism and romantic getaways. He calls Venice 'ambivalent' since its intricate system of canals and alleyways seems to belong neither to sea nor to land (2007b: 45). Existing in a kind of restless limbo, the city seems to bring faraway worlds closer and to make intimate experiences more distant. Venice is an exceptional place riddled by artifice, deception, and dreams, and its impressive palaces project the façade of a 'life that is dark, violent and relentlessly functional' (2007b: 44). The beauty of Venice is inspirational yet illusory, and its cheerful surfaces may well conceal a reality of disease and death, a tension dramatized by generations of poets, novelists, and movie directors (Podoksik 2012: 115–16). This city is ultimately unable to offer a home for the soul or a release from the weight of history, Simmel surmises, only the temptation to take on hazardous and exciting risks in the hopes of finding something new or experiencing something extreme. A trip to Venice is a unique adventure in itself, but it might also stand as an emblem for the modern experience as a whole.

In his essay 'The Adventure', from *Philosophical Culture* (discussed below), Simmel says that 'the philosopher is the adventurer of the spirit' (SC: 226). His former pupil, close friend, and lover, the art historian and poet Gertrud Kantorowicz (1876–1945), characterizes his thought as an adventurous search for alterity and novelty: 'All of Simmel's ultimate syntheses rest on the courage with which the unconditional development of a thought is pursued until, *reaching out for the "other" within it*, it transcends itself and performs that turn of axis in virtue of which the opposite poles meet and *a new truth emerges*' (Kantorowicz [1923] 1959: 4, emphasis added). This intriguing description is a worthy match for Simmel's own intricate prose in his later works, where he often seems to be 'reaching out for the "other" within' and struggling to bring a 'new truth' to light. The writings I discuss in this chapter all demonstrate this unique aspect of his thought. I begin with a consideration of his essay on the adventure, which appears in *Philosophical Culture* alongside the essay on fashion (which I discuss in chapter 6). The adventure magnifies certain aspects of the spatial and temporal sense of proximity and distance that is characteristic of modernity, as I note with reference to Simmel's remarks in the *Philosophy of Money* and *Sociology* and in an excursus on Harriet Martineau from England and Alexis de Tocqueville from France in their travel writings on America. The theme of out-of-the-ordinary experiences is then illustrated on an intimate scale in Simmel's discussions of the relations between the sexes, especially as they play out in flirtation and love affairs. Finally, the search for an otherness within that is *more-than-life* is evident in his metaphysical reflections on death and fate in *View of Life*, in his monograph on the paintings of Rembrandt Harmenszoon van Rijn (1606–1669), and in his later writings on the philosophy of history. Despite their eclectic appearance as a miscellany of topics – a 'mélange of relativist philosophy', as the title of the French translation of his collected essays from 1912 would suggest – I aim to show how Simmel's efforts in these lesser known writings are both systematic in their ambition and coherent in their structure and scope (Scaff 1990: 284).

Proximity and Distance in Sexual Relations and Love Affairs

Like the other essays in *Philosophical Culture*, 'The Adventure' begins with some general reflections on the outer appearance and inner depths of the cultural form under scrutiny before elaborating on its contemporary relevance and modern manifestations. As with fashion, the adventure may at first seem to be a superficial and uniquely modern cultural phenomenon. And yet by plumbing its depths we can recover its profoundly metaphysical sources: 'Each segment of our conduct and experience bears a twofold meaning: it *revolves around its own centre*, contains as much breadth and depth, joy and suffering, as the immediate experiencing gives it, and at the same time is *a segment of a course of life* – not only a circumscribed entity, but also a component of an organism' (SC: 221–2, emphasis added; also in ISF). The double significance that is at the core of all human experience consists in being simultaneously *centred* on itself and *decentred* by the act of separating itself from the stream of life. This latter 'eccentric' dynamic is distinctive to the adventure, which can be defined as an experience that entails 'dropping out of the continuity of life' (SC: 222). An adventure must have a clear beginning and a clear end, a time-frame that is sharply torn off from what came before it began and what comes after it is over. Although typically an adventure involves an encounter with 'something alien, untouchable, out of the ordinary', it nevertheless retains some connection to the character and identity of the person who embarks on it (SC: 223, 224). Simmel elaborates on many kinds of adventures and examines in detail the psychology and ethics of the adventurer, including gamblers, conquerors, artists, philosophers, dreamers, and lovers, each of whom combines a certain presence of mind with wanton self-abandonment. Although these character types are both extreme and extraordinary, they also reveal how the potential for peak experiences is inherent in the whole of the human condition: 'We are the adventurers of the earth; our life is crossed everywhere by the tensions which mark adventure' (SC: 232). If modernity can be defined as 'an incomparable experience' that has broken from the total context of historical life that came before it, then it might be called the quintessential age of adventure.

Before considering other examples in *Philosophical Culture*, we can picture the basic elements of this distinctive cultural form as a shift from *the course of everyday life* to *the experience of the adventure*. Figure 9 depicts what Simmel calls 'the stream of existence' as a temporal flow from the past through the present to the future, and also as a spatial displacement from now and here to elsewhere and thus to some other unknown 'nowhere' or 'now/here'. Ordinary experience is normally punctuated by the natural rhythms of night-time and daytime, of mealtime, work time, and rest time. When the tempo of these routines is suddenly disrupted, accelerated, or slowed down, however – by a chance encounter or an unexpected natural occurrence, for instance – then the conditions for an adventure are in place. The adventure also has a spatial dimension which entails a break from ordinary commonplaces, by taking a trip, for example, or by observing a world that is outside of one's own, such as the stars, the planets, or an eclipse. Figure 9 displays the connection between everyday and extraordinary experience in the shape of a telescope in order to highlight what Simmel calls the 'special relationship' between proximity and distance in modernity (Cantó-Milà 2016). As he argues in the final section of the *Philosophy of Money* (which I discuss in chapter 4), the modern money economy

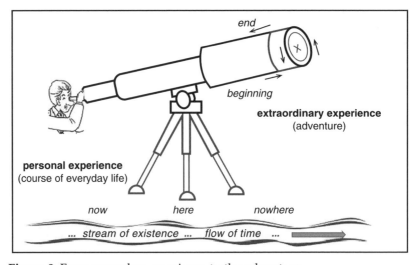

Figure 9 From everyday experience to the adventure

conquers spatial expanses by accelerating time, so that even the most remote people and faraway places are brought into intimate proximity. The new cultural technologies of magnification, such as the telescope which was invented in the early seventeenth century, draw attention to distances that in some sense have already been conquered: 'It is true that the infinite differences between ourselves and objects have been overcome by the microscope and the telescope; but we were first conscious of these distances only at the very same moment in which they were overcome' (PM: 475). In the chapter entitled 'Space and the Spatial Order of Society' in *Sociology*, this social-spatial sense of proximity and distance is located along a sliding scale between the familiar and the strange (the latter is marked in figure 9 by the X on the outer lens) and between concrete and abstract perspectives on life (S: 565–70; SC: 151–9). In other words, like the telescope which disrupts natural perception and broadens the sensible world, the adventure is an experience bound by time and space in which what was once far away now appears close, and what before seemed small or insignificant is magnified beyond its normal size and ordinary importance (a point Simmel develops further in VL: 3–4; see the 'Excursus on Spatiality and Temporality', pp. 166–9).

A less extraterrestrial and more mundane example can help us clarify the basic temporal and spatial parameters that make up the extraordinary experience of the adventure. Simmel acknowledges that nowadays the love affair has almost become synonymous with our sense of adventure (SC: 225–6). An encounter between lovers sweeps them away from the course of everyday life and displaces them into a suspended world with its own centre, if only for a moment (though it may seem like an eternity). However short-lived their liaison, the lovers feel the whole of life pulsating through them as its vehicle and fulfilment, fusing I and Thou in a relationship of complete intimacy. In a posthumously published fragment, 'On Love', Simmel describes the sexual drive as simply a life force leading in no particular direction, whereas erotic desire strives for more-life and even places itself at risk by reaching into the beyond for more-than-life: 'This self-negation, even if it is not an aggressive negation of life, is responsible for the hushed tragic music that intones before the door of love' (1984: 172; also in ISF). The tragic tones that foretell the end of a love affair reveal how men and women experience the erotic adventure differently, as Simmel suggests in this connection by referring to the notorious eighteenth-century Venetian adventurer Casanova: 'as a rule, a love affair is an "adventure" only for men' (SC: 227). While *he* pursues the erotic adventure with the zeal of a conqueror, *she* accepts the promise of happiness gracefully as a concession and a gift. Regardless of who initiates the flirtation or subsequently takes the lead in the courtship and the affair, in the end he needs to give only a part of himself while she is expected to give her all, sometimes with disastrous consequences.

In the essays on the philosophy of sexuality in *Philosophical Culture*, 'On the Relative and Absolute Problem of the Sexes' and 'Flirtation' (the latter discussed in chapter 6 above), Simmel highlights the ethical implications of this double standard in heterosexual relationships. Here he develops a decidedly *hetero* approach to sociological metaphysics of gender (as I note in chapter 4) and to the psychological ethics of sexuality as a binary reality. That is, in moving between absolute and relative perspectives on sexuality, his philosophical scheme allows him to consider only how two and *only two* sexes either oppose or complement each other. He does not imagine that there might be a third gender, a bisexual disposition, or polymorphous perversity. What he calls the problem of the sexes is assumed to be a product of either nature or history, even if these biological facts or cultural conventions might be ethically objectionable or socially constraining in some way. The 'problem of the sexes' is therefore partly an artefact of Simmel's own making, insofar as he assumes that the nature of masculinity and femininity is fixed rather than fluid and that these realities are *essentially* different rather than variable. Simmel asserts that *she* is the authentic human being in an unqualified sense while *he* remains 'half angel, half animal'; *her* metaphysical nature is fused in a direct way with her lived experience while *his* is disposed to transcendence and can be expressed in an impersonal idea and norm; and so on (1984: 112–13). In any event, he draws upon a mixture of metaphysical assumptions and quasi-sociological observations to emphasize the gendered character of all experience and the trans-sexual dimensions of cultural life. His larger point is that no human relationship is entirely neutral with respect to masculine and feminine values or completely void of sexual difference. Although in his essays on sexuality he seems incapable of imagining a female Casanova, a homosexual love affair, or an allosexual erotic encounter (neither hetero nor homo), his blindness to sexual variations at least allows him to focus on the masculine character of the iconic modern cultural form of the adventure.

Simmel's concern with the personal significance and intimate manifestations of modern culture inspired some of his most radical and enlightened students to expand his ideas in a political direction. As Ralph Leck's research has shown, Simmel inspired activists such as Kurt Hiller to agitate against heterosexual hegemony and the criminalization of homosexuals in the legal code and feminists such as Helene Stöcker to fight for political change against patriarchal norms and on behalf of the rights of single mothers (Leck 2000: 212–31; also Leck 2016: 177–8). Along with Georg Lukács and Siegfried Kracauer (discussed in Parts I and II), these students were part of a movement for spiritual-intellectual politics (*Geist-Politik*) that often embraced avant-garde aesthetic sensibilities and counter-cultural sexual ethics. Others also expressed their anti-bourgeois views or socialist opposition to commercialism, what Simmel calls 'mammonism' in *The War and Our Spiritual Decisions*, in which 'the worship of money and the monetary value of things … transplants itself into all kinds of ethical, aesthetic, and political ideologies' (quoted in Leck 2000: 183–4; GSG 16: 17–18). Many of these young people envisioned another world where the cult of commerce would be abolished in order to make way for a new world in which love, justice, and equality would prevail.

The young Ernst Bloch (1885–1977), who also attended Simmel's lectures and private seminars in Berlin before the war, is in some ways the true philosophical-political heir to Simmel's radical ethic of cultural subversion and intellectual engagement (Leck 2000: 284–304). Bloch was dispirited by Simmel's early enthusiasm for the reckless military adventures of imperial Germany, at first praising him as the 'finest mind among his contemporaries' but later condemning him bitterly as 'wholly empty and aimless, … a collector of standpoints which he assembles all around truth without ever wanting to possess it' (quoted in Maus 1959: 194). Nevertheless, he was still under Simmel's spell in 1915–16 when he set to work writing his masterpiece *The Spirit of Utopia*, a book which reads as a kind of messianic-Marxist fugue composed to accompany the birth of a future philosophical culture. Following Simmel's critique of mammonism, Bloch laments 'this dance around the golden calf' which has left only 'longing, and brief knowledge, but little deed' (Bloch 2000: 2). Perhaps inspired by Simmel's reflections on the handle (discussed in the previous chapter), he begins with an odd meditation on an old pitcher, which somehow allows him to imagine that 'everything … made out of love and necessity leads a life of its own, leads into a strange new territory, and returns with us formed as we could not be in life' (ibid.: 9; Adorno 1992). Reluctantly carried forth by the spirit of Simmel, Bloch seems intent on tracing the path of a utopian adventure which may ultimately lead nowhere but might also end in creating a more just and beautiful future where coercion and mediocrity have been conquered by compassion and freedom.

Death and Old Age in Art and Everyday Life

The most extraordinary experience imaginable would seem to be the afterlife, or immortality, or even death itself, assuming these are even *possible* experiences. In chapter 3 of the *View of Life*, on 'Death and Immortality', Simmel nevertheless makes a strenuous case against the conventional view that death is a decisive break with life. Death by accident, perishing as a result of some natural event, or being killed by someone or something are all typically thought of as 'the life-ending snip of the fates' (VL: 70; also in 2007b: 72–6). Although people and other living creatures all die in various ways, death and dying have a special significance for *mortal human beings*. We can only be certain about the fact that we will die, but not about when and how, and so we live life 'like people walking on a ship in the direction opposite its course' (VL: 70). Echoing ancient philosophies and anticipating later existentialist ideas on life and death, Simmel argues that human beings are compelled to die from within and in the course of maturing into their destiny as mortal beings (see Pyyhtinen 2018: 138–43 on Simmel's influence on Martin Heidegger in this connection). In other words, death is a formative moment shaping and directing the life-course of each individual from the beginning of life and not just at the end (VL: 70; Pyyhtinen 2012). He summarizes this view of death as an inherent condition of life in a key passage early on in the chapter: 'In every single moment of life we *are* beings that will die, and each moment would be otherwise if this were not our innate condition, somehow operative within it. Just as we are not already fully present in the instant of our birth, but rather something of us is continually being born, so too we do not die only in our last instant' (VL: 65). Human life takes on a certain form by virtue of its nature as mortal, and for this reason life is both bound to and shaped by death. The thought of immortality enters human culture at the point when the self imagines itself to be enclosed, saved, purified, or transcendent beyond any given moment of life. For this reason, the idea of immortality tends to be pictured as a world that is radically cut off from the everyday stream of existence. If death is essentially a mundane part of life that gives life shape and direction, then immortality may be thought to resemble an adventure, but one from which there is no return and that goes on forever. In Simmel's lyrical formulation, individuals can imagine something like an after-life or more-than-life insofar as they are 'equipped with the intimation of an intensive endlessness' (VL: 76).

Simmel's rather abstract reflections on dying and mortality sometimes sound almost mystical or 'metaphysical' in the conventional sense – that is, as speculative musings on ultimate realities that surpass ordinary experience or empirical understanding. Nevertheless, he clearly wants to describe death as integral to daily life and as informing each act or every moment as it takes shape within the ongoing stream of the life-course. In Simmel's view, in the final analysis death cannot be an adventure. His perspective on life and death is earthly and sensuous rather than supernatural and otherworldly, as vividly illustrated in the monograph he published in 1916 on the seventeenth-century Dutch painter Rembrandt. Here Simmel does not write as an art critic, sociologist, or historian examining the techniques, personal intentions, or social conditions that shaped Rembrandt's work, or as an enthusiast honouring the great master. Instead he offers a series of philosophical reflections on 'the phenomenon of Rembrandt' and on the art of painting as a point of access to inner experience and individuality (2005a: 3).

In a key section of the book Simmel expands upon the ideas on death he later developed in the *View of Life* (2005a: 70–9). He argues that the vibrancy and vitality of the figures in Rembrandt's paintings derive as much from their animated features and settings – in taverns, battles, and historical scenes where people work, play, fight, observe, rest, eat, drink, and so on – as from the silent presence of death that inhabits their life from the outset. Death is the inner and ever-present reality of each moment in Rembrandt's paintings, a reality which provides 'the coloration and shaping of life' (2005a: 74). In the language of his philosophical writings Simmel describes how Rembrandt's artistry lies in depicting the tragic character of death not as something mournful or sorrowful but, rather, as emerging exuberantly out of life's own law and meaning, fulfilling its most secret order (2005a: 76). Turning to the poetry of his friend Rainer Maria Rilke in the *Book of Hours*, he expresses how the unique

fate of death, which is anchored in each and every individual, is
mutely and effectively depicted in Rembrandt's paintings:

Oh Herr, gib jedem seinen eignen Tod,	Oh Lord, give to each a death of his own,
Das Sterben, das aus jedem Leben geht,	The dying that emerges out of that life
Darin er Liebe hatte, Sinn und Not.	In which he had love, meaning, and need.

(Rilke, quoted in Simmel 2005a: 78, 169)

For Simmel, as for Rilke and Rembrandt, 'death only reaches mac-
roscopic visibility at the moment of death' (2005a: 71). However, at
every other time in the course of our experience death shapes the
meaning of life without being noticed, just as it colours each of life's
moments in silence.

   If we cannot escape death and if, in fact, dying is present in every
lived experience, as Simmel argues, then we are confronted with
the question of whether this fateful condition leaves any room for
freedom. Simmel describes the fatalism in the common view of the
adventurer as someone who tempts fate and defies death in the
interests of freedom: 'it is just on the hovering change, on fate, on
the more-or-less that we risk all, burn our bridges, and step into the
mist, as if the road will lead us on, no matter what' (SC: 226). The
chapter on death and immortality in *View of Life* includes a short
digression on the general problem of fate with particular emphasis
on its meaning in the modern world (VL: 78–82; also in 2007b:
78–84). When a particular experience is understood as somehow
resulting from fate, Simmel argues, then we might say that '*a
sequence of objective occurrence*, proceeding purely causally, is woven
into *the subjective sequence of a life* determined in other respects from
within' (VL: 78, emphasis added). In other words, when something
happens that either violates or favours the intended or ideal direction of someone's life, it might be thought to be necessary, inevitable, or fateful. Simmel examines traditional notions of fate such as
the 'snip of the fates' already mentioned, a tragic destiny (*moira*)
controlled by the ancient gods, the divine providence of a sacred
being that predestines the lives of mortals, and the feeling of
impending doom. On a less grand scale, he also observes how
everyday occurrences – such as a chance encounter, an illness, or a
decision – can take on meaning as 'events' that determine the direction and outcome of someone's thoughts and actions: 'on the one
side we are held hostage to and ordered by cosmic dynamics, but

on the other side we feel and lead our individual existence from a personal center, as self-responsibility and somehow in self-enclosed form' (VL: 78). The distinctively modern notion of fate consists in emphasizing this personal dynamic, where individuals try to take fate into their own hands, often by renouncing any supernatural force that is separate from or alien to the meaning they give to their life (Button 2012). In the modern world, the sense of fate seems to be suffused with the scepticism of the adventurer, who combines uncertainty about the chances of survival or success with a firm belief that nothing is certain other than one's own inner strength and personal resolve (SC: 227; see also the discussion of scepticism in chapter 3).

As Simmel points out, the adventure tends to be 'a form of experiencing' that belongs not to the quiet lifestyle of old age but, rather, to the noisy restlessness of youth (SC: 229). The metaphysical underpinnings of this idea can also be illustrated with reference to his reflections on Rembrandt's paintings, especially the famous series of self-portraits as he grows old. Rembrandt's paintings of his aging self display the accumulation of changing facial features, moods, situations, and experiences of a life that has been lived to the maximum yet is still in the process of becoming. Rembrandt's self-portraits and his paintings of old people betray what Simmel grandiloquently calls 'the secret of life': 'that the whole life is in each moment, and yet each moment is unmistakably different from any other' (2005a: 12). Even the group portraits, such as his master-pieces *The Night Watch* and *The Anatomy Lesson*, achieve unity less as a result of their formal design than through the interactions between individual figures – that is, from 'the immediate inter-weaving of the vital forces that break out of each individual' (2005a: 47). With this idea in mind, Simmel argues that the painted portrait does not just convey the corporeal presence of the person depicted, as in a photograph, a movie, or some other mechanical reproduc-tion. In representing the perspective of the subject, the material reality of the painting also expresses the vision of the artist while at the same time reflecting back on the observing eye of the viewer. At one point 'the viewer Simmel' asks himself: 'What is it then that moves within the picture?' (2005a: 38). Of course, the painted figure does not move, and in a sense the painting breaks away from the reality of the subject by creating its own self-sufficient, framed, and two-dimensional world. In the cinema, by contrast, the images themselves move, while the spectators remain an immobile mass public settled in their seats with their attention fixed on the screen

(Frisch 2009: 131–42). By invoking this comparison, Simmel suggests that it is the imagination of the viewer that moves *within* the painting itself insofar as the viewer is aroused by the artist to complete the movement or gesture immanent in the painted figure both before and after the represented moment (2005a: 38). If Rodin can be described as the sculptor of bodies moving outwards towards the viewer (as I note in chapter 8), then Rembrandt might be called the painter of souls as they turn inward on themselves. In short, Rembrandt's portraits often seem to offer a glimpse into what an inward journey into the depths of one's own soul might look like.

Simmel's book on Rembrandt anticipates the more extensive philosophy of art that he was working on at the time of his death, unpublished fragments of which were unfortunately stolen on a train several years later (Rammstedt 2012: 303). The Rembrandt study also raises questions for the philosophy of history that preoccupied him throughout his career in that both projects are concerned with how we can understand the lives of historical persons and the historical events that affected them (Scaff 2005). In a letter to the philosopher Heinrich Rickert just as he was finishing *Rembrandt*, Simmel reports that he is also working on a new edition of his *Problems in the Philosophy of History*. This edition would be a 'completely different book with a different title' from one published in 1905, he writes, since his ideas 'have completely changed' (quoted in Backhaus 2003: 228; GSG 23: 579). In three essays written in his final years – 'The Problem of Historical Time' (1916), 'The Constitutive Concepts of History' (1917–18), and 'On the Nature of Historical Understanding' (1918) – Simmel considers how our understanding of contemporary people, events, and things may be extended to persons, places, or events in the past (these essays are translated in 1980). In the last of these studies, he writes that our perceptions of other people in both the past and the present are always motivated, pieced together from partial evidence, and yet ultimately caught up in the flow of experience and the stream of time: 'Historical understanding is only a variant of our *contemporaneous*, thoroughly quotidian understanding' (1980: 102). In the final analysis, our image of an historical personality and his or her actions is similar to how we know a personal acquaintance (Schwartz 2017). We could say, then, that it is possible to encounter Rembrandt himself through his paintings and to experience some of his life and times by reflecting on his art. Like the interaction between viewer and artwork, the relationship between a figure from the past and the reader or writer of history is analogous to the relationship between oneself and others. We experience an other person as a being-for-itself who is essentially different from us, as a life with 'an incomparable autonomy and sovereignty' of its own distinct from every other subject or object. And yet, as Rembrandt's paintings show us (and as Simmel's writings tell us), we also experience other people as sharing a life that is similar to or even the same as ours: 'we experience the other person, the Thou, both as the most alien and impenetrable creature imaginable, and also as the most intimate and familiar' (1980: 106). On a planetary scale we may indeed be 'adventurers of the earth', but everyday life is only rarely an adventure, an encounter with absolute otherness, or an extraordinary experience lived to the limit. More often, life is, instead, a series of ordinary moments and simple interactions that we connect together out of the flux and flow of time.

In a surprising way, one of Simmel's 'Snapshots under the Aspect of Eternity' (Momentbilder *sub specie aeternitatis*), from the series of brief anecdotes he published in the journal *Jugend*, prefigures some of these ideas on fate and the unintended consequences of an extraordinary experience. The snapshot called 'Relativity', published in 1902 (just three years before Albert Einstein's first paper on the general theory of relativity), begins with a citation from Goethe's *Elective Affinities*, a novel about a complex love quartet that forms when two young people suddenly enter into the lives of an older couple: 'Fate occasionally fulfills our desires, but only in its *own* way' (2007b: 275). In this short snapshot, Simmel recounts a story he overheard about a man who asks the devil to agree to make him the most intelligent man in the world. As is typical in stories about pacts with the devil, including several of Simmel's other snapshots as well as Goethe's classic *Faust* (discussed in the next chapter), the man does not quite get what he thought he had bargained for. The next day, he finds that his servants were now incompetent and had turned the household upside down; that his son had been punished at school for having understood nothing; and that even his wife, with whom he always shared everything, could not follow his usual report on his workday: 'Now the man was no more able to come to an understanding with those close to him than he could with those who were distant' (2007b: 276). The man then realizes that the devil had indeed kept his word, not by making him more intelligent, however, but rather by making everyone else more stupid! From this realization, another man listening to this story draws the conclusion that stupidity and intelligence are relative. What's more, the listener adds, people who are against public schooling or the enlightenment of the masses are really only trying to ensure that they are more intelligent than everyone else. In fact, however, they are simply paying homage to the principle of intelligence. As Simmel's readers might be wondering as they reach the end of this tale, if the fate of each of us is relative, and if fate does not always fulfil our desires as we had hoped or intended, then perhaps knowing our fate with certainty in advance may be among the stupidest things we could wish for.

Excursus on Spatiality and Temporality: Simmel after Martineau and Tocqueville

Simmel's remarks on space and time are among the most interesting and yet most unexplored aspects of his work. They have gone unnoticed in part because they are complex and difficult and in part because these writings are scattered in many places and only rarely considered together (see Scaff 2005, 2009; Pyyhtinen 2018: 85–8). At over 100 pages, the chapter in *Sociology* on 'Space and the Spatial Order of Society' begins by examining 'the fundamental qualities of the spatial form', followed by a discussion of 'the spatial determinations of the group'. In other words, Simmel first considers *how certain features of space take on the form of association* (*Vergesellschaftungsform*) before turning his attention to *how social life is realized as a spatial order*. He notes that a characteristic of social space is that it is physically limited, and then elaborates on this point in an excursus on social boundaries (S: 551–4; also in 2007b: 53–6). Another characteristic of social space consists in how people interact in relative proximity to or distance from one another, which he illustrates in an excursus on the sociology of the senses (S: 570–83; also in SC). Only a few commentators have noted that Simmel inserts the influential 'Excursus on the Stranger' into the chapter on space in a discussion of the social quality of geographic mobility and as an example of migration and settlement (S: 601–5; also in ISF; note that the digression on the stranger was written specially for this chapter). He describes the stranger as someone who 'comes today and stays tomorrow' – that is, as the movement through time of a settler who remains in a place rather than a nomad or wanderer who is passing through (S: 601; ISF: 143; see Levine 1985: 73–88). Considered together, these three accounts of how social life is spatialized and how time is socially animated – specifically with respect to boundaries, the senses, and strangers – can be considered among Simmel's most original contributions to modern thought.

Although he occasionally compares Europe and America in his writings, Simmel never travelled to the United States, having declined an invitation to accompany Max Weber and other German scholars to present papers at the 1904 World's Fair in St Louis (2015b; see Scaff 2011: 57). Nevertheless, his ideas on spatiality and temporality are vividly illustrated in the travel writings of two of his most important precursors in the history of the social sciences who wrote about their experiences in the US: Harriet Martineau (1802–1876), whose *Society in America* was published in two volumes in 1837, and Alexis de Tocqueville (1805–1855), whose *Democracy in America* appeared in two volumes in 1835 and 1840. Writing for different purposes and for different audiences – Martineau as a bourgeois feminist and socialist for a popular readership, Tocqueville as a liberal aristocrat for an educated French elite – they describe their American adventures in ways that substantiate Simmel's most compelling theoretical claims, although Simmel does not appear to have read either work (see Kemple 2011 for a more detailed analysis of the following examples).

A short passage in the section on 'Women' in *Society in America* recounts an incident reported to Martineau by a 'highly accomplished lady' who intervened in a dispute between an upper domestic and a poor woman of colour, both working in her household. The two servants were on good terms until 'one day, when there was to be an evening party, the upper domestic declined waiting on the company, giving as a reason that she was offended at being required to sit down at table with the coloured woman' (Martineau [1837] 1981: 302–3). The lady of the house was able to convince the servant to comply by pointing out that even her daughter and niece would be waiting on the company, but she also made one concession in silence: 'She had the colored woman come after dinner, instead of before.' This anecdote reveals how social boundaries between domestic servants of the same gender but different races are manifested in the social space of the middle-class kitchen table and at mealtimes. In her description of this conflict and its consequence, Martineau also alludes to the confidences shared to her as a foreigner by the lady of the house, echoing Simmel's point about the intimacy that is often afforded by anonymity (S: 590, 602–3). Elsewhere, she draws attention to her own deafness – Martineau could hear only with the aid of an ear-trumpet – and notes that this often gave her an advantage, since she was granted 'more *tête-à-têtes* than is given to people in general conversation' (1981: 54). In Simmel's terms, we can say that Martineau's vignette shows how racial and class tensions are expressed as *social and spatial boundaries*, and her account also shows how homosocial *encounters between strangers* unfold in what may be called the *acoustic space and time* of social life.

Tocqueville describes a comparable scene of inter-racial rivalry between women on a single page of the section of his book *Democracy in America*, 'The Three Races that Inhabit the Territory of the United States' (Tocqueville 1969: 320). While travelling through Alabama in the vicinity of the Creek territory, he rests beside a spring in the forest near the log cabin of a pioneer. A short while later, an Indian woman arrives holding the hand of a little Creole girl, presumably the daughter of the pioneer, followed by a Negro woman. Fascinated by this little 'tableau' of frontier life, Tocqueville observes how the little girl 'received the attentions of her companions with a sort of condescension'. At the same time, he notes, 'crouched down in front of the mistress, anticipating her every desire, the Negro woman seemed equally divided between almost maternal affection and servile fear, whereas even in the effusions of her tenderness [for the little girl], the savage woman looked free, proud, and almost fierce.' Suddenly this scene of idyllic peace and tranquillity is dissolved in an instant when the Indian woman and Tocqueville exchange glances: 'for she got up abruptly, pushed the child away from her, almost roughly, and giving me an angry look, plunged into the forest.' In hindsight Tocqueville can see that his presence as a stranger from Europe had magnified the tensions between the Indian woman and the Negro woman, both of whom are subordinate to the white pioneer and his Creole daughter: 'here a bond of affection united oppressors and oppressed, and nature bringing them closer together made the immense gap formed by prejudice and by laws yet more striking.' Again adapting Simmel's terms, we could say that Tocqueville's tableau exemplifies the way in which the contact zone between races is expressed as *a social and spatial boundary* between people, and also that his description of the scene shows how class and gender hierarchies are revealed within the *optical space of personal proximity* and over the *social time of an encounter between strangers.*

Writing a generation after Martineau and Tocqueville, Simmel formulates a theory of social space and historical time that yields insights into their ethnographic descriptions of race, gender, and class relations while at the same time lending conceptual coherence to their broad cross-cultural comparisons between Europe and America.

10

Conclusion: The Tragedy of Individuality

The two previous chapters consider Simmel's view of modernity as a fragmented age built on the broken shards of the past and as an extraordinary experience that seems to be almost entirely cut off from previous history. The problem that modernity poses to him is thus how to create a new unity out of what appears to be an infinite multiplicity, and whether it makes sense to long for synthesis and wholeness in a fractured and alienating world (Scaff 1990: 289). All his writings address this challenge primarily at the level of culture (*Kultur*) and intellectual life (*Geistesleben*). This task took on greater urgency after he moved from Berlin to Strasbourg in 1914 in the months just before the outbreak of the First World War. In a curious way, however, he had already discovered a solution to the modern problem of restoring unity to the broken world of nature and spirit through his meditations on Renaissance Florence. Among the three essays he wrote on the classic Italian cities, the piece on Florence, published in 1906, stands out as his song of praise for a time when nature has not surrendered to culture and as his portrait of a place where life itself has been perfected into a work of art and intellect: 'as each hill lifts itself up to a villa or a church, nature seems to rise everywhere toward the crowning of the mind' (2007b: 39). Unlike Rome and Venice, which are infused with a tragic sense of a lost world that can never be redeemed, Florence seems to gather together 'all that is ripe, cheerful and alive' by collecting the pieces of life into a gratuitous whole and shaping them into one graceful harmony (2007b: 40). As he writes in the last line of the essay: 'Florence is the good fortune of those fortunate human beings who have achieved or renounced what is essential in life, and who for this possession or renunciation are seeking only its form' (2007b: 41). By striking a balance between human purpose and objective function (as expressed in the apriority of commitment, discussed in my Introduction), and by creating the conditions of freedom for each individual to realize or reject what is essential in life, this city seems to succeed in reconciling the conflict between life and form. As Simmel confesses in a letter to the philosopher Edmund Husserl, with a copy of the essay enclosed: 'Florence is my country, the homeland of my soul' (quoted in Podoksik 2012: 102; GSG 22: 570). And yet, Simmel obviously writes not as a native but as a traveller passing through, and he stands in a long line of German visitors to Italy whose experiences are tinged with a romantic longing for a world that possibly never existed, as his essays on Germanic and Romanic styles and forms of individualism acknowledge (see the translations in 2007b). He admits frankly that 'Florence offers us no foundation in epochs in which one might want to start over again and to encounter the sources of life once more' (2007b: 41). No remembrance of times past can transform modern culture into the harmonious cultivation of self and things, and a brief holiday visit offers no model for a future world of unity in diversity.

This concluding chapter considers some of Simmel's late writings as a way of drawing up a balance sheet of his most important contributions and his most instructive failures. I begin with a discussion of his epic essay 'The Concept and the Tragedy of Culture', from *Philosophical Culture*, which presents the drama of modernity as a plot characterized by mounting tensions building up to a climax or catastrophe followed by an anticipated catharsis or possible redemption. Simmel imagines a few partial resolutions to this tragic view of the present world in his essays on the philosophy of religion and female culture. These writings form a kind of bridge to themes that preoccupied him throughout his life and also to the ideas of later twentieth-century thinkers, as I show in a digression on the work of the social psychologist George Herbert Mead, who reviewed Simmel's *Philosophy of Money* shortly after it was published, and the phenomenologist Edmund Husserl, who corresponded with Simmel for over a decade. Finally, I turn to writings where Simmel makes a strenuous effort to resolve the theoretical problems posed by the tragedy of modern culture, in particular the last chapter of the *View of Life*, 'The Individual Law', which I illustrate with the example of his remarks on dramatic acting and in his career-long writings on the philosopher Immanuel Kant and the poet, dramatist, novelist, and natural scientist Johann Wolfgang von Goethe. Even though Simmel's ideas sometimes seem antiquated to us today and his answers to perennial questions do not always satisfy us, I conclude that returning to him is still essential if the humanities and social sciences are to address the most pressing problems we face in the twenty-first century.

Bridges from Simmel, or Faust's Fate

Simmel's late works can be read as an attempt to imagine how the modern self makes connections on multiple scales and builds bridges between fragmentary modes of existence. In his earlier writings, he focuses on how the uniqueness of each person emerges from the expansion of the group, and how the experience of selfhood intensifies as subjective and objective interdependencies become ever more frequent and intricate. The opening sentence of 'The Concept and the Tragedy of Culture' dramatically portrays this problem as the latest manifestation of an ancient conflict and epic struggle of human beings with the forces of nature: 'Unlike animals, humanity does not integrate itself unquestioningly into the natural facticity of the world but tears itself loose from it, confronts it, demanding, struggling, violating and being violated by it – and it is with this first great dualism that the endless process between the subject and the object arises' (SC: 55). The challenge of becoming an individual in a fractured and violent world is not tragic in the traditional sense that it is doomed to end unhappily or in misfortune. Rather, human life is inherently tragic because the human subject can only express itself through objective cultural forms that are estranged from its very being: 'The paradox of culture is that subjective life, which we feel in its continual flowing ..., cannot achieve inner perfection on its own, but only by way of those selfsufficient crystalized configurations which have now become quite alien to its form' (SC: 58; GSG 14: 389). Mortality is a condition of human life just as the deepest layers of objective culture are destructive to personal expression: 'it is often as if the creative movement of the soul were dying from its own product' (SC: 59). Like the other essays in *Philosophical Culture*, Simmel's argument here is for the most part pitched at a general level and occasionally focuses on distinctive features of modern culture such as contemporary art and morality, science and technology, religion and the law. In the closing pages, he describes what he calls the 'inner developmental logic' by which modern individuals become overburdened with material culture and yet also poor in spirit: they have everything but possess nothing – *omnia habientes, nihil possidentes* (SC: 73; see chapter 7 above). He places particular emphasis on the subjective experience of this uneven state of affairs: 'The infinitely growing stock of the objectified mind makes demands on the subject, arouses faint aspirations in it, strikes it with feelings of its own insufficiency and helplessness, entwines it into total constellations from which it cannot escape as a whole without mastering its individual elements' (SC: 73). With a stress on this personal perspective, Simmel resorts to literary, dramatic, and allegorical imagery by formulating his concept of culture as 'the path of the soul from itself as incomplete to itself as the completed essence' (SC: 75).

Despite this almost religious and mystical way of expressing the concept of culture, Simmel's argument can be thought of in simple terms both as a two-way street between self and other and as a path connecting subject and object. Figuratively speaking, human endeavours such as science, work, artistic production, and religious ritual are ways of building worldly bridges between ourselves and others and from human subjects to non-human objects. As he puts it in the *Philosophy of Money*, our intentions require objective mediation in order to be realized: 'our actions are the bridge that makes it possible for the content of the purpose to pass from its psychology to a real form' (PM: 206). In *Sociology* he describes in detail how our senses construct connections to others in part through the act of imagining our fellow human beings as objects: 'what I see, hear, feel of the other is simply the bridge over which I would get to where that person is an object to me' (S: 570). In the closing pages of that book he breaks down these relationships analytically in terms of their social, individual, human, and natural dimensions (S: 671–5; ISF: 36–40; see chapter 7 above). Using the image of the bridge, figure 10 depicts how these four dimensions intersect in space and interact over time. To adapt the Latin expressions Simmel was so fond of using, the self can be considered the *terminus a quo* or starting point in a journey outwards to other human beings (marked with an X in figure 10), such as the infant's bond with a particular mother that eventually extends to others in general. In the course of seeing the (m)other and oneself as an object – of desire, attraction, language, or knowledge, for instance – the self can then begin the return journey to its *terminus ad quem* – its destiny or end point – as a conscious and creative subject. In other words, the self becomes individuated and socialized only by 'passing over' into the realization of itself

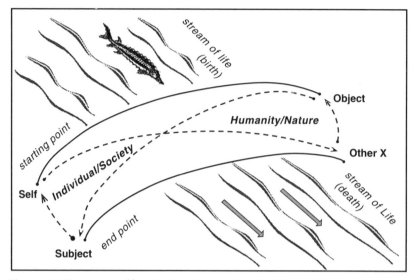

Figure 10 Between self and other, beyond subject and object

as a human and natural being. We could say, then, that Simmel's concept of culture outlines both a social psychology of self–other interactions and a phenomenology of subject–object relations (see the 'Excursus on Identity and Difference', pp. 185–7).

The bridge metaphor can also be taken literally as referring to an historically specific cultural technology that unites in reality what is conceived as separate in the mind (Siegert 2015). As Simmel argues in his short essay 'Bridge and Door' (discussed in my Introduction) human beings are uniquely equipped to make such distinctions and connections: 'we must first conceive intellectually of the merely indifferent existence of two river banks as something separated in order to connect them by means of a bridge' (SC: 174). The next step in this cultural and mental development consists in imagining a passageway and constructing a solid structure across this fluid mass and undifferentiated movement: 'The people who first built a path between two places performed one of the greatest human achievements' (SC: 171). The bridge both symbolizes and materializes the human conquest of nature and the extension of the human will over space. In a sense, this cultural technology interrupts or suspends the flow of life passing from more-life (through the birth of new life-forms, for example) to more-than-life (life ending in death). Ancient worlds and traditional communities tend to view rivers as transportation waterways, as links between settlements, or as the focal point for cultural activities (marked with the sturgeon in figure 10, one of the oldest endangered species on earth). As the cultural theorist Zoe Todd (Red River Cree) points out, for millennia indigenous philosophers have been engaged 'with sentient environments, with cosmologies that enmesh people into complex relationships between themselves and all relations, and with climates and atmospheres as important points of organization and action' (Todd 2016: 6–7). In contrast to this integrated cosmic vision of the web of life and the stream of existence, modern societies tend to view the river as a boundary separating territories or as an obstacle that must be overcome. From this perspective, the bridge is not just a metaphysical emblem of social and cultural life but also a crowning achievement of Western civilization. The bridge is a feat of engineering that facilitates traffic and forges connections between people as well as securing borders and enforcing divisions between nature and culture. Insofar as Simmel's meditations on the bridge leave aside the tragic implications of this logic of historical development, the limits of his thought are also the limits of his cultural and social world.

The tragic interpretation of culture implies a narrative that begins with an original worldly plenitude and leads to the dissolution of this world into fragments. Simmel's vision does not stop there, however, but goes on to imagine the possible emergence of a new unity-in-diversity that projects an alternative to the fractured cultures of modernity (SC: 56). For this reason, it is misleading to characterize Simmel himself as a tragic figure or as a philosopher of tragedy, since he also anticipates overcoming the gulf between subjective and objective culture and rising above fate rather than capitulating to this broken state of affairs or retreating into the self (Leck 2000: 298–301; Scaff 1990: 293). As he once wrote to the famous literary scholar and poet Friedrich Gundolf (1880–1931), his 'metaphysics of the individual' is only one side of his philosophy of life and culture, since the other side is 'a metaphysics of this world', which in any case should not be considered 'an absolute key that opens all doors' (GSG 22: 872). In 'The Conflict of Culture', his sweeping lecture on the current crisis, Simmel describes how the modern age seems to have demolished the bridge between past and future, thus leaving only formless life to fill the gap. He highlights some of the latest attempts to forge cultural links across the abyss in order to 'create new forms appropriate to present energies': in expressionist painting and music, in the philosophy of pragmatism, in the liberal ethics of prostitution and open marriages, and in the persistence of mysticism and spiritualism (SC: 80–90; GSG 16: 190–207).

The last of these is the topic of two essays on the philosophy of religion in *Philosophical Culture* which give new focus to his career-long writings on religious questions (see the translations in 1997b and SC: 275–95). 'The Problem of Religion Today' asks whether religiosity is in decline in a world ruled by empirical science, and whether the religious soul can regain the metaphysical value that it once projected onto transcendent objects. Simmel's answer is that contemporary spiritualist and mystical movements give expression to a full range of feelings – hope and despair, humility and dependence, longing and wonder, devotion and desperation – in ways that cannot be completely explained away rationally or resolved scientifically: 'The religious mode of existence is not simply a static, tranquil state; [it is] *a form of life in all its vitality*, a way in which life vibrates, expresses itself, and fulfills its destinies' (1997b: 14, emphasis added). In 'The Personality of God' Simmel defines religious belief as a dynamic state of faith that takes shape in the relationship between oneself and a transcendent being: 'Faith is, as it were, the sensory organ by which this being is conveyed to us' (1997b: 46). Anticipating the influential ideas of his young friend Martin Buber (1878–1965), the theologian who published Simmel's philosophical and sociological study *Religion* in the book series he edited, Simmel argues that this sensibility emerges through a dialogue between oneself and a personal spiritual being: 'For in that "*interaction*" which is the essence of all that is alive and all that is mental, *self-consciousness – by which the subject becomes its own object* – achieves its absolute form' (1997b: 58, emphasis added). In Simmel's view, a possible resolution to the fragmentary character of modern life and selfhood may lie in the unity envisioned in the relationship between I and Thou and in the mutual reflection of an absolute Self and an absolute Other on macrocosmic and microcosmic scales. He suggests that perhaps a renewed religious culture emerging from within modernity may yet offer some salvation for the soul on its path through life and beyond the ruins of modernity.

Simmel reserves his most forceful expression of hope in the possibility of redeeming the tragedy of modern culture in the last essay of *Philosophical Culture*, 'Female Culture'. As I note in chapter 5 from a sociological perspective, he is inspired by the achievements of the modern feminist movement in expanding women's personal participation in the production and consumption of cultural goods. Despite these advances, he believes this movement has yet to result in the creation of new cultural values, social forms, intellectual capacities, and aesthetic sensibilities. What he calls 'the cultural capital [*Kulturbesitz*] of an era' – the complex combination of objective forces and subjective ideals – has been controlled and defined by men and continues to pose a threat to the development of an autonomous female culture (1984: 64; GSG 14: 417; also in SC). He asks whether there is a fundamental discrepancy between female nature and objective culture as such and wonders whether an objectively female culture may even be a contradiction in terms (1984: 100). As I point out in the previous chapter, the impasse Simmel encounters in his writings on women and sexuality may lie in the narrowly heterosexual philosophical schema he assumes in posing these questions. As he once remarked in conversation, 'there are too few categories, just as there are too few sexes' (Lukács 1991: 147). Here again we can see how Simmel himself seems to be able to sense the limits of his thought but without fully surpassing them.

Simmel's lifelong preoccupation with the psychology, sociology, and metaphysics of womanhood is akin to Goethe's metaphysical notion of 'the eternal feminine', and is often inflected with Nietzsche's critical reflections on essential differences between the sexes (see Derrida 1979: 83–95). In the unpublished fragment 'On Love', Simmel acknowledges that the title character in Goethe's drama *Faust*, who sold his soul to the devil for more knowledge, pleasure, wealth, and power – in short, for more-life – experiences his love for the doomed Gretchen as his first great adventure, an episode in the dramatic epic of his life in which he is the hero and in which she lives on only as the metaphysical sublimation of her immortal nature as Everywoman (1984: 177). Faust 'was unfaithful to women because he was faithful to himself' and because he obeyed the higher law of his own life, as Simmel says about Goethe (GSG 15: 211). By idolizing female culture, Simmel himself sometimes seems to echo the Chorus Mysticus that concludes Goethe's epic tragedy:

Alles Vergängliche	All that is changeable
Ist nur ein Gleichnis;	Is but refraction;
Das Unzulängliche,	The unattainable
Hier wird's Ereignis;	Here becomes action.
Das Unbeschreibliche,	Human discernment
Hier ist's getan;	Here is passed by;
Das Ewig-Weibliche	Woman Eternal
Zieht uns hinan.	Draw us on high.

(Goethe 1986: 214; 1976: 308)

Simmel's metaphysics of sexuality and his philosophy of love likewise conceive of female culture as a transcendent ideal that unifies I and Thou, as a bridging principle connecting subjective and objective culture, and thus as a possible alternative to the tragedy of the broken cultures of modernity. Despite his close relations with the exemplary women around him – including Marianne Weber, Gertrud Kantorowicz, Margarete Susman, and his wife Gertrud – he does not envision the practical feminization of such male-dominated domains as work, law, science, and art (with a few exceptions), nor does he call for the participation of men in domestic activities and the transformation of home life. Like Faust's dramatic personal journey that leads from his study into the depths of hell, Simmel's notion of the tragedy of culture ultimately finds resolution either in the fleeting shape of an analogy (*Gleichnis*) with art and literature or in the life of a singular individual thinking and acting alone.

Back to Simmel!, or Faust's Study

Throughout his life Simmel was preoccupied with the limits and possibilities of individual freedom in the modern world, not only as a personal concern for himself but also as a sociological reality and psychological experience for everyone, and ultimately as an aesthetic, ethical, metaphysical problem that must be addressed on a cosmic scale. His early monographs *On Social Differentiation*, *Introduction to the Science of Morality*, and *Philosophy of Money* all include chapters reflecting on the creativity and liberty of the individual. The last chapters of both *Sociology* and *Fundamental Questions of Sociology* also consider how personal autonomy is both enhanced and inhibited by the expansion of mass society. These questions are taken up from a philosophical perspective in later writings, such as the posthumous fragment 'Freedom and the Individual' (ISF: 217–27), and in the concluding paragraph of *Main Problems of Philosophy*, where he discusses the conflict of duties and demands placed on individuals: 'the ideal demands of the world in us and of us in the world are deeply bound together; ... between them lies what one might call the view of life [*Lebensanschauung*]' (GSG 14: 157). Although he had planned for many years to write a work on metaphysics, he completed his *View of Life* only in the final weeks before he died, in September 1918. As he wrote in the spring to his friend the philosopher Hermann Graf Keyserling (1880–1946), if he can finish his ethical and metaphysical investigations, 'they will be my testament. I am at an age where the harvest must be brought in, and no further delay is allowed' (VL: x; GSG 23: 928; note that this remark echoes the fable of the dying man that Simmel recounts in *Philosophical Culture*, discussed in chapter 1; SC: 36). And in his final days he wrote to his friends Max and Marianne Weber: 'My life presents itself to me as an unexpected closure .... I leave at the right moment without any regret or resignation' (GSG 23: 1024). The last chapter of the *View of Life*, 'The Individual Law', thus seems to be his last philosophical statement on life as a whole and on the difference between a singular life both as it is and as it ought to be lived.

Simmel's metaphysics of life is at the same time an ethics of human being. His argument is that our lived experiences are integral to and a product of our circumstances. And yet our sense of self also hopes to reach beyond any particular place and time. Thus each one of us is constantly engaged in an inner dialogue between the person I am and the person I strive to be, just as we are all constantly comparing the world as we know and live it with the world as we imagine it will become. Through our relationships with ourselves and with others we must act on 'what the day demands' (Goethe 1989: 294; quoted in VL: 109), and each one of us must find and obey 'the demon that holds the threads of one's life' (Weber 2004: 31). In Simmel's view, the task of every person is to discover and enact the individual law that springs from the very sources of his or her life: 'the law of the individual – developing from the same root from which the individual's (perhaps utterly diverging) reality springs – … is nothing other than *the totality or centrality of life itself, unfolding as obligation*' (VL: 126, emphasis added). The life that pulses through every individual is concentrated in every action in such a way that what is experienced as a matter of life and death becomes a singular obligation: 'life, proceeding in its totality as Ought, means law for the very same life that proceeds in its totality as actuality' (VL: 107). Rather than formulating an abstract moral rule that could then be applied to each individual equally – such as Kant's categorical imperative to act according to a maxim that one could will to be a universal law – Simmel imagines a law 'that is particular to each individual and applies universally to all the individual's activities' (Lee and Silver 2012: 125). With this idea in mind, he tries to think beyond the old slogans that all individuals are created equal or that each individual is unique (as discussed in 'The Metropolis and Mental Life' and *Fundamental Problems of Sociology*, for instance; SC: 174, 184–5; 1950: 81–3). Rather, the individual law implies a form of individualism emerging from the flux of historical life that is not subjected to the laws of the market, civil society, or nature (Podoksik 2010: 135–43; Pyyhtinen 2010: 152–4). Simmel's final reflections on this theme seem to search not just for a philosophy of life in general but also for the concept of 'a life', a singular being that strives to transcend boundaries but is also immanent in the process of becoming (Deleuze 1997; Joas 2000: 69–83). Rather than resorting to an ancient scholarly doctrine about what exists beyond the plane of the physical world or embracing newfangled beliefs about the mystical basis of reality, Simmel strives to imagine how a life develops and effervesces into more-life, and how life as a whole ultimately augments and overcomes itself by becoming more-than-life.

I have noted that Simmel's late writings often have a fragmentary and essayistic quality even as they strive for systematic coherence by converging on the idea of life. In this sense, his thought might itself be considered tragic in part because he could not fully realize his ambitious intentions. And yet this failure may be less a personal shortcoming than an inherent feature of modern culture itself. As his own career demonstrates, the tragedy of individuality is evident in the life of the intellectual just as it also finds expression in other cultural spheres of modernity. In the essay 'The Dramatic Actor and Reality', for instance, published in 1912, he laments the 'deep social tragedy' that lies at the heart of contemporary art. Perhaps reflecting back on his life as a scholar as well, he notes that the masses have more access than ever to cultural institutions and yet 'an abyss without bridges cuts off the majority from insight into the essence of art forms' (1968: 91). The dramatic arts are especially remarkable for the way they transcend both the literary script of the playwright and the technical demands of reality, such as staging, lighting, and props: 'the actor does not transform the dramatic work of art into reality; on the contrary, he makes use of reality, and transforms the reality which has been assigned to him into a work of art' (1968: 93). The dramatic actor is neither the puppet of the director nor simply a person interacting directly with the audience but, rather, an artist who creates 'a complete unity with its own laws' (1968: 96). Whether or not we would agree with Simmel that acting is a distinctively feminine art, as he suggests in the essay 'Female Culture' (1984: 85–90), it is interesting that the great actresses of his day impressed him with their ability to perform to perfection according to their own 'individual law', even on those evenings when they were 'tired and indisposed'. As Simmel marvels in one of his 'Snapshots *sub specie aeternitatis*', on a bad night La Duse – as the celebrated

Italian actress Eleonora Duse (1858–1924) was called – can still reveal the unity of her life and her public image along with the totality of her body and soul through the beauty of her movements (2007b: 276–7). Insofar as 'the task which confronts the present age [is] to replace mechanism with life processes', he remarks, then one of the lessons he has learned from the theatre and from philosophy is that every instant and every action realizes something of the life of the whole (1968: 96; VL: 132). To be sure, he also acknowledges that such a realization is not possible for everyone and may only be within reach of a few.

Despite the mind-expanding breadth of his *View of Life* and the profoundly new directions of thought to which this book points, perhaps Simmel's essay 'Kant and Goethe: On the History of the Modern *Weltanschauung*' might also stand as his final 'testament' and as a valiant attempt to resolve the conflict between mechanism and vitalism. Beginning as a short piece published in 1899, the essay was expanded in 1906 into a beautifully designed coffee-table book with twelve illustrations – portraits of philosophers, artists, and great works of art – ending with a photograph of the statue 'The Thinker' by Rodin, to whom the book was dedicated (GSG 10: 481–93). In the augmented version published in 1916, Simmel added the subtitle and rededicated it 'To the Jastrow Household in Lasting Friendship'. Here Simmel situates his own thought both within the worldview of the modern age and between the two spiritual models that guided his intellectual life and also acknowledges his cherished friends, neighbours, and colleague (see the illustration p. x). Since the Renaissance, he argues, human beings have come to see themselves as fundamentally dualistic beings and the world itself as divided between nature and mind, often by setting scientific objectivity against the inner meaning of life (2007a: 159). Kant and Goethe each place themselves beyond the opposition between materialism and spiritualism and somewhere between sensualism and rationalism, ultimately by reflecting on how knowledge and experience are grounded in the unity of body, mind, and soul (2007a: 167, 175).

Simmel's book *Kant*, a collection of his university lectures that is the culmination of his lifelong interest in this great philosopher, was his most popular work, going through four editions with significant additions and revisions up to the year he died. In the preface he states that his aim is to interpret the scholastic concepts of Kant's philosophy not just as an academic exercise but also as an expression of his image of the world (GSG 9: 7). In 'Kant and Goethe', this expansive approach to the life of the mind becomes a full-fledged theory of the modern worldview, which Simmel defines as an open-ended perspective on unity-in-diversity and on the cultural spheres that make up contemporary existence. Kant's achievement was to raise the subjectivism of the modern age to a total principle and a comprehensive worldview, while at the same time upholding the scientific interpretation of the natural world as consisting of mechanical laws and spatial relationships: 'Neither materialism, which aims to explain the mind through the body, nor spiritualism, which explains the body through the mind, are admissible', Simmel asserts. 'Each has to be explained in terms of laws applicable only to itself' (2007a: 162). For Kant, the absolute limit of knowledge is nature – that is, the non-human and objective 'things-in-themselves' that can only be represented through the separate faculties of the free and creative mind.

Beginning with his doctoral dissertation, Simmel became more critical of Kant's intellectualist interpretation of the world even as he developed a deeper appreciation for his emphasis on the *activity* of representation by the *whole* person, not just the mind (Podoksik 2016: 10, 28; GSG 9: 61, 86). Nevertheless, he became increasingly dissatisfied over how little this philosophy has to say about sensuous or lived experience (*Erlebnis*), religious faith, the ethics of altruism and lying, particular works of art, or other social and cultural topics that interested Simmel. In a letter to Count Keyserling he asks: 'When will the genius appear who will emancipate us from the spell of the subject in the same way that Kant liberated us from that of the object? And what will this third category be?' (quoted in Backhaus 2003: 227; GSG 22: 66–7). Simmel's answer would be not the philosophies of the will developed by Schopenhauer and Nietzsche but, rather, the radical ideas of Bergson and Husserl (GSG 12: 383–5), and above all Goethe for his novel conceptualization of *Leben* (Life) as a creative and transformative force.

As in his book on Rembrandt, Simmel's 1913 monograph *Goethe* sets out on a vitalist quest for 'the spiritual meaning, … the archetype or primary phenomenon (*Urphänomen*), … [and] the idea of Goethe', rather than simply to provide a biography of the man or an appreciation of his work (GSG 15: 9–10). Since Goethe does not have a well-developed philosophy, there can only be a kind of philosophizing *about* Goethe on the basis of his literary, scientific, and autobiographical writings (2007a: 163). As expressed in his poem 'Allerdings: Zum Physiker' ('All Things Considered: To the

Physicist'), Goethe's worldview unites nature and spirit and comprehends object and subject *within* rather than against the realm of appearances:

Nature hat weder Kern	Nature neither has core
Noch Shale,	Nor outer rind
Alles ist sie mit einem Male.	It is all at the same time.
	(Quoted in 2007a: 165)

For Goethe, the inner and outer states of the individual are essentially 'alternating pulse beats' of the all-encompassing life of Nature, like the rhythm of a body breathing in and out: 'the principle of *Leben*, which is apparent in nature, also applies to the human soul' (2007a: 166). Human beings are fundamentally connected to all things and their knowledge of the world is a natural function of life itself. Unlike Kant, Goethe fully appreciates the great tragedy of human life, which lies in how it cannot realize its inner potential and fullest expression within the prevailing conditions. This tragic view is dramatized in the life of Faust, who becomes aware that 'his unrealized energies would destroy him' if he were to remain a scholar in his study: 'The pact with Mephisto and the completion of his life's work with the help of demonic powers is merely the positive rendition' of this fate (2007a: 187). Fortunately, neither Goethe nor Simmel needed supernatural intervention for their energies to find full expression in this world, only the theatre, the lecture hall, and the writing desk, as well as the good company of family, friends, and colleagues.

In the dramatic final paragraph that Simmel added to the 1916 edition of 'Kant and Goethe' he suggests that the worldview of the epoch that is now coming to an end might best be expressed in the slogan: 'Kant *or* Goethe!' (2007a: 190). Nevertheless, he adds that in the coming age the two warring camps designated by these names might well unite 'under the sign of Kant *and* Goethe'. In other words, the future worldview would not entail mediating between these conflicting perspectives or reconciling their differences; rather, it would involve 'negating them through the fact of the lived experience of them' (2007a: 190). Simmel certainly hoped that his own writings would serve as a sign illuminating the future and indicating a third way beyond the standoff between the scientific-mechanistic worldview represented by Kant and the aesthetic-vitalistic worldview embodied in Goethe (Levine 2012). He recalls that in the 1870s the science-oriented solution to the problem of life found inspiration in the catchphrase 'Back to Kant!', which quickly prompted a reply in the realm of aesthetics: 'Back to Goethe!' (2007a: 163–4). Perhaps today the social sciences and humanities might find a new motto that might draw attention to their differences and conflicting perspectives: 'Back to Simmel!'

In our own time, there has been a growing sense of the need to return to Simmel, as if we are rediscovering in him our own preoccupations or somehow meeting him again as he returns from a point we are still struggling to reach (Duncan 1959: 108; Habermas 1996: 403; Pyyhtinen 2018: 4; Scaff 1988: 21). Shortly after his death one of his most influential students, Georg Lukács, called Simmel 'the most significant and important transitional figure in the whole of modern philosophy' and went on to characterize his teacher as a playful thinker whose ideas 'must remain a labyrinth and cannot become a system' (Lukács 1991: 145, 148). Against the grain of this influential viewpoint, I have portrayed Simmel as a methodical thinker who speaks to our deepest concerns and calls out to us across the abysses of place and time – sometimes obscurely and occasionally poignantly, as in a poem he wrote in 1901:

> *Es war ein Abgrund zwischen allem Sein und Dir,*
> *So brückenlos, – wie Ja und Nein es von einander sind,*
> *Dass Sehnsucht selbst nicht weiss, wohin die Arme strecken.*
> *Und wie Du mich erblicktest, der ich traurig ging*
> *Und liebend – und Dich ein Erröthen überkam,*
> *Der warmen Welle, die Dir auf zum Herzen stieg,*
> *Abglanz und Scham – ich wusst' es, ach, so gut und tief:*
> *Es war doch nur, dass plötzlich Dich die Hoffnung regte,*
> *Ich sei vielleicht die Brücke – nur die Brücke.*

> There was an abyss between all existence and You,
> So bridgeless – just as Yes and No are from one another,
> That longing itself does not know what the arms reach out for.
> And as You glanced at me, I who walked sadly by
> And loving – and the blush that came over You,
> A reflection and embarrassment from the warm wave
> That rose up in your heart – alas, I knew it quite well and deeply:
> It was just a hope that suddenly stirred You,
> Perhaps I might be the bridge – only the bridge. (2012: 269, 271)

A century after his death we may still find in Simmel the bridge to many of the questions we have almost forgotten how to ask.

Excursus on Identity and Difference: Simmel across Mead and Husserl

Simmel's later writings might be approached as an elaboration on the thesis he proposed earlier in 'The Metropolis and Mental Life': the human is 'a being that makes distinctions' (SC: 176; GSG 7: 116). From infancy onwards we learn to distinguish between self and (m)other, and the fabric of social and natural relationships is woven out of the sense we make of these primary differences. At the same time, Simmel's later works can also be said to expand on the paradox he formulated in the *Philosophy of Money*: the human is 'the indirect being' (PM: 211; GSG 6: 265). We do not become aware of our place in the world all at once or by mapping a straight path through it but only by following a circuitous route that passes through the objects of our desire and the intentions of other people. In the difficult opening page of the chapter on 'The Individual Law' in *View of Life*, Simmel imagines how these two perspectives – the distinction between self and other and the indirect relationship of subject and object – somehow intersect with one another. He states that an object is called 'actual' when it appears to have a certain consistency and identity that are distinct from everything subjective, and yet one object appears to be the exception to this rule: 'namely, the subject's own life' (VL: 99). In other words, my own life consists of something necessary, desirable, intentional, and even obligatory that stands both *between* myself and others and *beneath* the split between subject and object. Simmel's final writings thus seem to stretch across both a social psychology of social and individual identity and a phenomenology of subjective and objective difference.

As evidence for this idea, consider the posthumously published lectures titled *Mind, Self, and Society* by the American philosopher and social psychologist George Herbert Mead (1863–1931). Mead does not seem to have met Simmel while he studied psychology and economics at Berlin University from 1889 to 1891. However, he did write an early review of the *Philosophy of Money* that focuses on how processes of exchange separate objective relations from subjective feelings (see Frisby in PM: li–lii). In the section of the lectures on 'Self', Mead elaborates on this basic scheme by arguing that the individual experiences itself not directly, but only indirectly, by adopting the particular standpoints of other members of the same social group, and also objectively, by interacting with the social group as a whole. I become an object to myself only by taking up the attitudes of other individuals towards myself. Thus, the self is not just a subjective experience but also 'a social structure' (Mead 1934: 140). At the play stage of early childhood, for example, a child becomes a 'me' through interaction with particular others – responding to its mother or siblings – as distinct from the child's agency as an 'I' with its own sense of freedom and initiative. In the course of these interactions, 'the "I" both calls out to the "me" and responds to it' (ibid.: 178). Through the exchange of gestures and by using significant symbols, the child eventually enters a game stage characterized by a more structured set of rules and roles. We divide ourselves up into different selves with reference to those around us, with whom we relate against a general field of meaning and relevance. For Mead as for Simmel, the self is not simply a personal experience but above all an object that interacts with and takes up the attitude of others. Since a person's identity is always divided between 'I' and 'me', an individual is less a fixed entity than a fluid element – what Simmel calls the 'soul' – where inner and outer worlds are either distinguished from or dissolved into one another.

Simmel's later perspective on the relationship of human subjects and natural objects also finds expression in the early work of his friend and fellow philosopher Edmund Husserl (1859–1938). The thesis that guides the two volumes of Husserl's *Logical Investigations*, published in 1900 and 1901, asserts that objects do not simply exist apart from our intellectual constructions or vague intuitions of them. They also inhabit our field of consciousness and intentions in ways that give us partial access to the things themselves: 'Meanings inspired only by remote, confused, inauthentic intuitions – if by any intuitions at all – are not enough: we must go back to "the things themselves"' (Husserl 1970: 252). We do not have to build a mental bridge between the world 'in here' and the world 'out there', as modern philosophy has assumed since the seventeenth century (Backhaus 2003: 224–5). Rather, our intentions are oriented towards objects just as our perceptions are directed towards others in various ways. Our bodies and minds turn to things and people in the act of placing some of them in the foreground while relegating others into the background. The shift in attention that we experience in the everyday world between our subjective intentions and the objective world is rarely simple and straightforward. Rather, this experience is always a bit queer or skewed by the inevitable differences between the presence or absence of things and our attitudes towards them, and by the angle in which others and objects appear or hide themselves from us (Ahmed 2006: 25–6). Objects and other people ultimately surpass our knowledge of them because they are made up of multiple relations and because their manifold qualities subsist within the infinite flow and flux of experience. Husserl later expands on these ideas in a way that complements Simmel's thoughts on the internal consciousness of time, which he refines in his conception of the lifeworlds of predecessors, contemporaries, and successors who relate to one another with different degrees of intimacy and anonymity (Schutz 1971).

In 1911 Simmel sent Husserl a copy of his *Main Problems of Philosophy*, boasting that the book must have hit a nerve in the 'philosophical culture' of the age since it sold 13,000 copies in ten weeks, even though it makes 'no concession to popularity' (GSG 22: 940–1). Rather than drawing Husserl's attention to the chapter 'On Subject and Object', as we might expect, Simmel highlights his discussion of Hegel in 'On Being and Becoming', which focuses on the idea that 'being accomplishes itself, so to speak, only in this endless path of becoming' (GSG 14: 76; Simmel's posthumous essay on Hegel in GSG 24 develops this argument further). The dynamic principle of modern thought as represented by Hegel may have inspired Simmel to reformulate his 'apriorities' in a final attempt to move beyond the transcendental philosophy of Kant by expanding on the concepts of identity and difference. (Compare the three main chapters of the *Fundamental Questions of Sociology* and three sections of 'On the Nature of Historical Understanding'.)

In his final years, Simmel often seems to be struggling to imagine a new intellectual path across his own predecessors and contemporaries and in the direction that Mead and Husserl mapped out towards a philosophical sociology of individual, social, cultural, and natural life.

Suggestions for Further Reading

Simmel's writings in English have been steadily accumulating since the 1950s. The most accessible are the anthologies edited by Donald N. Levine, *Georg Simmel: On Individuality and Social Forms* (1971; ISF) and by David Frisby and Mike Featherstone, *Simmel on Culture* (1997a; SC). These volumes include selections from many of Simmel's writings that I discuss, including pieces from his major books: *The Philosophy of Money* (2004; PM); *Sociology* (2009; S); and *The View of Life* (2010; VL). The sporadic, incomplete, and scattered character of translations can nevertheless leave us with the impression that Simmel's writings are more fragmentary and less systematic than they actually are. For example, since there is no complete English translation of *Philosophical Culture*, one has to consult several sources: the essays on fashion and the adventure (in ISF and SC); on the ruin and the handle (1959); on female sexuality, flirtation, and the problem of the sexes (1984); on religion in the modern world and the personality of God (1997b); on the tragedy of culture (SC and 1959); and on the Alps, Michelangelo, and Rodin (forthcoming). This last volume, Austin Harrington's collection *Simmel on Art and Aesthetics*, will finally bring together several dozen essays on portraiture, theatre, painting, literature, and other topics, most of which have not been translated before. Elsewhere, I have compiled itemized chronologies of all Simmel's writings in English to date, along with their sources, in the German edition of Simmel's collected works (Harrington and Kemple 2012; Kemple and Pyyhtinen 2016). An updated and expanded version of this list is forthcoming in *Simmel Studies*.

For classroom use and for those who are new to Simmel, I recommend reading each chapter of this book along with two or more pieces by Simmel or by a thinker referred to in the excursus. For example, chapter 1 could be read with 'How is Society Possible?' (in ISF) and 'Bridge and Door' (in SC), perhaps with a selection from Herbert Spencer (1972). Olli Pyyhtinen's *The Simmelian Legacy* (2018) provides an excellent introduction to Simmel's core concepts and an illuminating discussion of the reception of Simmel in the English- and German-speaking worlds. Works by David Frisby, Horst Helle, and Donald N. Levine listed in the References also offer accessible overviews of Simmel's main ideas, with an emphasis on his social theory, as do the introductions and editorial notes to many of the translations. More advanced discussions of particular topics can be found in anthologies (Coser 1965; Kaern et al. 1990; Kemple and Pyyhtinen 2016; Kim 2006; Wolff 1959) and special issues of journals such as *Theory, Culture & Society* (1991; 2007b; 2012), the *Journal of Classical Sociology* (Dodd 2013), and *Simmel Studies*. Among the new Simmel scholars publishing in English I especially recommend the work of Natália Cantó-Milà, Eduardo de la Fuente, Nigel Dodd, Gregor Fitzi, Elizabeth Goodstein, Austin Harrington, Ralph Leck, Ephraim Podoksik, Olli Pyyhtinen, and Daniel Silver.

The twenty-four volumes of Simmel's collected works, *Georg Simmel Gesamtausgabe* (GSG), were completed under the editorial direction of Otthein Rammstedt in 2016 (see Rammstedt 2012 on the genesis of this project). I estimate that at least half of what might be considered Simmel's 'essential works' have not yet been translated into English, including key philosophical essays and occasional pieces, selections from his correspondence, and the monographs *On Social Differentiation*, *Introduction to Moral Science*, *Kant*, *Main Problems of Sociology*, and *Goethe*. Recent German scholarship on Simmel has been based largely on the GSG, often by editors and students of Rammstedt. Several anthologies and monographs offer illuminating discussions of Simmel's scholarly networks, intellectual sources, and key concepts (Cécile and Papilloud 2009; Böhringer and Gründer 1976; Christian 1978; Dahme and Rammstedt 1984; Fitzi 2002; Großheim 1991; Härpfer 2014; Köhnke 1996; Lichtblau 2011; Mičko 2010; Tyrell et al. 2011; and Ziemann 2000).

Among the most useful online resources worth checking out I recommend the Georg Simmel homepage in German, English, and French (http://socio.ch/sim/), the Centre Georg Simmel in French (http://centregeorgsimmel.ehess.fr/en/), the Red Simmel in Spanish and English (http://www.redsimmel.org), and the e-appendix to Pyyhtinen 2018, 'Works by and on Simmel' (www.palgravehighered.com/pyyhtinen).

References

Works by Georg Simmel in English Translation

To the best of my knowledge, all Simmel's writings for which there is an English translation are published in the sources listed below. Some translations are partial or appear in more than one version. See the Suggestions for Further Reading above for more information on specific texts.

(1950) *The Sociology of Georg Simmel*, ed. and trans. K. H. Wolff. Glencoe, IL: Free Press.

(1959) *Georg Simmel, 1858–1918*, ed. and trans. K. H. Wolff. Columbus: Ohio State University Press.

(1964) *Conflict & The Web of Group Affiliations*, trans. K. H. Wolff and R. Bendix. New York: Free Press.

(1968) *The Conflict in Modern Culture and Other Essays*, ed. and trans. K. P. Etzkorn. New York: Teachers College Press.

(1969) On Social Medicine, trans. J. Casparis and A. C. Higgins, *Social Forces* 47(3): 330–4.

(1971) *Georg Simmel: On Individuality and Social Forms*, ed. D. N. Levine. Chicago: University of Chicago Press [abbreviated in the text as ISF].

(1976) *Georg Simmel: Sociologist and European*, ed. and trans. P. A. Lawrence. Sunbury-on-Thames: Nelson.

(1977) *The Problems of the Philosophy of History*, trans. G. Oakes. New York: Free Press.

(1980) *Georg Simmel: Essays on Interpretation in Social Science*, ed. and trans. G. Oakes. Manchester: Manchester University Press.

(1984) *Georg Simmel: On Women, Sexuality, and Love*, ed. and trans. G. Oakes. New Haven, CT: Yale University Press.

(1986) *Schopenhauer and Nietzsche*, trans. H. Loiskandl, D. Weinstein, and M. Weinstein. Urbana: University of Illinois Press.

(1991) *Theory, Culture & Society* 8(3), Special Issue on Georg Simmel, ed. M. Featherstone.

(1994a) *Georg Simmel: Critical Assessments*, ed. I. D. Frisby. London: Routledge.

(1994b) The Picture Frame: An Aesthetic Study, trans. M. Ritter, *Theory, Culture & Society* 11(1): 11–17.

(1997) *Simmel on Culture*, ed. D. Frisby and M. Featherstone. London: Sage [abbreviated in the text as SC].

(1997) *Georg Simmel: Essays on Religion*, ed. and trans. H. Helle. New Haven, CT: Yale University Press.

(1998) On the Sociology of the Family, trans. M. Ritter and D. Frisby, *Theory, Culture & Society* 15(3–4): 283–93.

(2004) *The Philosophy of Money*, trans. T. Bottomore and D. Frisby. London: Routledge [abbreviated in the text as PM].

(2005a) *Rembrandt: An Essay on the Philosophy of Art*, trans. A. Scott and H. Staubmann. London: Routledge.

(2005b) Europe and America in World History, trans. A. Harrington, *European Journal of Social Theory* 8(1): 63–72.

(2007a) Kant and Goethe: On the History of the Modern *Weltanschauung*, trans. J. Bleicher, *Theory, Culture & Society* 24(6): 159–91.

(2007b) *Theory, Culture & Society* 24(7–8), Special Issue: Simmel on Aesthetics, Ethics and Metaphysics, ed. T. Kemple, trans. T. Kemple, U. Teucher, J. Bleicher, and A. Harrington.

(2008) *Englischsprachige Veröffentlichungen 1893–1910* [English language publications 1893–1910], *Georg Simmel Gesamtausgabe*, Vol. 18, ed. D. Frisby. Frankfurt am Main: Suhrkamp.

(2009) *Sociology: Inquiries into the Construction of Social Forms*, 2 vols, ed. H. Helle, trans. A. J. Blasi, A. K. Jacobs, and M. Kanjirathinkal. Leiden: Brill [abbreviated in the text as S].

(2009–10) The Tale of the Color, trans. A. Schuster, *Cabinet Magazine* no. 36, http://cabinetmagazine.org/issues/36/simmel.php.

(2010) *View of Life: Four Metaphysical Essays with Journal Aphorisms*, trans. J. A. Y. Andrews and D. N. Levine. Chicago: University of Chicago Press [abbreviated in the text as VL].

(2012) *Theory, Culture & Society* 29(7–8), Special Issue: Georg Simmel's 'Sociological Metaphysics': Money Sociality and Precarious Life, ed. and trans. A. Harrington and T. Kemple.

(2015) On Art Exhibitions, trans. A. Harrington, *Theory, Culture & Society* 32(1): 87–92.

(forthcoming) *Georg Simmel: On Art and Aesthetics*, ed. and trans. A. Harrington. Chicago: University of Chicago Press.

Other Works Cited

Adorno, T. W. (1992) The Handle, the Pot, and Early Experience, in *Notes to Literature*, Vol. 2, ed. S. W. Nicholsen. New York: Columbia University Press, pp. 211–19.

Ahmed, S. (2006) *Queer Phenomenology: Orientations, Objects, Others*. Durham, NC: Duke University Press.

Arvidsson, A. (2016) Facebook and Finance, *Theory, Culture & Society* 33(6): 3–23.

Backhaus, G. (1998) Georg Simmel as an Eidetic Social Scientist, *Sociological Theory* 16(3): 260–81.

Backhaus, G. (2003) Husserlian Affinities in Georg Simmel's Later Philosophy of History: The 1918 Essay, *Human Studies* 26(2): 223–58.

Barbour, C. (2012) The Maker of Lies: Simmel, Mendacity and the Economy of Faith, *Theory, Culture & Society* 29(7–8): 218–36.

Barthes, R. (1989) *Sade, Fourier, Loyola*, trans. R. Miller. Berkeley: University of California Press.

Barthes, R. (2005) *The Language of Fashion*, trans. A. Stafford. London: Bloomsbury.

Baudelaire, C. (1964) *The Painter of Modern Life and Other Essays*, trans. J. Mayne. London: Phaidon Press.

Bayatrizi, Z., and Kemple, T. (2012) Un problème de chiffres: l'utilisation des connaissances empiriques en statistique dans la théorie sociale classique, trans. J. Maertens, *Sociologie et sociétés* 44(2): 45–73.

Beller, J. (2006) *The Cinematic Mode of Production: Attention Economy and the Society of the Spectacle*. Hanover, NH: Dartmouth University Press.

Benjamin, W. (1978) Paris – Capital of the Nineteenth Century, trans. E. Jephcott, in *Reflections*. New York: Schocken Books, pp. 146–62.

Bergson, H. (1998) *Creative Evolution*, trans. A. Mitchell. New York: Dover.

Bloch, E. (2000) *The Spirit of Utopia*, trans. A. A. Nassar. Stanford, CA: Stanford University Press.

Blumenberg, H. (2012) Money or Life: Metaphors of Georg Simmel's Philosophy, trans. R. Savage, *Theory, Culture & Society* 29(7–8): 249–62.

Böhringer, H., and Gründer, K. (eds) (1976) *Ästhetik und Soziologie um die Jahrhundertwende: Georg Simmel*. Frankfurt am Main: Klostermann.

Borch, C. (2010) Between Destructiveness and Vitalism: Simmel's Sociology of Crowds, *Conserveries mémorielles* no. 8, http://cm.revues.org/744.

Bourdieu, P. (1998) *Practical Reason: On the Theory of Action*, trans. R. Nice. Stanford, CA: Stanford University Press.

Burke, K. (1989) Irony and Dialectic, in *On Symbols and Society*, ed. J. R. Gusfield. Chicago: University of Chicago Press, pp. 247–60.

Button, R. W. (2012) Fate, Experience and Tragedy in Simmel's Dialogue with Modernity, *Theory, Culture & Society* 29(7–8): 53–77.

Cantó-Milà, N. (2005) *A Sociological Theory of Value: Georg Simmel's Sociological Relationism*. Bielefeld: Transcript.

Cantó-Milà, N. (2013) Gratitude: Invisibly Webbing Society Together, *Journal of Classical Sociology* 13(1): 8–19.

Cantó-Milà, N. (2016) On the Special Relation between Proximity and Distance in Simmel's Forms of Association and Beyond, in *The Anthem Companion to Georg Simmel*, ed. T. Kemple and O. Pyyhtinen. London: Anthem Press, pp. 81–100.

Cécile, R., and Papilloud, C. (eds) (2009) *Soziologie als Möglichkeit: 100 Jahren Georg Simmels Untersuchungen über der Formen der Versgesellschaftung.* Wiesbaden: Springer.

Christian, P. (1978) *Einheit und Zwiespalt: Zum heglianisierenden Denken in der Philosophie und Soziologie Georg Simmels.* Berlin: Duncker & Humblot.

Clarke, J. (2005) Capitalism, in *Keywords: A Revised Vocabulary of Culture and Society*, ed. T. Bennett et al. Oxford: Blackwell, pp. 22–6.

Coser, L. A. (ed.) (1965) Introduction, in *Georg Simmel*. Englewood Cliffs, NJ: Prentice-Hall.

Dahme, H.-J., and Rammstedt, O. (eds) (1984) *Georg Simmel und die Moderne: Neue Interpretationen und Materialen.* Frankfurt am Main: Suhrkamp.

de la Fuente, E. (2016a) Frames, Handles and Landscapes: Georg Simmel and the Aesthetic Ecology of Things, in *The Anthem Companion to Georg Simmel*, ed. T. Kemple and O. Pyyhtinen. London: Anthem Press, pp. 161–84.

de la Fuente, E. (2016b) A Qualitative Theory of Culture: Georg Simmel and Cultural Sociology, in *The Sage Handbook of Cultural Sociology*, ed. D. Inglis and A.-M. Almila. London: Sage, pp. 78–90.

Deleuze, G. (1997) Immanence: A Life …, *Theory, Culture & Society* 14(2): 3–7.

Derrida, J. (1979) *Spurs: Nietzsche's Styles*, trans. B. Harlow. Chicago: University of Chicago Press.

Derrida, J. (1981) Freud and the Scene of Writing, trans. J. Mehlman, *Yale French Studies* no. 48: 74–117.

Dodd, N. (2012) Simmel's Perfect Money: Fiction, Socialism and Utopia in *The Philosophy of Money, Theory, Culture & Society* 29(7–8): 146–76.

Dodd, N. (ed.) (2013) Special Issue: Georg Simmel and David Frisby, *Journal of Classical Sociology* 13(1).

Dodd, N. (2014) *The Social Life of Money*. Princeton, NJ: Princeton University Press.

Dodd, N. (2016) *Vires in Numeris*: Taking Simmel to Mt Gox, in *The Anthem Companion to Georg Simmel*, ed. T. Kemple and O. Pyyhtinen. London: Anthem Press, pp. 12–40.

Du Bois, W. E. B. (1999) *The Souls of Black Folk*, ed. H. L. Gates Jr. and T. H. Oliver. New York: W. W. Norton.

Du Bois, W. E. B. (2000) Sociology Hesitant, *boundary* 27(3): 37–44.

Du Bois, W. E. B. (2006) Die Negerfrage in den Vereingten Staaten *(The Negro Question in the United States (1906)*, trans. J. Fracchia, *New Centennial Review* 6(3): 241–90.

Duncan, H. D. (1959) Simmel's Image of Society, in *Georg Simmel, 1858–1908*, ed. K. H. Wolff. Columbus: Ohio State University Press, pp. 100–18.

Durkheim, E. ([1895] 1951) *Suicide: A Study in Sociology*, trans. J. A. Spaulding and G. Simpson. Glencoe, IL: Free Press.

Engels, F. (1972) *The Origin of the Family, Private Property and the State*. New York: International Publishers.

Fitzi, G. (2002) *Soziale Erfahrung und Lebensphilosophie: Georg Simmels Beziehung zu Henri Bergson*. Konstanz: UVK.

Fitzi, G. (2016) Modernity as Solid Liquidity: Georg Simmel's Life-Sociology, in *The Anthem Companion to Georg Simmel*, ed. T. Kemple and O. Pyyhtinen. London: Anthem Press, pp. 59–80.

Francis, M. (2007) *Herbert Spencer and the Invention of Modern Life*. Ithaca, NY: Cornell University Press.

Freud, S. (1976) *The Interpretation of Dreams*, trans. J. Strachey. Harmondsworth: Penguin.

Frisby, D. (1985) Georg Simmel: First Sociologist of Modernity, *Theory, Culture & Society* 2(3): 49–67.

Frisby, D. (1986) *Fragments of Modernity: Theories of Modernity in the Work of Simmel, Kracauer, and Benjamin*. Cambridge, MA: MIT Press.

Frisby, D. (1992) *Simmel and Since: Essays on Georg Simmel's Social Theory*. London: Routledge.

Frisby, D. (2001) *Cityscapes of Modernity: Critical Explorations*. Cambridge: Polity.

Frisby, D. (2002) *Georg Simmel*. London: Routledge.

Frisch, D. (2009) *Georg Simmel im Kino: Die Soziologie des frühen Films und das Abenteuer der Moderne*. Bielefeld: Transcript.

Gassen, K., and Lassmann, M. (eds) (1958) *Buch des Dankes an Georg Simmel*. Berlin: Duncker & Humblot.

Gilman, C. P. (1989) *The Yellow Wallpaper and Other Writings*, ed. L. S. Schwartz. New York: Bantam Books.

Gilroy, P. (1993) *The Black Atlantic: Modernity and Double Consciousness*. Cambridge, MA: Harvard University Press.

Goethe, J. W. von (1976) *Faust: A Tragedy*, trans. W. Arndt. New York: W. W. Norton.

Goethe, J. W. von (1986) *Faust: Der Tragödie zweiter Teil*. Stuttgart: Reclam.

Goethe, J. W. von (1989) *Wilhelm Meister's Journeyman Years*, trans. K. Winston. Frankfurt am Main: Suhrkamp.

Goodstein, E. S. (2002) Style as Substance: Georg Simmel's Phenomenology of Culture, *Cultural Critique* no. 52: 209–34.

Goodstein, E. S. (2016) Sociology as a Sideline: Does it Matter that Georg Simmel (Thought He) Was a Philosopher?, in *The Anthem Companion to Georg Simmel*, ed. T. Kemple and O. Pyyhtinen. London: Anthem Press, pp. 29–58.

Goodstein, E. S. (2017) *Georg Simmel and the Disciplinary Imaginary*. Stanford, CA: Stanford University Press.

Green, B. S. (1988) *Literary Methods and Sociological Theory: Case Studies of Simmel and Weber*. Chicago: University of Chicago Press.

Gross, M. (2001) Unexpected Interactions: Georg Simmel and the Observation of Nature, *Journal of Classical Sociology* 1(3): 395–414.

Großheim, M. (1991) *Von Georg Simmel zu Martin Heidegger: Philosophie zwischen Leben und Existenz*. Bonn: Bouvier.

Habermas, J. (1996) Georg Simmel on Philosophy and Culture: Postscript to a Collection of Essays, trans. M. Deflem, *Critical Inquiry* 22(3): 403–14.

Härpfer, C. (2014) *Georg Simmel und die Entstehung der Soziologie in Deutschland: Eine netzwerksoziologische Studie*. Wiesbaden: Springer.

Harrington, A. (2016) *German Cosmopolitan Thought and the Idea of the West: Voices from Weimar*. Cambridge: Cambridge University Press.

Harrington, A., and Kemple, T. (2012) Georg Simmel's 'Sociological Metaphysics': Money, Sociality, and Precarious Life, *Theory, Culture & Society* 29(7–8): 7–25.

Harrington, A., and Kemple, T. (2013) An Interview with Thomas Kemple and Austin Harrington on Simmel, *Theory, Culture & Society* blog, https://www.theoryculturesociety.org/interview-with-thomas-kemple-and-austin-harrington-on-simmel/.

Hart, K. (1986) Heads or Tails? Two Sides of the Coin, *Man* 21(4): 637–56.

Helle, H. J. (2013) *Messages from Georg Simmel*. Chicago: Haymarket Books.

Helle, H. J. (2015) *The Social Thought of Georg Simmel*. Thousand Oaks, CA: Sage.

Herrington, S. (2013) *Cornelia Hahn Oberlander: Making the Modern Landscape*. Charlottesville: University of Virginia Press.

Howell, J. (2016) How Thinking Became Work: The Mental Work Problem in Nineteenth-Century Europe, unpublished MA thesis, University of British Columbia.

Huey, L., and Kemple, T. (2007) 'Let the Streets Take Care of Themselves': Making Sociological and Common Sense of 'Skid Row', *Urban Studies* 44(12): 2305–19.

Husserl, E. (1970) *Logical Investigations*, trans. J. N. Findlay. London: Routledge & Kegan Paul.

Jaworski, G. D. (1997) *Georg Simmel and the American Prospect*. Albany: State University of New York Press.

Joas, H. (2000) *The Genesis of Values*, trans. G. Moore. Chicago: University of Chicago Press.

Kaern, M., Phillips, B., and Cohen, R. S. (eds) (1990) *Georg Simmel and Contemporary Sociology*. Dordrecht: Kluwer.

Kantorowicz, G. ([1923] 1959) Preface to Georg Simmel's *Fragments, Posthumous Essays, and Publications in His Last Years*, in *Georg Simmel, 1858–1918*, ed. K. H. Wolff. Columbus: Ohio State University Press, pp. 3–8.

Kemple, T. (1995) *Reading Marx Writing: Melodrama, the Market, and the 'Grundrisse'*. Stanford, CA: Stanford University Press.

196 *References*

Kemple, T. (2007) Allosociality: Bridges and Doors to Simmel's Social Theory of the Limit, *Theory, Culture & Society* 24(7–8): 1–19.

Kemple, T. (2009) Weber/Simmel/Du Bois: Musical Thirds of Classical Sociology, *Journal of Classical Sociology* 9(2): 187–207.

Kemple, T. (2010) Thomas Kemple introduces 'David Frisby on Georg Simmel and Social Theory', *Theory, Culture & Society* special e-issue on David Frisby: www.theoryculturesociety.org/thomas-kemple-introduces-david-frisby-on-georg-simmel-and-social-theory/.

Kemple, T. (2011) The Spatial Sense of Empire: Encountering Strangers with Simmel, Tocqueville and Martineau, *Journal of Classical Sociology* 11(4): 340–55.

Kemple, T. (2013) Allegories of the End: Classical Sociologies of Economic Sustainability and Cultural Ruin, *Journal of Historical Sociology* 26(3): 365–82.

Kemple, T. (2014a) *Intellectual Work and the Spirit of Capitalism: Weber's Calling*. Basingstoke: Palgrave Macmillan.

Kemple, T. (2014b) Mannheim's Pendulum: Refiguring Legal Cosmopolitanism, *UC Irvine Law Review* 4(1): 273–95.

Kemple, T. (2016) Simmel and the Sources of Neoliberalism, in *The Anthem Companion to Georg Simmel*, ed. T. Kemple and O. Pyyhtinen. London: Anthem Press, pp. 141–60.

Kemple, T., and Harrington, A. (2016) Dialogue fictif entre Weber et Simmel: le conflit, en quatre époques, trans. R. Dion, *Sociologie et Sociétés* 48(1): 213–19.

Kemple, T., and Pyyhtinen, O. (2016) Editors' Introduction – Thinking with Simmel, in *The Anthem Companion to Georg Simmel*, ed. T. Kemple and O. Pyyhtinen. London: Anthem Press, pp. 1–12.

Kim, D. D. (ed.) (2006) *Georg Simmel in Translation: Interdisciplinary Border Crossings in Culture and Modernity*. Newcastle: Cambridge Scholars Press.

Köhnke, K. C. (1996) *Der junge Simmel in Theoriebeziehungen und sozialen Bewegungen*. Frankfurt am Main: Suhrkamp.

Kracauer, S. (1995) *The Mass Ornament*, trans. T. Y. Levin. Cambridge, MA: Harvard University Press.

Kracauer, S. (1998) *The Salaried Masses*, trans. Q. Hoare. London: Verso.

Landmann, M. (1958) Bausteine zur Biographie, in *Buch des Dankes an Georg Simmel*, ed. K. Gassen and M. Landmann. Berlin: Duncker & Humblot.

Lash, S. (2005) *Lebenssoziologie*: Georg Simmel in the Information Age, *Theory, Culture & Society* 22(3): 1–23.

Lash, S. (2010) Intensive Sociology: Georg Simmel's Vitalism, in *Intensive Culture: Social Theory, Religion and Contemporary Capitalism*. London: Sage, pp. 21–42.

Latour, B. (2005) *Reassembling the Social: An Introduction to Actor-Network Theory*. Oxford: Oxford University Press.

Latour, B., and Lépinay, V. A. (2009) *The Science of Passionate Interests: An Introduction to Gabriel Tarde's Economic Anthropology*. Chicago: University of Chicago Press.

Leck, R. M. (2000) *Georg Simmel and Avant-Garde Sociology: The Birth of Modernity, 1880–1920*. Amherst, NY: Humanity Books.

Leck, R. M. (2016) *Vita Sexualis: Karl Ulrichs and the Origins of Sexual Science*. Urbana: University of Illinois Press.

Lee, M., and Silver, D. (2012) Simmel's Law of the Individual and the Ethics of the Relational Self, *Theory, Culture & Society* 29(7–8): 124–45.

Levine, D. N. (1985) *The Flight from Ambiguity: Essays in Social and Cultural Theory*. University of Chicago Press.

Levine, D. N. (2012) *Soziologie* and *Lebensanschauung*: Two Approaches to Synthesizing 'Kant' and 'Goethe' in Simmel's Work, *Theory, Culture & Society* 29(7–8): 26–52.

Levine, D. N., Carter, E. B., and Gorman, E. M. (1976) Simmel's Influence on American Sociology, Parts I & II, *American Journal of Sociology* 81(4): 813–45; 81(5): 1112–32.

Lichtblau, K. (1991) Causality or Interaction? Simmel, Weber and Interpretive Sociology, *Theory, Culture & Society* 8(3): 33–62.

Lichtblau, K. (2011) *Die Eigenart der kultur- und sozialwissenschaftlichen Begriffsbildung*. Wiesbaden: VS Verlag für Sozialwissenschaften.

Lukács, G. (1971) *History and Class Consciousness*, trans. R. Livingstone. London: Merlin Press.

Lukács, G. (1991) Georg Simmel, trans. M. Cerullo, *Theory, Culture & Society* 8(3): 145–50.

Mannheim, K. (1936) *Ideology and Utopia: An Introduction to the Sociology of Knowledge*, trans. L. Wirth and E. Shils. New York: Harcourt, Brace & World.

Mannheim, K. (1952) The Problem of Generations, in *Essays on the Sociology of Knowledge*, ed. P. Kecskemeti. London: Routledge & Kegan Paul.

Mannheim, K. (2012) Soul and Culture, trans. A. Wessely, *Theory, Culture & Society* 29(7–8): 286–301.

Martineau, H. ([1837] 1981) *Society in America*, ed. S. M. Lipset. New Brunswick, NJ: Transaction Books.

Marx, K. (1977) *Karl Marx: Selected Writings*, ed. D. McLellan. Oxford: Oxford University Press.

Marx, K. (1988) *Das Kapital*, Vol. 1, Marx–Engels Werke, Vol. 23. Bonn: Dietz.

Maus, H. (1959) Georg Simmel and German Sociology, in *Georg Simmel, 1858–1918*, ed. and trans. K. H. Wolff. Columbus: Ohio State University Press.

Mauss, M. (1967) *The Gift: Forms and Functions of Exchange in Archaic Societies*, trans. I. Cunnison. New York: W. W. Norton.

Mead, G. H. (1934) *Mind, Self, and Society*, ed. C. W. Morris. Chicago: University of Chicago Press.

Mičko, M. (2010) *Walter Benjamin und Georg Simmel*. Wiesbaden: Harrassowitz.

Morris, A. D. (2015) *The Scholar Denied: W. E. B. Du Bois and the Birth of Modern Sociology*. Berkeley: University of California Press.

Morris-Reich, A. (2003) The Beautiful Jew is a Moneylender: Money and Individuality in Simmel's Rehabilitation of the 'Jew', *Theory, Culture & Society* 20(4): 127–42.

Naegele, K. D. (1958) Attachment and Alienation: Complementary Aspects of the Work of Durkheim and Simmel, *American Journal of Sociology* 63(6): 580–9.

O'Neill, J. (1973) On Simmel's Sociological Apriorities, in *Phenomenological Sociology: Issues and Applications*, ed. G. Psathas. New York: Wiley.

O'Neill, J. (2001) 'Oh My Others! There is No Other!' Capital Culture, Class and Other-wiseness, *Theory, Culture & Society* 18(2–3): 77–90.

Papilloud, C. (2002) Critical Relations: Anthropology of Exchange in Georg Simmel and Marcel Mauss, *Simmel Studies* 12(1): 85–107.

Park, R. E. ([1928] 1950) Human Migration and the Marginal Man, in *Race and Culture*. Glencoe, IL: Free Press.

Park, R. E., and Burgess, E. W. (eds) (1969) *Introduction to the Science of Sociology*. Chicago: University of Chicago Press.

Park, R. E., Burgess, E. W., and McKenzie, R. D. (1967) *The City*. Chicago: University of Chicago Press.

Partyga, D. (2016) Simmel's Reading of Nietzsche: The Promise of 'Philosophical Sociology', *Journal of Classical Sociology* 16(4): 414–37.

Podoksik, E. (2010) Georg Simmel: Three Forms of Individualism and Historical Understanding, *New German Critique* 37(109): 119–45.

Podoksik, E. (2012) In Search of Unity: Georg Simmel on Italian Cities as Works of Art, *Theory, Culture & Society* 29(7–8): 101–23.

Podoksik, E. (2016) Neo-Kantianism and Georg Simmel's Interpretation of Kant, *Modern Intellectual History* 13(3): 597–622.

Poggi, G. (1993) *Money and the Modern Mind: Georg Simmel's Philosophy of Money*. Berkeley: University of California Press.

Pyyhtinen, O. (2009) Being-With: Georg Simmel's Sociology of Association, *Theory, Culture & Society* 26(5): 108–28.

Pyyhtinen, O. (2010) *Simmel and 'the Social'*. Basingstoke: Palgrave Macmillan.

Pyyhtinen, O. (2012) Life, Death and Individuation: Simmel on the Problem of Life Itself, *Theory, Culture & Society* 29(7–8): 78–100.

Pyyhtinen, O. (2014) *The Gift and its Paradoxes: Beyond Mauss*. Farnham: Ashgate.

Pyyhtinen, O. (2015) *More-than-Human Sociology: A New Sociological Imagination*. Basingstoke: Palgrave Macmillan.

Pyyhtinen, O. (2016) The Real as Relational: Simmel as Pioneer of Relational Sociology, in *The Anthem Companion to Georg Simmel*, ed. T. Kemple and O. Pyyhtinen. London: Anthem Press, pp. 101–20.

Pyythinen, O. (2018) *The Simmelian Legacy*. Basingstoke: Palgrave Macmillan.

Rammstedt, O. (1991) On Simmel's Aesthetics: Argumentation in the Journal *Jugend*, 1897–1906, *Theory, Culture & Society* 8(3): 125–44.

Rammstedt, O. (2012) On the Genesis of a Collected Edition of Simmel's Works, 1918–2012, *Theory, Culture & Society* 24(7–8): 302–16.

Scaff, L. A. (1988) Weber, Simmel, and the Sociology of Culture, *Sociological Review* 36(1): 1–30.

Scaff, L. S. (1990) Georg Simmel's Theory of Culture, in *Georg Simmel and Contemporary Sociology*, ed. M. Kaern, B. Phillips, and R. S. Cohen. Dordrecht: Kluwer, pp. 283–96.

Scaff, L. A. (2005) The Mind of the Modernist: Simmel on Time, *Time & Society* 14(1): 5–23.

Scaff, L. S. (2009) The Vision of the Social Theorist: Simmel on Space, in *Soziologie als Möglichkeit*, ed. R. Cécile and C. Papilloud. Wiesbaden: Springer, pp. 45–61.

Scaff, L. A. (2011) *Max Weber in America*. Princeton, NJ: Princeton University Press.

Schutz, A. (1971) Husserl's Importance for the Social Sciences, in *Collected Papers I: The Problem of Social Reality*, ed. M. A. Natanson and H. L. van Breda. The Hague: Martinus Nijhoff.

Schwartz, B. (2017) How is History Possible? Georg Simmel on Empathy and Realism, *Journal of Classical Sociology* 17(3): 213–37.

Shapin, S. (2007) Man with a Plan: Herbert Spencer's Theory of Everything, *New Yorker*, 13 August.

Siegert, B. (2015) *Cultural Techniques: Grids, Filters, Doors, and Other Articulations of the Real*, trans. G. Winthrop-Young. New York: Fordham University Press.

Simmel, H. (1958) Auszüge aus den Lebenserinnerungen, in *Ästhetik und Soziologie um die Jahrhundertwende: Georg Simmel*, ed. H. Böhringer and K. Gründer. Frankfurt am Main: Klostermann.

Sombart, W. (2001) *Economic Life in the Modern Age*, ed. N. Stehr and R. Grundmann. New Brunswick, NJ: Transaction Books.

Sombart, W. (2005) Technology and Culture, in *Sociological Beginnings: The First German Conference of the German Society for Sociology*, ed. and trans. C. Adair-Toteff. Liverpool: Liverpool University Press.

Spencer, H. (1972) *On Social Evolution*, ed. J. D. Y. Peel. Chicago: University of Chicago Press.

Spivak, G. C. (1987) Scattered Speculations on the Question of Value, in *In Other Worlds*. London: Methuen.

Stewart, J. C. (1999) Georg Simmel at the Lectern, *Body & Society* (5)4: 1–16.

Susman, M. (1992) *Das Nah- und Fernsein des Fremden: Essays und Briefe*, ed. I. Nordman. Frankfurt am Main: Judischer Verlag/Suhrkamp.

Swedberg, R. (2016) Can You Visualize Theory? On the Use of Visual Thinking in Theory Pictures, Theorizing Diagrams, and Visual Sketches, *Sociological Theory* 34(3): 250–75.

Tarde, G. ([1888] 1969) The Laws of Imitation, in *On Communication and Social Forms*, ed. T. N. Clark. Chicago: University of Chicago Press.

Tarde, G. (2016) Sociology and Monadology, in *The Social after Gabriel Tarde*, ed. M. Candea. Abingdon: Routledge.

Tocqueville, Alexis de ([1835/1840] 1969) *Democracy in America*, trans. J. P. Meyer. New York: Doubleday.

Todd, Z. (2016) An Indigenous Feminist's Take on the Ontological Turn: 'Ontology' is Just Another Word for Colonialism, *Journal of Historical Sociology* 29(1): 4–22.

Tyrell, H., Rammstedt, O., and Meyer, I. (eds) (2011) *Georg Simmels große 'Soziologie'*. Bielefeld: Transcript.

van Vucht Tijssen, L. (1991) Women and Objective Culture: Georg Simmel and Marianne Weber, *Theory, Culture & Society* 8(3): 203–18.

Varul, M. Z. (2016) Waste, Industry and Romantic Leisure: Veblen's Theory of Recognition, *European Journal of Social Theory* 9(1): 103–17.

Veblen, T. (1953) *The Theory of the Leisure Class*. New York: New American Library.

Weber, Marianne (1988) *Max Weber: A Biography*, trans. H. Zohn. New Brunswick, NJ: Transaction Books.

Weber, Marianne (1998) Excerpts from 'Selections from Marianne Weber's *Reflections on Women and Women's Issues*', trans. E. Kirchen, in *The Women Founders*, ed. P. Madoo Lengermann, and J. Niebrugge-Brantley. Boston: McGraw-Hill.

Weber, Max (1978) *Economy and Society*, Vol. 1, ed. G. Roth and C. Wittich. Berkeley: University of California Press.

Weber, Max (2001) *The Protestant Ethic Debate: Weber's Replies to his Critics, 1907–1910*, ed. D. J. Chalcraft and A. Harrington. Liverpool: Liverpool University Press.

Weber, Max (2004) *The Vocation Lectures*, trans. D. Owen and T. B. Strong. Indianapolis: Hackett.

Weber, Max (2005) Remarks on Technology and Culture, trans. B. Zumsteg and T. Kemple, *Theory, Culture & Society* 22(4): 23–38.

Weber, Max (2009) *The Protestant Ethic and the Spirit of Capitalism, with Other Writings on the Rise of the West*, trans. S. Kalberg. Oxford: Oxford University Press.

Weber, Max (2012) *Max Weber: Collected Methodological Writings*, trans. H. H. Bruun and S. Whimster. London: Routledge.

Weingartner, R. H. (1960) *Experience and Culture: The Philosophy of Georg Simmel*. Middletown, CT: Wesleyan University Press.

Weinstein, D., and Weinstein, M. A. (1991) Georg Simmel: Sociological *Flâneur* Bricoleur, *Theory, Culture & Society* 8(3): 151–68.

Weinstein, D., and Weinstein, M. A. (1993) *Postmodern(ized) Simmel*. London: Routledge.

Wilde, O. (1985) *The Importance of Being Earnest and Other Plays*. Harmondsworth: Penguin.

Wolff, K. H. (ed. and trans.) (1959) *Georg Simmel, 1858–1918*. Columbus: Ohio State University Press.

Zelizer, V. A. (1994) *The Social Meaning of Money: Pin Money, Paychecks, Poor Relief, and Other Currencies*. Princeton, NJ: Princeton University Press.

Ziemann, A. (2000) *Die Brücke zur Gesellschaft: Erkenntniskritische und topographische Implikationen der Soziologie Georg Simmels*. Konstanz:Unversität sverlag Konstanz

Index

Page numbers in italics refer to illustrations

'Adornment, Excursus on' (from *Sociology*) 88–90
'Adventure, The' (from *Philosophical Culture*) 57, 154–7
aesthetics 23–4, 106–8, 138–44, 146, 148, 178, 184
  and art 4, 7, 20, 39, 92, 135, 178, 180–2
  see also 'Art Exhibitions'; Goethe; Meunier; 'Philosophy of Landscape'; 'Picture Frame'; *Rembrandt*; 'Rodin'; 'Ruin'; 'Sociological Aesthetics'
'Alps, The' (from *Philosophical Culture*) 146–7
American Journal of Sociology 2, 8, 128, 129
analogies xiv, 18, 101
Année sociologique 2, 8, 40
apriorities (preconditions of social life) 11–18, *16*, 127, 187
  first apriority 14, 17, 25
  second apriority 14–15, 17, 78, 103, 116
  third apriority 15, 17, 135, 171

Archiv für Sozialwissenschaft und Sozialpolitik 130–1
'Art Exhibitions, On' 107–8
association (*Vergesellschaftung*) 4, 10–11, 13, 16, 20, 134
  forms of 78, 80–3, 107, 111–12, 166

Baudelaire, Charles 104
Benjamin, Walter 104
Bergson, Henri 3, 19, 97, 110–13, 182
Berlin 37, 53, 77, 92, 98, 102–3, 107–8, 115
  entertainment and art 107–8, 125, 137
  Simmel's life in xi–xii, 24, 51, 69, 89, 112, 115, 129, 131, 159, 170, 185
  see also Simmel, Georg
'Berlin Trade Exhibition, On the' 28, 37
'Beyond Beauty' 148–9
blasé attitude 64, 80, 85, 99, *100*, 108
Bloch, Ernst 3, 89, 136, 159–60

Bouglé, Celestin 76
boundaries and limits 83–4, 88, 107, 175
see also 'Social Boundary'
bricoleur xv, 110
'Bridge and Door' 16–17, 33–4, 174–5
Buber, Martin 3, 176
Burgess, Ernest 128

capitalism 43–4, 55–9, 64–5, 97
Casanova 157–8
causality 83, 133
causes 10–11, 15, 18, 25, 29–31, 40, 58, 71, 86, 135, 162
see also interaction
class conflict 9, 55, 64, 71–5, 115
competition 9, 20, 37, 56, 59–60, 65, 124
'Concept and the Tragedy of Culture, The' (from *Philosophical Culture*) 74, 136, 171–3, 178
'Conflict' (from *Sociology*) 65–7, 82
'Conflict in Modern Culture, The' 134, 175–6
'Constitutive Concepts of History, The' 164
consumption and consumerism 9, 25, 30, 32, 35, 37, 55–6, 61–4, 66, 70–3, 105–8, 139–40, 150–1
Cooley, Charles Horton 2, 8
Coser, Lewis 8
crypto-currencies 48
culture (*Kultur*) 11–12, 26, 55, 66–7, 89, 134–9, 141, 143, 148, 170–1, 174–5
capitalist 59–64, 69–72, 104
human 19, 24, 29–30, 33, 95, 135, 143, 160, 175
modern 27, 36–7, 66, 68, 73–4, 115, 133–9, 153–9, 171–2
objective and subjective 17, 66–7, 92–4, 99–102, 135, 172–3
urban 88, 106, 108–9, 112, 124

see also aesthetics; 'Concept and the Tragedy of Culture'; 'Conflict of Modern Culture'; 'Female Culture'; *Philosophical Culture*
cynicism 11, 27, 43, 59, 66

Dante 2, 6, 7, 137
Darwin, Charles 2, 8, 19–20
Descartes, René 6
desire 20, 29, 32, 34, 37, 41, 52, 61, 63, 64, 72, 74, 108, 126, 157, 165–6
see also value
'Differentiation and the Principle of Saving Energy' (from *On Social Differentiation*) 54–5
Dilthey, Wilhelm 2, 8, 111
distance
and proximity 133, 154–7, 166
social 9, 17, 59, 61, 64, 79, 86, 89, 104, 109, 115–16, 121–3
spatial or temporal 32–3, 38, 59, 67, 101
Dodd, Nigel 49–50
'Domination and Subordination' (from *Sociology*) 44, 58, 123
'Dramatic Actor and Reality, The' 180–1
Dresden 7, 77
Du Bois, W. E. B. 2, 8, 20, 115, 129–31
Durkheim, Émile 2, 3, 8, 19, 26, 28, 35, 40–2, 76, 91, 101
Duse, Eleanora *see* 'La Duse'

Enckendorff, Marie Luise *see* Simmel, Gertrud
energy 19, 29, 54–5, 60–1, 79, 86
Engels, Friedrich 26, 60, 74, 91, 95, 126
Ernst, Max 3
'Ethnological and Psychological Studies in Music' 2, 6, 20, 39

exchange   25, 27–35, 40, 44–53,
   60–2, 67, 69, 72–4, 85–7, 150–2,
   185–6
   see also interaction; value
'Expansion of the Group and the
   Development of Individuality,
   The' (from *Sociology*)   82, 103

'Fashion' (from *Philosophical
   Culture*)   154–5, 103–8
fate and fatalism   38, 73, 119, 154,
   160–6, 167, 176
   see also 'Adventure'; View of Life
Faust   165, 177–8, 183
   see also Goethe
'Female Culture' (from
   Philosophical Culture)   92, 171,
   176–7
feminism   3, 8, 74, 77, 83, 91–5
'Fidelity and Gratitude, Excursus
   on' (from *Sociology*)   150, 152
First World War   xii, 135–6
flâneur   xv, 97, 110
'Flirtation' (from *Philosophical
   Culture*)   97, 107, 138, 158
'Florence'   137, 153, 170–1
form(s) *see* association; causality;
   culture
'Fragmentary Character of Life,
   The'   139, 147
freedom   17, 85–5, 94, 107, 109,
   113, 115, 160, 162, 171
   academic   xii
   individual   9, 27–30, 35–8, 43–4,
      75–6, 133, 178, 186
   of the poor person   123–4
'Freedom and the Individual'   178
Freud, Sigmund   3, 5, 21–2
Friedländer, Julius   2, 6
Frisby, David   78, 133
Fundamental Questions of Sociology
   3, 12, 76, 84–5, 112, 178

George, Stefan   3
Gilman, Charlotte Perkins   2, 8,
   19, 95

Goethe   ix, xv, 3, 136, 182
Goethe, Johann Wilhelm von   ix,
   xii, xv, 136–7, 165, 172, 177,
   179, 181–4
   see also 'Kant and Goethe'
Goodstein, Elizabeth   176
Gundolf, Friedrich   175

'Handle, The' (from *Philosophical
   Culture*)   143, 159
Hegel, G. W. F.   4, 8, 76, 187
Heidegger, Martin   160
Heidelberg   3, 7, 69, 77, 112, 136,
   139, 140
Hiller, Kurt   3, 77, 159
'How is Society Possible?,
   Excursus on the Question'
   (from *Sociology*)   4, 12–8, 82
   see also apriorities
Husserl, Edmond   3, 111, 171, 182,
   186–7

individual, individuality,
   individualism *see* freedom
'*Infelices Possidentes!*'   108, 125
interaction (*Wechselwirkung*)   10–
   13, 15, 24–5, 29–36, 41, 47–50,
   58, 176
   aesthetic   163–4
   between propertied and
      poor   115–23
   cultural   134, 140, 142, 150–2
   social   66, 78–83, 87, 89–90, 106,
      174
'Intersection of Social Circles,
   The' (from *Sociology*)   76,
   99–102
Introduction to Moral Science   2, 4,
   7, 20, 76
irony   18, 89, 104, 109, 121, 149

Jastrow, Ignaz and Anna   xi–xii,
   136, 181
jewellery   48–9, 88–9, 92, 105
   see also 'Adornment, Excursus
   on'

Jews, Jewishness   7–8, 14, 64, 127, 129
Jugend   2, 7, 38, 91, 148, 149, 165
  see also 'Beyond Beauty'; 'Only a Bridge'; 'Snapshots *sub specie aeternitatis*'

Kant   2, 76, 181–4
Kant, Immanuel   2, 3, 4, 6, 8, 11–13, 17, 39, 171, 179, 181–4, 187
'Kant and Goethe'   3, 181–4
Kantorowicz, Gertrud   93, 154, 178
Keyserling, Hermann Graf   178, 182
Kracauer, Siegfried   3, 89–90, 101, 108, 125, 159

'La Duse'   180–1
Lazarus, Moritz   6
Leck, Ralph M.   8, 159
lies, lying   87, 90–1
  see also 'Maker of Lies'; 'Secret and the Secret Society'
life-philosophy, life-sociology   13, 59, 111–12, 138, 175, 180
  see also 'Kant and Goethe'; metaphysics; *View of Life*
Logos   3, 139
London   77, 85, 98, 131, 137
'Love, On'   157, 177–8
Lukács, Georg   3, 69–70, 89, 112, 136, 159, 177, 184

Main Problems of Philosophy   3, 11, 178, 187
'Maker of Lies, The'   91
Mannheim, Karl   97, 112–13
Martineau, Harriet   154, 167–9
Marx, Karl   2, 8, 26, 31, 35, 47, 54, 56, 60–1, 64, 67–8, 71–4, 91
Marxism   69, 159
Mauss, Marcel   121, 139, 150–2
Mead, George Herbert   171, 185–7

mental work   26, 54–5
  see also prostitute
metaphor   16–17, 23, 24, 40 101
  see also analogies; irony; metonymy; synecdoche
metaphysics   10, 12, 18–21, 26, 72–3, 111, 138, 141–2, 145, 175, 179–80
  sociological   76, 148, 158
  see also life-philosophy; *Philosophical Culture*; *View of Life*
metonymy   18, 105
'Metropolis and Mental Life, The' (the metropolises essay)   3, 7, 135, 185, 179
  sociology of cities   75, 77–8, 83–6, 98–9, *100*, 104, 108–11, 114, 124–8
Meunier, Constantin   144
'Michelangelo' (from *Philosophical Culture*)   138, 143–4
miser and spendthrift   63–4
modernity   18, 60, 76, 78, 104–5, 133–45, 148, 153–6, 175–6, 180
Mommsen, Theodor   6
'Money Alone Doesn't Bring Happiness'   28, 39
money economy   5, 12, 16, 19, 78, 85–8, 99–105, 109, 114, 125, 134, 151, 156–7
  philosophy of   25–6, 28–9, 33–8, 43–71
  see also capitalism; exchange; value
'Money in Modern Culture'   28, 36
more-life, more-than-life   145–7, 154, 157, 174, 180
  see also life-philosophy; metaphysics; *View of Life*

nature   11–12, 16–17, 21, 26, 93, 146, 148, 153, 182–3
  and culture   28–9, 33, 68, 134–5, 138–43, 170–5
  see also 'Alps'; 'Philosophy of Landscape'; 'Ruin'

'Nature of Historical
    Understanding, On the' 164–
    5, 187
'Negativity of Collective Modes of
    Behavior, Excursus on' (from
    Sociology) 127
Nietzsche, Friedrich xv, 2, 3, 4, 8,
    76, 108–9, 111, 126, 177, 182
    see also Schopenhauer and
    Nietzsche

'Only a Bridge' 184

Paris 1, 77, 98, 103, 104, 137, 144
Park, Robert E. 3, 77, 115, 128–31
'Personality of God, The' (from
    Philosophical Culture) 138,
    176
pessimism 27, 43, 59, 66, 80
Philosophical Culture 3, 11, 136,
    138, *141*
    'Introduction' 18–19, 138, 179
    see also titles of specific essays
philosophical sociology 12, 21,
    76, 112, 187
    see also metaphysics
'Philosophy of Landscape,
    The' 147–8
Philosophy of Money 3, 21, 23–4,
    28, *30*, 33, 38, 68, 76–80, 101,
    173, 178, 185
    'Preface' 25, 29–30, 71
    Chapter 1: 'Value and
        Money' 28–34
    Chapter 2: 'The Value of Money
        as a Substance' 50–5
    Chapter 3: 'Money in the
        Sequence of Purposes' 60–4
    Chapter 4: 'Individual
        Freedom' 35–8
    Chapter 5: 'The Money
        Equivalent of Personal
        Values' 44–9
    Chapter 6: 'The Style of
        Life' 64–70, 115, 156

'Picture Frame, The' 31, 143
'Poor Person, The' (from
    Sociology) 116–25, 131
poverty 53, *82*, 115–16, 118–19,
    121, 125, 131
'Problem of Historical Time,
    The' 164
'Problem of Religion Today, The'
    (from *Philosophical
    Culture*) 176
'Problem of Sociology, The' (from
    Sociology) 11–12, 81, *82*
*Problems in the Philosophy of
    History* 2, 7, 11, 76, 164
prostitute, prostitution 14, 44, 50,
    52–3, 63, 72, 92
'Psychology of Money, On
    the' 51, 63
Pyyhtinen, Olli 120–1

'Quantitative Conditioning of the
    Group, The' (from
    Sociology) 34, 40, 82, 85

race, race relations 41, 95, 115,
    127–9
rationality, rationalism 65–6, 79,
    85
reciprocal cause and effect *see*
    causality; interaction
reification 47, 60, 69, 73–4
    see also Lukács
relationism, relativism 10–11,
    33–4, 39, 48, 92, 149, 154
    individual, social, human, and
        objective relations 120–1
'Relative and Absolute Problem of
    the Sexes, The' (from
    Philosophical Culture) 92–3
'Relativity' 165–6
religion 11, 41, 76, 92, 135, 142,
    147, 171, 172, 176
Religion 3, 176
Rembrandt xv, 3, 101, 136, 156,
    161–5, 182

Rickert, Heinrich   3, 164
Rilke, Rainer Maria von   3, 161–2
'Rodin' (from *Philosophical Culture*)   xv, 138, 144–5, 148, 154
Rodin, Auguste   3, 181
'Rome'   137–8
'Ruin, The' (from *Philosophical Culture*)   136, 138–41, 146

Sachs, Hans   27
Schopenhauer, Arthur   xv, 2, 8, 111, 182
Schopenhauer and Nietzsche   xv, 3, 76, 109
scepticism   11, 59, 66, 86, 163
Schäfer, Dietrich   7
Schmoller, Gustav   6, 51, 129
science   9, 21, 25, 28, 56, 59, 92, 135, 147, 172–3, 176, 178, 184
'Secret and the Secret Society, The' (from *Sociology*)   80, *82*, 87–8
'Self-Preservation of the Group, The' (from *Sociology*)   *82*, 112, 140, 150
sex, sexuality   25, 50, 52–5, 73–5, 77, 91–5, 97, 141, 154, 157–9, 177–8
   see also feminism; 'Female Culture'; Gilman; prostitute; 'Relative and Absolute Problem of the Sexes'; Weber, Marianne
Simmel, Georg
   biographical notes on   xi–xii, 1–9, 23–4, 76–7, 134–6
   see also Jastrow; Kantorowicz; Susman; Weber; and *titles of specific works*
Simmel, Gertrud (*née* Kinel)   xi, 2, 6, 93, 136, 178
Simmel, Hans   xi, 1, 2, 6, 24, 135
Small, Albion   8, 128

'Snapshots *sub specie aeternitatis*'   39, 91, 165, 190
   see also *Jugend*; 'La Duse'; 'Maker of Lies'; 'Money Alone Doesn't Bring Happiness'; 'Relativity'
'Sociability'   106–7
   see also *Fundamental Problems of Sociology*
'Social Boundary, Excursus on the' (from *Sociology*)   166
Social Differentiation, On   2, 4, 7, 20, 40, 55, 76, 178
social evolution   5, 17, 20, 134
   see also Darwin; Spencer
social media see technology
socialism   8, 24, 43–4, 108
'Sociological Aesthetics'   76, 106, 148
Sociology   3, 28, 77–8, 80–3, *82*, 109–10, 134
   see also *titles of specific chapters*
'Sociology of the Meal, The'   140–1
'Sociology of the Senses, Excursus on' (from *Sociology*)   120, 166–7
Sombart, Werner   8, 26, 44, 56, 58
'Some Contemporary Problems of Philosophy, On'   111–12
'Some Remarks on Prostitution in the Present and in Future'   53
soul   6, 27, 38, 65, 75, 89, 94, 100–1, 113, 130–1
   and culture   143–4, 147, 154, 164, 171–3, 176–7, 181, 183, 186
'Space and the Spatial Ordering of Society' (from *Sociology*)   120, 166–7
Spencer, Herbert   2, 4, 5, 8, 19–21
statistics   28, 40–2
   see also 'Quantitative Conditioning of the Group'
Steinthall, Heymann   6
Stöcker, Helene   3, 77, 159

'Stranger, Excursus on the' (from *Sociology*) 121–2, 166–7
Strasbourg xii, 3, 136, 170
subjectivism 11, 59, 71, 45, 182
Susman, Margarete 5, 21, 93, 178
sustainability 149–50, 152
   see also 'Self-Preservation of the Group'
synecdoche 18

'Tale of the Color, The' 1–4
Tarde, Gabriel 2, 8, 11, 19, 26, 28, 40–2
technology 9, 17, 56, 61, 172
   cultural technologies and social media 64, 140, 125, 174
'Tendencies in German Life and Thought since 1870' 9
time and space 6, 13–17, 25, 67–8, 133, 140, 157, 166–9, 173
Tocqueville, Alexis de 154, 167–9
Tönnies, Ferdinand 2, 8, 109
tragedy of culture see 'Concept and the Tragedy of Culture'
Treitschke, Heinrich von 6
tropes see irony; metaphor; metonymy; synecdoche

value and valuation 10–11, 29–30, 32–4, 43–4, 49–50, 61–3
   exchange value 72–3
   exhibition value 37–8, 61
   functional value 47–8
   personal worth 30, 44–8, 50–5
   value and price 27–8, 31, 51–2
   value-judgements 94, 109, 126
   see also culture; desire; exchange; Marx

Veblen, Thorstein 2, 8, 19, 139, 150–2
'Venice' 137, 153–4
View of Life 3, 111, 136, 138, *141*, 142, 178, 181
   Chapter 1: 'Life as Transcendence' 145, 157
   Chapter 2: 'The Turn toward Ideas' 147
   Chapter 3: 'Death and Immortality' 147, 160–2
   Chapter 4: 'The Law of the Individual' (individual law) 171–2, 185

War and Our Spiritual Decisions, The 159
Washington, Booker T. 130
Weber, Marianne ix, 93–5, 178, 179
Weber, Max 2, 3, 7, 8, 19, 26, 69, 91, 94, 101, 112, 131, 139, 179
   commentary on Simmel 44, 56–8, 77, 87, 123
Wirth, Luis 128
women see 'Female Culture'; feminism; 'Relative and Absolute Problem of the Sexes'; sexuality
'Women's Congress and Social Democracy, The' 92
'Written Communication, Excursus on' (from *Sociology*) *82*, 90

yodelling see 'Ethnological and Psychological Studies in Music'